The Mythology of
the Superhero

The Mythology of the Superhero

ANDREW R. BAHLMANN

McFarland & Company, Inc., Publishers
Jefferson, North Carolina

LIBRARY OF CONGRESS CATALOGUING-IN-PUBLICATION DATA

Names: Bahlmann, Andrew R., 1979– author.
Title: The mythology of the superhero / Andrew R. Bahlmann.
Description: Jefferson, North Carolina : McFarland & Company, Inc., Publishers, 2016. | Includes bibliographical references and index.
Identifiers: LCCN 2016012698 | ISBN 9781476662480 (softcover : acid free paper) ∞
Subjects: LCSH: Comic books, strips, etc.—United States—History and criticism. | Superheroes. | Classical literature—Influence. | Superheroes in literature. | Heroes in literature.
Classification: LCC PN6725 .B27 2016 | DDC 741.5/97 3—dc23
LC record available at https://lccn.loc.gov/2016012698

BRITISH LIBRARY CATALOGUING DATA ARE AVAILABLE

ISBN (print) 978-1-4766-6248-0
ISBN (ebook) 978-1-4766-2518-8

© 2016 Andrew R. Bahlmann. All rights reserved

No part of this book may be reproduced or transmitted in any form or by any means, electronic or mechanical, including photocopying or recording, or by any information storage and retrieval system, without permission in writing from the publisher.

Front cover image of superhero © 2016 yogysic/iStock

Printed in the United States of America

McFarland & Company, Inc., Publishers
Box 611, Jefferson, North Carolina 28640
www.mcfarlandpub.com

To Heidi

Acknowledgments

First and foremost, I owe a great debt to my wife, Heidi. She has walked with me through all the highs and the lows that have led to this moment. Also, to my four sidekicks, who have shared in the sacrifice.

Because this book began with my Ph.D. work, thanks go out to my committee chair, Dr. Felicia Campbell, who has been nothing but encouraging from the first. Also, I owe thanks to committee members Dr. Joseph McCullough, Dr. John Unrue and Dr. Lawrence Mullen. All have been willing participants and generous with their time as I developed my work from idea to dissertation to book. I would be remiss if I didn't mention Susan Summers, who helped me chart a new course when I was floundering.

As this work grew, so did the list of people who deserve thanks. My entire family has been encouraging and supportive despite the fact that this was something a little bit different for them—and for me.

Special thanks go out to my readers. Firstly, to the person I'm going to call the Reader. I'm pretty sure I did uncover your secret identity, as you suggested I might, but I enjoy the idea of your superhero persona in the context of this book enough that I just wanted to leave it at this. Considering how much you did to help this book become better, you certainly deserve recognition. Dealing with your hundreds of suggestions made me a better writer and a more humble scholar. Thanks for that. Thanks to Christopher Weitrick for his help with Chapter 2 and Alison Rubin for her feedback on Chapter 3. I especially want to acknowledge those who helped me when I struggled with the final chapter—and I hope you approve of what you see—Scott Bahlmann, Tim Moungey, Aaron Woods, Jessica McCall, and Chris Yi.

There are so many people beyond this who have been supportive, kind and understanding and who deserve recognition. However, most people don't read this part of a book and those who do tend to move on once they've found their names. To avoid feeling ungrateful, though, I want to thank all of those who have helped me to survive and thrive long enough to see something like this come to fruition.

Table of Contents

Acknowledgments — vii

Preface — 1

Introduction: Superheroes as a New Mythology — 3

1. Building a Framework: The Lexicon of Superhero Mythology — 25
2. Green Arrow as an Exemplar of the Superhero Myth Structure — 95
3. Buffy Summers and the Superhero Myth: Reading a Popular Culture Icon Through a Mythological Lens — 112
4. Finding the Superhero: Reading SyFy's *Alphas* Through the Mythological Lexicon — 132
5. The Superhero Before the Superhero: Finding Superhero Mythology in the Old English *Beowulf* — 150
6. The Superheroic Structure: Examining the Mythological Character of the Superhero — 168

Appendix: Superhero Tropes — 181

Chapter Notes — 185

Bibliography and Television Shows and Films — 195

Index — 201

Preface

This book began life as a dissertation, the idea growing out of a recognition of some of the similarities between early epics like *Gilgamesh* and *Beowulf* and romances, including *Gawain and the Green Knight*. As I explored these similarities I began to see the underpinnings of a mythology that shared something with these older works while still being something new. The more that I read, the more I realized that many people talk about a superhero mythology, but there was little that explained what the mythology is and how it looks. The dissertation grew out of a desire to fill that gap in the conversation.

The bibliography includes many works that helped inform the ideas behind this one. Peter Coogan's *Superhero: The Secret Origin of a Genre* and Richard Reynolds' *Super Heroes: A Modern Mythology* served as early foundational works to understand the superhero as it has been discussed in similar ways. Texts like Roland Barthes' *Mythologies* and William Doty's *Mythography* created a greater understanding of how myth works and why it matters, Barthes especially in terms of popular culture and mythology.

Because superheroes are such a dominant force in popular culture, there is a need to be able to address their existence in our society and the way they inform our culture. Coogan's generic distinction is a valuable part of that conversation and his definition of the superhero still serves for most conversations about what a superhero is. My own explanation in Chapter 6 relies heavily on the groundwork he established, and should be considered a variation on the theme rather than a new creation.

The book is designed to help us understand and appreciate the framework of superhero mythology. Certainly, it can play a part in discussions about who is and is not a superhero. Certainly, it can be a tool in discussing the popularity and psychological impact superheroes have on us. The hope is that it will become a valuable tool in myriad conversations about superheroes. But at its core, the book is simply supposed to help us be able to articulate the structure of the superhero myth to better be able to talk about its presence and import in cultures wherein it is found.

Introduction: Superheroes as a New Mythology

What follows is not the first mention of the superhero as a mythological figure. The idea has been bandied about for several years. In fact, the superhero has become an integral part of popular culture of the last few years. In her introduction to a collection of Wonder Woman comics, Gloria Steinem argues for the mythic status of Wonder Woman and proclaims, "Mythology is a collective human memory."[1] From the time *X-Men* hit screens in 2000, superheroes have become a part of mainstream culture in a way they haven't been for decades. The blockbusters since that time have included multiple films centered on superheroes and their mythology. Outside of film, events like the death of Superman, the revelation of the origins of the Marvel character Wolverine, and DC's reboot have all been commented upon in mainstream news outlets. Though the superhero has existed within the society at the least since Superman's first appearance in *Action Comics*, the character's recent rise to prevalence is largely unprecedented in the history of the myth.

This work is not an examination of the genre of the superhero or a psychological examination of the how and why we need superheroes. Both ways of reading superheroes has been covered in several other books dealing with superheroes. Many of them are quite good and were used in creating this work. What this book is is an effort to explain the superhero as a mythological construct. By creating a framework of basic elements, referred to as tropes or mythemes, this work seeks to build a system that can be used to identify the characteristics of superhero mythology. This system will allow for more careful and cooperative discussions of the myth and how it functions in the various formats that contribute to the broad scope of the mythology.

There is no intent to have this work be the last word on this construct. The hope is that this work will open the doors to a fruitful conversation that will lead us to a viable and valuable way of talking about the myth of the superhero that will make our efforts to explore the superhero and the way the character influences our society more productive. The result of this conversation will be a system of framing the myth that will help us articulate what the superhero myth means in our society and how it affects popular culture.

This work presents a brief, concise explanation of what myth is and how it functions. It further examines several of the mythemes that form the framework of the mythos, drawing on the way Roland Barthes presents his own study *Mythologies*. Based on the supposition that signs create meaning through the interaction of the signifier and the signified, Barthes argues that current mythologies can be identified by the way they give a shared cultural meaning to a society. Because superheroes have become more and more recognizable over the years, they are uniquely placed to give a modern society a mythological framework of secular gods and heroes through which societal ideals can be discussed, examined and complicated. More so than the parts of society in Barthes' study, the superhero has become a shared touchstone for American culture. There are no claims herein to definitively explain why the superhero has become the new mythology of American culture. Rather, the focus is on exploring how the myth is recognized. The lexicon gives a structure whereby we can recognize superhero mythology in popular culture. By recognizing the mythology, we can more clearly articulate its impact on our modern world.

Simplistically, everything that follows in this book is designed to shed light on one basic question: why? Throughout popular culture, the superhero moniker has been applied to a diverse number of characters, from the Teenage Mutant Ninja Turtles to Buffy the Vampire Slayer. Even Harry Potter has been compared to tights clad heroes found frequently in the pages of comics. This book avoids arguing whether any of these characters is a superhero. Instead, it proposes a framework that explains why diverse characters are connected to superhero myth. This framework is also a tool that can be used to explore the development of the superhero, including how and where it exists in societies, and can help us discuss its role in the cultural fabric where the superhero is found.

In the first issue of *Action Comics* published in 1938, a character was presented that changed the face of comics and introduced a new mythology into the American consciousness. Created by Jerry Siegel and Joe Shuster, Superman bore a strong resemblance to mythic characters that preceded him. He was strong like Samson, quick like Hermes, and had the chiseled features frequently associated with gods and heroes.

> Siegel seems to have touched upon a mythic theme of universal significance. Superman recalled Moses [...] and also Jesus, sent from above to redeem the world. There are

parallel stories in many cultures, but what is significant is that Siegel [...] had created a secular American messiah.[2]

However, Superman was also markedly different than these characters that preceded him. Siegel and Shuster both admit to being devoted fans of the science fiction magazines being published in the 1930s.[3] Many of these adventure stories and others published in the pulp magazines of the era contributed to the kinds of stories told about and the costume of Superman, and by extension the superhero myth in general. Hailing from another planet, Superman could "leap an eighth of a mile," lift enormous weights, and run with superspeed.[4] Rather than comparing these abilities to Hermes or Samson, perhaps more traditionally mythic sources, Jerry Siegel and Joe Shuster explain the source of Superman's abilities in terms more familiar to science fiction. He is not some demigod. He is an alien sent here from the dying planet Krypton, a last ditch effort on the part of his parents to save him from a global apocalypse. This new messiah is found in a space pod and raised by a farming couple rather than being pulled from a reed basket on the Nile and raised by the daughter of the pharaoh. He does have mythic abilities above and beyond even the most impressive of his predecessors in the pulp novels. However, Siegel and Shuster opt to compare his leaping ability to that of a grasshopper and his tremendous strength to "the lowly ant [which] can support weights hundreds of times its own," using scientifically based comparisons rather than comparing him to characters from traditional mythology.[5]

It is significant to note that Superman's first foray did not fill the whole of *Action Comics* first issue. Though he appeared on the cover, his first story was only one of several that shared the pages. Early superhero stories were short and shared space with other genres. Even when only superheroes graced the pages, it was incredibly rare for a story to carry through the whole of the book. Superhero stories began, then, as extremely closed and episodic. The sweeping, cross-story arcs that proliferate today would have been unheard of in early comics. The shorthand necessary to provide complete stories in six pages or less resulted in the development of many of the tropes of the superhero. The gaudy, primary color costumes; the cackling supervillain; the larger than life, black and white, good versus evil stories; all come from both this short storytelling origin and from the precursors to the superhero. The penny dreadfuls and pulp novels included starkly defined characters. Epics and medieval romances developed larger than life heroes of nobility and character. Even early myths contributed superhuman abilities and struggles that could stretch from story to story, even as each story was a narrative whole unto itself.

Shortly after Superman, a plethora of superheroes began to appear on the scene. The father of Zatanna Zatara shared the same debut issue of Action Comics as Superman. The year after Superman's first appearance, Marvel produced Namor, who would become a major player in their superhero universe. DC also created a character that was in many ways the antithesis of the Man of Steel. A dark figure willing to commit acts of violence, Batman had no powers to parallel Superman's. His costume was originally only shades of gray and black and seemed to draw from the macabre works of Edgar Allan Poe more than of the circus strongmen who inspired Superman's costume and poses. By the end of 1941, roughly three and a half years after the debut of the Man of Steel, the pages of comics were teeming with superheroes including many names still recognizable today. Several names have become popular in sometimes drastically different forms, including early forms of Daredevil, Quicksilver, the Human Torch, and Red Tornado.[6] Others are still very recognizable from their early years. Wonder Woman, Captain Marvel (a.k.a. Shazam), Catwoman, Robin, Green Arrow, and Captain America all originated in this developmental window of time.

At the time superheroes entered comics, they were by no means the only sorts of story found in the books. Comics was a thriving medium that included westerns, war stories, romance, thrillers, horror comics, satire, as well as juvenile fare and funny stories. This thriving variety continued for decades. However, it didn't take long for comics to draw criticism. As early as 1940, national critics were condemning the effect comics had on juveniles.[7] This criticism eventually led to the convening of a judiciary subcommittee on juvenile delinquency in 1954. Fredric Wertham of *Seduction of the Innocent* fame served as a witness for the committee. Though the committee claimed that it formed with "no preconceptions" and even recognized that "the majority of comics were 'as harmless as soda pop,'" the testimonies were carefully controlled to show comics in a bad light.[8] "When it was all over, the comic book industry closed ranks and adopted a self-regulatory code" to avoid government oversight.[9]

In the wake of the hearing and implementation of the code, several comics publishers went out of business, though in some cases it was not due to the changes brought about by the code.[10] Eventually, what was left was "funny animal, teen, and romance comics," but that wasn't enough to keep comics going.[11] So, in an effort to bolster sales, comics launched what became known as the Silver Age of superheroes.[12] Since then, though their popularity has ebbed and flowed, superheroes have been a part of the fabric of popular culture. Marvel began challenging the typical iconic heroes of DC lore almost immediately with the Fantastic Four, their turbulent take on the *superteam*. However, the superhero was still a character that vanquished evil, saved the damsel, and generally fought along clear lines of right and wrong. The "white hat" attitude regarding superheroes changed with the onset of the Bronze Age, when the lines between right and wrong were complicated. Emblematic of this shift was the addition of Green Arrow to the Green Lantern title by Denny O'Neil and Neal Adams. Green Arrow exposed the titular character to a host of social ills and emphasized the idea that, at least up to that point, superheroes were not only *ineffective against real world problems*, but didn't even pay attention to the gray areas between right and wrong. As muddy as the waters of morality may be in superhero comics, there is a tacit understanding that characters like Batman and Superman would never cross their moral lines and that the villain would always end up behind bars by the last panel.

The development of the superhero, indelibly linked with the birth of Superman, marked a new branching in the mythology of the hero. Over the years, the change led to the development of a unique mythology. Though the myth of the superhero shares some elements in common with romantic, epic, and adventure tales, the combination of shared and unique mythemes as described in Chapter 1 manifest something new, something different. Superheroes were founded on the principles of science fiction. From Batman's "wonderful toys" to the powers of Thor,[13] in many ways superheroes seem to be the literal embodiment of Arthur C. Clarke's claim that "any sufficiently advanced technology is indistinguishable from magic."[14] Superhero mythology, while supposedly grounded in more scientific notions than other pantheonic mythologies, is still full of pseudo-scientific magical happenings. Indeed, in the film *Thor*, the hero explains, "Your ancestors called it magic, and you call it science. Well, I come from a place where they're one and the same thing."[15] Throughout the film, and in much of Thor's history in comics, the powers of Asgard are explained as advanced science, or different science, rather than as straight up magic. The phrase *different science* is meant to cover the fact that while we have yet to uncover the scientific laws that govern the workings of Mjolnir, to the Asgardians, Thor's mighty hammer follows a clear set of presumably understandable, pseudo-scientific, standards. To them, it is science, just science that humans are incapable of understanding.

It is also interesting, and significant to note that it has been revealed in the comics that Superman's invincibility offers no protection from the forces of magic, because there is room for magic in superhero mythology. The shift away from the mystical toward the scientific, though incomplete,[16] was a natural growth from the emphasis on technology and the sciences in the popular culture that inspired Superman's creators. Brought about as American society adjusted to the new world precipitated by the industrial revolution and advances in scientific inquiry, one response from popular culture was the development of science fiction as a genre in the pulps of the early 1900s. These changes led to a new sort of storytelling, one that prompted Siegel and Shuster to create Superman and motivated others to follow in their footsteps, creating godlike characters straddling the lines between the supernatural and the rational worlds. This mythology is overtly fictional, but deeply meaningful in the society that produces, consumes, and embraces tales of superheroes.

The study of mythology goes back decades. In Lord Raglan's *The Hero: A Study in Tradition, Myth, and Drama*, he argues that pre-literate societies don't have the capacity for complex thought that would be required for the creation of these kinds of myth. While elitist, his work does posit an interesting idea that has perpetuated in the study of myth by suggesting that one who believes in the supernatural already has notions about how the supernatural works. This set of predetermined rules disallows the subject the ability to create new myths outside of any preexisting belief system. The belief system and the mythology build upon each other and are inextricably connected. Concept begets rules of functionality that in turn influence the concepts as the myth evolves and changes within the culture. Essentially, people engaged in a mythology cannot create it *ex nihilo*. They must build it from within and based on rules largely beyond their control.

J. R. R. Tolkien proposes that "myth is alive at once and in all its parts, and dies before it can be dissected. It is possible, I think, to be moved by the power of myth and yet to misunderstand the sensation, to ascribe it wholly to something else."[17] Assuming Tolkien's analysis of myth to be accurate, any study like this runs the risk of killing the very thing it seeks to analyze. Analysis can, at times, take away something of the vitality in the application of the mythology. Richard Slotkin further suggests that one of the critical problems "which lies at the source of every study of myth in history and literature [is] the problem of defining myth and of distinguishing between archetypal myth, folk legends, and artistic mythopoesis."[18] Though there is something about myth that can make it difficult to analyze, in part because it is so interwoven and sublimated by the community that produces the myth, it is important to do what we can if we are to find evidence of mythology in superhero stories and to be able to comprehend its role in society. A large part of the challenge of working with mythology is the plethora of ways that we view myth.

In his wide-ranging book *Mythography: The Study of Myths and Rituals*, William G. Doty explains that he "has developed a list of more than fifty" definitions of myth.[19] He does recognize that many of the definitions he has encountered include elements that appear with some frequency. He lists the following:

- myth as aesthetic device, narrative, literary form.
- subject matter having to do with the gods, an "other world."
- explaining origins (etiology).
- as mistaken or primitive science.
- myth as the words to rituals, or myth dependent upon ritual, which it explicates.
- making universals concrete or intelligible.
- explicating beliefs, collective experiences, or values.
- "spiritual" or "psychic" expression.
- the ideological framework for a culture.[20]

His book considers several specific approaches to defining and studying myth, while resisting any sort of overarching, central definition of the term. The closest he comes is to posit a comprehensive list of elements pertaining to what he calls a "mythological corpus."[21] He states that anything belonging to the body of myth will include:

> (1) a unusually [sic] complex network of myths that are (2) culturally important, (3) imaginal (4) stories, conveying by means of (5) metaphoric and symbolic diction, (6) graphic imagery, and (7) emotional conviction and participation (8) the primal, foundational accounts (9) of aspects of the real, experienced world and (10) humankind's roles and relative statuses within it.
>
> Mythologies may (11) convey the political and moral values of a culture and (12) provide systems of interpreting (13) individual experience within a universal perspective, which may include (14) the intervention of suprahuman entities as well as (15) aspects of the natural and cultural orders. Myths may be enacted or reflected in (16) rituals, ceremonies, and dramas, and (17) they may provide materials for secondary elaboration, the constituent mythemes (mythic units) having become merely images or reference points for a subsequent story, such as a folktale, historical legend, novella, or prophecy.[22]

It should be readily apparent that the superhero corpus is strongly connected to Doty's mythological corpus.

In American culture, superheroes are especially significant in recent years, and their stories are told most frequently through media that includes a strong visual—or imaginal—component. They are certainly complex and communicate through metaphor and symbol. In stories like Marvel's *Civil War*, the *Avengers* films, and DC's recent films, graphic imagery is used to connect to the real world, to our place therein, and to comment on the political and moral climate of the time. They invoke a strong emotional response from their adherents and are not infrequently used as means to interpret the role of the individual in the broader world. Superheroes themselves practically epitomize the idea of suprahuman intervention embodied in muscles and costumes within a cultural construct usually recognized as some version of American society. Events like Comic-Con have a ritualistic flair to them, however, the frequency in which superheroes are incorporated into weddings, birthdays, and the like evidence that the myth of the superhero has been integrated into our rituals and ceremonies. The incorporation of superheroes into other stories, their cameos in *The Lego Movie* and the depiction of political figures in superhero tales as brief examples, manifest in a small part the way superheroes have been coopted and removed from their generic constraints into other stories.

Of course, this rationale still needs a full definition of myth. Robert A. Segal has synthesized a working definition that serves to explicate some of the central tenets Doty recognizes as communal in people's definitions of myth. In his explanation of myth, he focuses on four points: the myth is communicated through story; it contains personified characters, frequently with supernatural components; it must be significant in the culture; and that the myth must be pervasive yet fictional. Segal suggests that these four elements define all myth, regardless of the theoretical approach.[23]

Segal begins by proposing that myth is a story: "Theories that read myth symbolically rather than literally still take the subject matter, or the meaning, to be the unfolding of a story."[24] While myth is story driven, the stories are *about* characters. Abstract concepts like truth and honesty may be a part of the story, but it is the concretes that make the story happen, not the abstracts. Even though frequent conversations about myth deal more with tropes and ideas derived from the myth, all of these concepts are presented within the context of the stories. The powers of Thor's hammer, in both Norse and superhero mythology, are communicated through stories in which he uses the hammer.

In Segal's definition, the second requirement is that the subject of myth must be people or personified non-humans, and are most often super-human in some manner. Again, abstract concepts may be communicated through myth, but the story of the myth is related through the personification if the characters that exist within the tales rather than through abstract philosophizing and heavy moralization. Even when animals are present in the myth, if they are integral to the story, they tend to be anthropomorphized.

In one Native American story explaining how the animals got their names, Coyote determines that he wants to be first in line to receive a strong name like Bear or Eagle. He explains his aspirations to his wife, Mole, who fears he will leave her if he gains more notoriety and respect. So she lets him sleep until the sun rises high. By the time Coyote makes it to the naming place, the Creator has given away all the good names and even the little names. The creature is left with the name Coyote. However, the despondent trickster is consoled by the Creator. He explains that Coyote's role will be to teach the new human creatures all the skills they will need to know. He is also imbued with the ability to come back to life, to understand the speech of the other animals and humans, and to change his shape.[25] Coyote is one of several animals that seem to have more in common with humans than with the world of the wild animals within their mythological stories. Humans, or recognizably human-like figures, predominate in myth narratives.

Perhaps the most important aspect of Segal's definition is the third premise, which proposes that "myth accomplishes something significant for adherents."[26] Whether those who support a myth believe it to be factual or not, they do believe it is significant in some meaningful way. This truth may not be of an empirical or factual nature. Frequently it takes the form of more abstract concepts like freedom and choice. One of the greatest challenges in this regard is the fact that the significant something of myth is commonly left unarticulated, especially by the originators of the myth. The messages, the truths expressed, are built into the story but left to the listener to parse out and gain individually. American professional wrestling serves as an example of this concept in practice.

Over fifty years ago, Roland Barthes wrote an analysis of wrestling. Significantly, he proposes that "[t]rue wrestling," the subject of his essay, is different than "fake wrestling," even though his essay is clearly talking about what we now call professional wrestling.[27] He argues, "Wrestling is not a sport, it is a spectacle."[28] Though his focus is on the type of wrestling he saw in France, the idea of a mythology of wrestling has continued to present day professional wrestling. In wrestling, "the wrestler's function is not to win but to perform exactly the gestures expected of him. [....] Once the adversaries are in the Ring, the public is entrusted with the obviousness of the roles."[29] Thus, wrestling is not about victory or defeat, but about the nearly caricature like nature of the athlete/performers. From the different iterations of Hulk Hogan, Sting, the Rock, Kane, to John Cena, professional wrestling is populated with performers who have developed an established personality that drives the way they act in the ring. Devotees of the myth are less engaged with victory and defeat, and more with the development of the concepts embodied by the figures they follow. The challenge with myth is to recognize there is frequently more to a given tale than just the meaning we find therein and to let these meanings coexist without discounting or diminishing them.

Segal's fourth point is perhaps the least satisfying. He argues that a myth is "a conviction false yet tenacious."[30] Even if the idea of myth as false holds generally, it frequently leads to more conflict than is worth when dealing with devout adherents of a mythology. For a Roman Catholic, the doctrine of transubstantiation is not of necessity any more false than the theory of evolution is to science or a rule regarding verb conjugation is to grammarians.

For this reason we must accept the possibility that myth can be and usually is true, but not in an empirically satisfying way. While it would be impossible to talk of a myth with any degree of empiricism the same way we discuss and accept scientific tenets, those who adhere devoutly to a myth will hold to that perceptual truth with the same tenacity that scientists do to theirs. Though we may believe a myth to be fallacious, to insist adherents' convictions are false is to severely deter any opportunity to engage in meaningful and revealing conversation regarding their engagement with that myth. It also belies the idea that what is important to a myth has less to do with veracity and more to do with the depth of belief therein. Adherents will not engage meaningfully in conversation about their myth when it is discounted offhandedly, nor should they.

To an extent, this is true of those who are acolytes of the myth of the superhero. While there are almost none[31] who believe that there are superheroes in life like those found at the core of the myth, many still hold to the truth in concept of the myth. There are also those who have attempted to bring the superhero out of the pages of the comics, off of the screen and into the streets. The Real Life Superhero (RLSH) movement is populated with people who wear the trappings of the superhero mythology, complete with colorful tights, stylized armor and masks, and gadgets. These people believe they are interacting with superhero mythology in a real and meaningful way. Most satisfy themselves by dressing in the vestments of the superhero and engaging in public service, reaching out to the homeless and providing neighborhood watch. However, some do take it a step further. Master Legend, an RLSH from Florida, claims to have "superspeed, high endurance, sight beyond sight, healing powers, [and] superhuman strength."[32] His perception of the reality of his abilities has not led to any major conflicts with the police. In fact, Master Legend bears the distinction of being one of the few RLSH to have received a commendation from the local authorities. The commendation came from the Orange County Sheriff's Department for aid rendered in the aftermath of Hurricane Charley.[33] The truth or fiction of Master Legend's superabilities is practically inconsequential in the broader scope of the mythology.

Ultimately, Segal explains that "to qualify as a myth, a story, which can of course express a conviction, be held tenaciously by adherents." This story draws its main players from human and other personified characters.[34] In this sort of culminating definition, Segal himself has wisely moved away from suggesting that a myth is, of necessity, fallacious. He also presents less conviction in expressing the need for myth to have an absolute meaning for those who celebrate it. Even when, or perhaps especially when, a myth's meaning is obscure and hard to articulate that meaning still exists on some level in the eyes of those who celebrate the mythology, even if they themselves cannot articulate what that meaning is. Segal's single line definition of myth seems to synthesize the general consensus among scholars. It is simple enough to cross through the various disciplines without being simplistic enough to be of no value.

In his work, *Regeneration Through Violence*, Richard Slotkin develops a definition of myth designed to help explicate the way myth works in American history. At the outset of his explication, he states, "A mythology is a complex of narratives that dramatizes the world vision and historical sense of a people or culture, reducing centuries of experience into a constellation of compelling metaphors."[35] The impact of the "myth-tale recapitulates that people's experience in their land, rehearses their visions of that experience in its relation to their gods and the cosmos, and reduces both experience and vision to a paradigm."[36] Vitally, Slotkin explicates that there is a difference between what he calls the "mythopoeic mode of consciousness" and the "myth-artifact."[37] "[M]ythopoeic perception [...] is mystical and religious, drawing heavily on the unconscious and the deepest levels of the psyche, defining relationships between human and divine things, [...] temporalities and ultimates."[38] In fact, Slotkin suggests, "A myth that ceases to evoke this religious response, this sense of total identification and collective participation, ceases to *function* as myth."[39] On the other hand, the myth-artifact "symbolically embodies the mythopoeic perception and makes it concrete and communicable."[40] The mythopoeic exists in abstraction and this abstraction is the part of myth that is difficult to conceptualize, sometimes even for adherents to the mythology. The artifacts, which almost inevitably contain "narrative, character, imagery, [and] values"[41] function as windows into the mythology. "The myth-artist [...] uses the artifacts of myth to evoke the [myth's] complex of affirmations to the audience,"[42] intended usually for the adherents to the myth; but for the uninitiated, the artifacts are the way to engage with unfamiliar mythologies.

Though communicated largely through narrative artifacts, myth transcends any single story. Mythic characters exist in stories, certainly, but also in images, symbols, anecdotes and—perhaps most importantly—in the minds of the adherents of the myth. No matter what the story, we know that if Zeus is in the story at some point he will attempt to seduce a mortal and the resultant offspring will be superhuman and that Hera will oppose the child. We know that Coyote will function as the trickster any time he appears in plains myth. We know that Kane will function in an antagonistic role when he steps onto the stage at a wrestling event. For the purposes of this work, perhaps the most appropriate example of the way mythological characters are transferable is that of the Norse pantheon, specifically the character of the god Thor. Most of the stories from the sagas bear little resemblance to the Marvel character and his exploits. The comics take the supernatural exploits of Thor and place them within trappings that make sense in the context of superhero mythology. However, he is still recognizable as a member of both mythological traditions. His characteristics and relationships with Odin, Loki, and Frigga are similar in the Norse tales and in Marvel's works. They aren't mirror images, but much of this comes about because the two mythologies suggest different "relationship[s] of hero to universe and of man to God [....] It is the narrative which gives the images life by giving them a mode of interaction."[43] Thus, characters can be interchanged, settings can alter, but the overarching body of narratives within the myth creates the windows, or lenses, by which people can come to an understanding of a mythological corpus, or mythopoeic perception.

The approach taken in this book is similar to the way Roland Barthes discusses myth in *Mythologies*. He begins by stating "that myth is a system of communication, [...] it is a message."[44] He expounds on this simple definition, stating that myth "is a mode of signification, a form" defined by "the way in which it utters [its] message."[45] Key to an understanding of Barthes' framework for mythology is the concept of the sign. Barthes draws on Ferdinand de Saussure's work in semiology to explain how myth works. The concept at work comprises of the interrelation between signifier and signified. At a basic level, an example will help explain the terms and how they relate to each other. The four letters that make up the word cape have no direct connection to the thing they represent. They comprise a word, a signifier that has no real meaning until we connect it to a signified. The cape may be a simple red that connects us to Superman. It may be black with scalloped edges, bringing to mind Batman. It could be a vampiric cape with a raised collar, the extremely high collared cape of Dr. Strange, or even the off the shoulder small cape worn by Shazam. When we connect that signifier to one of these ideas, we find a signified for the signifier. The interaction of these two forms a sign, something that has meaning and form. Barthes calls this basic level of semiology "the language."[46]

However, Barthes suggests that mythology exists on a second level of communication, which he terms "the metalanguage."[47] At this level of communication, the linguistic sign—for example, Batman's cape—becomes the signifier to be filled again with a signified. Batman's cape invokes a sense of brooding darkness, of justice, of loss, and other aspects of the character that have no direct correlation to a black scalloped cape, but have become almost inextricably connected with that sort of clothing within the mythology of the superhero. Thus, the sign of the cape becomes a signifier in this second level of linguistic meaning that becomes the sign of Batman. Another issue that complicates the idea of a sign deriving from a signifier and a signified is that a single signified can connect to multiple signifiers. Again, the idea, the "signified," of Batman can be invoked by more than just the cape as a signifier. The bat symbol is perhaps the strongest signifier, but the cowl itself, the Batmobile, even just an ordinary bat for some, invokes the sign of Batman in the mind of the receiver of the signifier. Thus, on multiple levels, signifiers are the form by which a signified is invoked to create a sign. The signification that creates mythology is tied to specific historical moments that tend to lend themselves poorly to changes in society. According to Barthes no myth lasts forever, and the development of each myth is tied specifically to signs already created in the culture. This is why superheroes have characteristics and traits that are familiar outside of the mythology. When the culture changes, the myth must change as well or be replaced by a new set of signs that meet the mythological needs of the society. The first time a basic set of characteristics was combined in a new and distinct way was in that first issue of Action Comics when Siegel and Shuster presented Superman as a new type of action hero. This was a moment that indicated a collection of new signs that developed to fulfill the need for a different kind of American mythology.

Because comics are a visual medium and this medium is almost indelibly tied to superheroes, the entire context of iconicity used in comics applies generally to superheroes as well. Scott McCloud explains in his groundbreaking work *Understanding Comics*, "while comic colors were less than expressionistic, they were fixed with a new iconic power. Because costume colors remained the same, panel after panel, they came to symbolize characters in the mind of the reader."[48] Accompanying the explanation is an illustration that includes a patch of purple between two swatches of green. Not only does this signify the Hulk, it also immediately brings to mind transformative rage, destruction, and for a great many, the phrase, "Hulk smash!" The signifier, a specific grouping of colors, signifies a superhero character which in turn becomes a signifier for the specific kind of superhero he is and for how he interacts with the world of the superhero. The specificity that demonstrates through simplistic drawings of superheroes manifests their iconicity and the way in which the signs of the superhero mythos are perhaps unique. These sorts of "images or *signs* used to refer to mythical concepts or myths" are called mythogram by Doty.[49]

What, then, is myth and how does it function in regards to this work? Based on the variety of approaches, the following distills the concept of myth to something that we can use to comprehend superheroic mythology and the lexicon that follows. Despite the fact that Barthes fails to recognize this in his work, myth is conveyed through narrative. This narrative can be implied or expressed, but the artifacts of myth have a narrative component to them. There is almost always an anthropomorphization of key non-human elements. The events and characters that matter all connect in some clear way to the human experience. Myth confronts the challenges, struggles, and key elements of its society usually through metaphor and symbolism. The cultural struggles are given a mask through which a society can examine and reexamine key issues and attempt, even fictionally to find resolution or understanding. The fact that myth deals in metaphor and symbolism lead some to dismiss it as fictional, but a key aspect of mythology is that it is true in ways that matter whether or not the elements of the myth are factual. Myth must matter regardless of its veracity. Myth derives its essence from elements extant in the society. It uses pieces of the cultural fabric to create meaning, and in so doing forms a construct that is shifting and changing until it no longer serves a purpose in its society. These smaller components, recognizable as Barthes' metalinguistic signifiers, are mythemes. Doty defines the mytheme as "an easily identifiable, small unit of a complex myth."[50] Chapter 1 delivers a list of key mythological elements, mythemes, that form the framework of superhero mythology. Other parts of mythology and how the superhero fits within the definition can be discussed easily, but the framework that allows us to identify the myth requires further exploration.

The superhero and cultural interactions with the character, genre, and surrounding constructions have strong connections with the variety of approaches to defining and applying mythology. Whether it is comics, film, television, novels, or online communications, the primary means for communicating the superhero myth is through stories. These can be full-length graphic novels, two-hour films, animated cartoons, or brief anecdotes shared in chat rooms and at comic shops and conventions. Furthermore, these stories are nearly exclusively about humans or humanoid-type characters. The vast majority of superheroes look very much like idealized humans. Even those who can shift their shape, like J'on J'onzz the Martian Manhunter, tend to adopt a more humanoid appearance. Even the non-human characters still tend to express themselves through human means and have very recognizable issues.

In *JLA: Heaven's Ladder*, written by Mark Waid with art by Bryan Hitch and Paul Neary, the Earth itself is literally hijacked and incorporated into a giant machine which forms a double helix. As the Justice League seeks to save the earth from its new place as part of a strand of cosmic DNA, they discover the creators of the machine are afraid of a very familiar thing. This highly advanced race fears death. They have gathered various worlds to try to learn about what comes after death. Their entire effort is the same as many here on earth, to find a peace regarding whatever may come after the current reality ceases. In the case of *Heaven's Ladder*, this alien race takes on human form only when it aids in communication. For most of the story they appear as comet-like blue or red lights. Despite this unusual appearance and their incredibly advanced technology, their fears are all too human.

The fact that these aliens still share our same problems seems significant. Perhaps we gain a sense of fitting in with the cosmos ourselves. Perhaps we gain confidence in humanity's ability to meet all comers because it is the very human Ray Palmer, the Atom, who establishes a working relationship with the aliens in *Heaven's Ladder*. Ultimately, the meaning drawn from this story is largely dependent on what the reader brings into it, despite any intended meaning on the part of Waid. And this is the case with many superhero stories. In fact, the very nature of superheroes seems tied to opening up an opportunity to create meaning via a collaborative effort between creators, artists, readers, fans, and producers. There is no doubt to those who share in the myth that superheroes have meaning, but what that meaning is can be difficult to define. There are certainly stories, especially of children, finding security and inspiration from superheroes. A significant example is that of a young boy who got separated from his parents at Comic-Con in 2011. He went up to a man dressed as the DC superhero the Flash because, according to reports, "he knows him."[51] The Flash cosplayer helped the boy connect with security and find his parents. The RLSH movement also certainly draws its inspiration from the superhero mythos. Whether they form a neighborhood watch in costumes, like the Black Monday Society in Salt Lake City, Utah, or focus their efforts on aiding the homeless, like Zetaman, these characters draw inspiration for their efforts, their language, their dress, and their directives from the shared mythology found in the superhero.

Tom Hiddleston, currently most known for his depiction of the supervillain Loki in both *Thor* and *The Avengers*, explains the appeal of the superhero myth:

> [S]uperhero films offer a shared, faithless, modern mythology, through which [...] truths can be explored. In our increasingly secular society, with so many disparate gods and different faiths, superhero films present a unique canvas upon which our shared hopes, dreams and apocalyptic nightmares can be projected and played out. Ancient societies had anthropomorphic gods: a huge pantheon expanding into centuries of dynastic drama; fathers and sons, martyred heroes, star-crossed lovers, the deaths of kings—stories that taught us of the danger of hubris and the primacy of humility. It's the everyday stuff of every man's life, and we love it. It sounds clichéd, but superheroes can be lonely, vain, arrogant and proud. Often they overcome these human frailties for the greater good. The possibility of redemption is right around the corner, but we have to earn it.[52]

Hiddleston focuses on film, and with good reason. The myth was created in the pages of comics but has exploded into the public consciousness through television and film. For our society, film and television have become the de facto medium through which our shared cultural consciousness is expressed.

In *The Meaning of Superhero Comic Books*, Terrence Wandtke suggests that so many people consider superheroes to be a type of mythology, which he explains is "something that naturally grows from the means by which stories are shared but that varies from culture to culture," because of the way superheroes interact with American society.[53] He explains that "the superhero seems to change and yet reactivates a supposedly transcendent mythic sensibility."[54] He pushes this further in his work, comparing superhero stories to pre-literate oral epics. As he works through the concept, he posits that superheroes are an exemplary part of what he terms "new traditionality," a term which Wandtke describes at one point as "a self-conscious love of variation," that has risen through the development of new media, specifically television and the internet.[55] Wandtke focuses primarily on the comic book as the medium through which the myth of the superhero was built. He admits to the import of television, radio and movies on the way the myth exists today, but for him the roots will always remain within the pages of graphic novels and comics.

Wandtke's new traditionality draws from studies of oral culture. He explains that the oral society functions in several ways that are different than literate societies. Citing Walter Ong, Wandtke expresses that oral cultures value

> (1) repetition rather than innovation, (2) aggregation rather than analysis, (3) participation rather than objectivity, (4) the situation rather than the abstract, and (5) addition to rather than advancement beyond existing ideas.[56]

Along with these points, he highlights the nature of orality to favor the most recent rendition of a myth over any sense of an original source. Simplistically, the oral tradition approaches storytelling and knowledge in ways that may seem at odds to a literate society. The "readers" in an oral culture expect to engage with and influence the story and the way it unfolds. They "turn outward to group thought rather than inward to individual thought."[57] The ideas of "fixity, originality, and primacy" that are more integral to literary culture tend to be used as the basis for arguing for literature as high culture and new forms of media less invested in these ideals—such as comic books—as low culture.[58] Because orality tends to be directly linked to pre-literate cultures, new media and other works that share commonalities with orality have been dubbed secondary orality. The primary difference between early and secondary orality is that the latter is more of an intentional choice, an orality of kind in a post-literate world. Whether they are aware of their efforts or not, creators of new orality in the media intentionally favor the sorts of storytelling associated with communal activity articulated by the points and approaches of oral societies.

Wandtke shifts the term from secondary orality to new traditionality largely due to the sort of reading required by comics in general. He proposes that though the term "oral literature" has been applied to the ability to read comics it is "awkward and confusing [in its] implications."[59] Furthermore, it and other terms that imply a literacy of any sort manifest a subconscious preference for the written text on a page over the image.

> Although the importance of each and their reliance upon one another will vary from one comic book work to another, [word and image] are inseparable within the medium; in fact, the coexistence/codependence of word and image in comic books is what usually forms the basis of the definitions that theorists use to distinguish comic books from other mediums.[60]

This cooperative dichotomy within comics, according to Wandtke, emphasizes the oral, new traditional nature of the comics. He argues that epics frequently contain extremely graphic descriptions of the visual. These descriptions serve "to close the gap between what is already said and what is later said."[61] The all-encompassing nature of visuality allows for, and encourages multiple meanings to coexist in a text, in a more immersive experience than tends to exist in literature. The term traditionality also allows for "greater critical specificity in a culture that uses literacy in ways that have little to do with the typical parameters of orality and literacy."[62]

Wandtke also argues that the visuality produced by oral cultures is similar in kind and function to superhero images. He proposes that traditional art is almost never simply for ornament or for functionality, but usually functions as both simultaneously. "The images [...] are almost always tied to a story that may be made clear in the course of the work but usually does not need to be" because the story is already encoded in the society.[63] Images will be exaggerated to call attention to pertinent details. They are frequently presented in sequence to indicate the development of a narrative. The images are also stylized, creating "visual clichés" or symbols for the culture.[64] All of this creates a visual that works with the story to invite participation in an already known cultural story. All of these elements are also readily apparent in superhero comic books, and by extension are common in film, book, and television manifestations of the mythology. "[S]uperhero comic books remain the best example of a resurgence of oral culture and the concomitant resurgence of traditionality in illustration."[65]

Regarding terminology, there are some who prefer the term *super hero* as two separate words. Super can frequently be use adjectivally to modify the noun hero. In this case, experience shows that society has no difficulty in using the term "super hero" as a descriptor of those who are frequently considered to be heroes who go above and beyond. In *Superhero: The Secret Origin of a Genre*, Peter Coogan suggests the following differentiation. "A super hero is a hero who is super or superior to other kinds of heroes (typically by virtue of physical abilities)" whereas superheroes are "the protagonists of superhero-genre narratives."[66] Thus, for Coogan, superheroes can only exist within the superhero genre. Any narrative outside of the genre would not include superheroes. By extension, the same could apply to superhero as myth. Any collective narrative that exists essentially outside of superhero mythology would not include superheroes as characters.

Generally, we can and frequently do apply the term "hero" to those who serve in the military, on police forces, and as paramedics and firefighters. For many, there are those within these professions who go above and beyond and should be considered more than heroes. For example, Medal of Honor recipients like the Spec 4 Leslie H. Sabo, Jr. On May 10, 1970, in Cambodia, Specialist Sabo charged an ambush of enemy combatants, killing several and drawing their fire from his platoon. In the same conflict, he charged a flanking force. When he needed to resupply his ammunition, he ran to the side of an exposed wounded comrade. "As he began to reload, an enemy grenade landed nearby. Sabo picked it up, threw it, and shielded his comrade with his own body, thus absorbing the brunt of the blast and saving his comrade's life." Though critically wounded, Sabo then crawled toward the enemy position and took them out with a grenade of his own.[67] Identifying people like Sabo as super heroes is not without merit, but to put them in the same category as Superman and Batman, utilizing the term superheroes, seems disingenuous. Superhero, as a single word, is largely unique to the genre. Though it has been used outside of the mythology, in scholarship surrounding this particular myth and genre that using the term superhero exclusively as a reference for the sorts of characters found fairly exclusively in the superhero genre will be of great benefit in making clear delineations between these and other heroes.

The following chapters articulate and explore the major and many of the minor tropes that serve as signifiers of the superhero mythology. From elements dealing with character development to relations and from origins to story arcs, these tropes are an integral and necessary part of understanding and locating the superhero myth in popular culture today. To exemplify the way these tropes articulate the existence of the mythos within a work, subsequent chapters will expound a tropological reading of a few different kinds of texts that share in the mythology of the superhero. Examinations will extend from the traditional superhero to the potentially superheroic character known as Buffy, she who slew vampires in the 1990s television series. Others that will be examined include a short-lived television series, *Alphas*, and the ancient Old English epic known by the name of the main character, the Geatish Beowulf. Ultimately, the focus of the work is in the list of mythemes, a lexicon that will help to establish a structure for examining the mythology of the superhero. In order to understand what this book is attempting to do, it is integral to understand that the myth of the superhero is only one level of myth that exists within the overarching concept of superheroes.

This framework is specifically and solely designed to examine the largest circle of mythology surrounding the superhero. On smaller levels, specific heroes have a mythology that has grown up around their character and compatriots. Batman, Superman, and Spider-Man all have individual mythos[68] that exist somewhat independent of their part of the larger mythology. Further, superhero teams like the X-Men, the Justice League, and the Green Lantern Corps frequently have an independent mythos. Significant companies dealing with superheroes also have a specific shared mythos. Marvel and DC both have a mythos that is divergent from each other. Image Comics has developed their own shared universe. All of these layers interact with each other in ways that create a flux in the shared mythology. This work attempts to move away from these individual, specific mythologies and to look at the largest circle of the myth that deals with superheroes.

The intention of this work is to foster a more carefully articulated discussion of the superhero while avoiding strong arguments for or against specific readings. Having an articulated, central, scholarly based collection of the tropes that make up the framework of this mythology is valuable in assessing both how far reaching the myth extends and what the elements contribute to the myth at its core. Others have given thought-out definitions of the character and the genre of the superhero, but there has been very little done with developing an understanding of the myth of the superhero as it has developed. The framework in this book will help to establish how superheroes are formed and why we sometimes recognize superheroes even when they don't wear tights. As we see mythemes from superhero mythology in characters and events around us, the mythology sometimes extends beyond the bounds of "canonical" superheroes. This work is to be a starting point in a new way of discussing the popular culture phenomenon of superheroes, why they matter, and how they function in our societies. The fact that new traditionality allows for fluid and ever-changing realities remains a challenge when we attempt to formalize a structure that recognizes the changes inherent in the myth without being so free of structure as to be completely invaluable.

This lexicon attempts to create a comprehensive structure by which we can discover, articulate, and discuss the myth of the superhero as it is found in modern, new traditional culture. Every other scholarly text written on the superhero seems to take for granted that certain tropes or mythemes are part of the superhero structure. Most studies focus on a small handful of tropes as sufficient to encompass the whole of the superhero. Other than the all-inclusive wiki found at tvtropes.org, there has been no effort to articulate the broader body of tropes of the superhero and what they might mean within the mythology. The lexicon at tvtropes.org is incredibly valuable in understanding the vast number of tropes associated with superheroes, in both general and specific ways. They include basic tropes like the Retcon (and the Cosmic Retcon) as well as beautifully named tropes like By the Power of Grayskull. Their exhaustive list was instrumental in creating the list of mythemes in this Introduction.

What follows is a lexicon which seeks to address a lack of focus on the key aspects of the construct of superhero mythology and, at the least, create a starting point from which a real discussion of the mythemes of superheroes and how they function both within and without of the superhero as a genre. In this lexicon, there is little to no effort to exclude characters, stories, or works from the mythology. The work approaches the idea of the superhero myth as potentially pervasive in ways similar to that of the literary trope of the messiah figure. The figure of the messianic character is referenced in as varied works as *Cool Hand Luke*, *The Matrix*, and *The Lord of the Rings*. While very few, if any, of these messianic characters are directly comparable to the Christian figure, they share in the myth in interesting and valuable ways. This book works in a comparable manner in regards to superhero mythology. Nobody is left out, yet, from engaging in the superhero myth. The weeding out of the non-superhero is something to engage with after the mythology has been established and discussed in context of the given tale. Even then, Peter Coogan admits that "ruling characters in or out of the superhero genre is a bit of a parlor game"[69] and the same frequently holds true for superhero mythology.

Working from the conceit that superhero mythology is unique in its own right, this work focuses on developing the parameters of that mythology. The main effort of this work is not to argue for or against any given interpretation of the superhero mythology, but to present in a way that has been absent from the discussion, a clear lexicon of the mythemes that give structure to the myth. Traditionally, mythemes are the smallest unit of a myth. They serve as the base unit of which all unified myths are comprised. As such, though not all individual stories share the mythemes presented herein, the terminology holds insofar that these base elements are the most fundamental elements identified to explicate the mythology. In the chapters that follow, significant components of the myth of the superhero will be identified and defined as they apply to the broader scope of the mythology. These mythemes, largely synonymous with the literary concept of tropes, form a scaffolding of sorts within which the stories that create the mythology function.

The term *trope* is used in the context of this book as roughly synonymous with mytheme, that of an archetype or device or character that is recognizable as part of generic or, in this case, mythological conventions. This is largely done to avoid redundancy in terminology and I recognize that there are other uses and meanings of the trope that bear no relation to the way the term is used in this work. The tropes vary in importance and value, but all serve to interact and create expectations in the minds of those who interact with the myth. The greater the quantity of mythemes, the stronger an individual story becomes tied in to the larger mythology. However, even a few tropes are frequently significant enough for those familiar with the mythology to draw connections to tales that function on the outskirts of the myth. These tropes also serve in helping identify new superheroic tales and to connect the mythology with its predecessors. The purpose of examining these mythemes without making an effort to completely circumscribe the myth is to allow these fringe stories to exist within the broader myth so that their interaction with the myth can be more clearly recognized and discussed. Frequently, it is at the fringes that we find the clearest commentary regarding what goes on at the core.

1

Building a Framework
The Lexicon of Superhero Mythology

In Peter Coogan's *Superhero: The Secret Origin of a Genre*, he goes to great lengths to articulate the superhero as a generic convention, including precursors to the superhero and why certain characters, like Buffy, fall outside of the genre. Coogan explains that "[c]onventions—particularly those of plot, setting, character, icon, and theme—combine to create genre."[1] These conventions "must be present for a specific story or character to be considered an example of the genre."[2] The key characteristics of the superhero genre are encompassed by "mission, powers, and identity [...] and provide the basis of [his] definition of the genre."[3] "The superhero's mission is prosocial and selfless, which means that his fight against evil must fit in with existing, professed mores of society and must not be intended to benefit or further his own agenda."[4] The powers of the superhero "are one of the most identifiable elements of the superhero genre" and tend to "emphasize the exaggeration inherent in the superhero genre."[5] For Coogan, "[t]he identity element comprises the codename and the costume, with the secret identity being a customary counterpart to the codename."[6] All of the aspects that create the superhero genre fit within these three conventions. Coogan explains that the character of the superhero cannot exist outside of the genre. The two are invariably intertwined. Because of this, characters like Buffy cannot be superheroes because they exist outside of the genre. However, there is connectivity between Buffy, Beowulf, and others like them and the superhero. Accordingly, the superhero mythology must be broader, allowing for mythemes to suggest that superheroic elements can and do exist outside of generic constraints.

Before the mythemes and their definitions and discussions are presented, a note on how they work within superhero mythology may be necessary. At the outset, though perhaps obvious, it is important to express that no superhero is going to be found in possession of all the mythemes of the superhero. The more tropes present, the more obvious the character and story will appear to fit within the myth of the superhero. In a way, these mythemes serve as a way of determining a character's or story's position on a target. The more mythemes there are present, the closer the narrative or image is to the center and more like the stereotype of the superhero. Fewer mythemes would push the character or story to the edges of the target, but still potentially engage with and be part of the superhero mythology. Coogan admits a similar system exists in genre switching characters, "A solar system can serve as a useful metaphor in thinking about genre switching characters [...] At the center of the genre system, the formula burns hottest and the gravity is strongest, keeping conventions and formula rigid [....] As one moves out to the gas giants, the genre shifts and the formula carries less influence [...] but the stories are still recognized as being within the genre."[7] However, there is less flexibility in the conventions of the genre than is ideal for connecting to the grand fabric of characters and concepts that have been connected to the superhero myth in various ways.

Granted, this reading is much more inclusive than exclusive, allowing for much more interaction between superheroes and those figures influenced by or that draw on the superhero genre. However, this wide-ranging approach is one necessary way of looking at superheroes in order to comprehend the way the mythology can and does inform popular culture. Furthermore, in the following lexicon, an attempt has been made to avoid too much in the way of analysis regarding *why* certain mythemes are more important than others or even what these mythemes might say about the superhero mythology and its role and commentary on our society. While this is a potentially valuable question, this book seeks to set up the framework of superhero mythology rather than to spend time discussing the import of the individual mythemes.

By way of demonstration, Superman, Batman and Wonder Woman form three points of an equilateral triangle that has its center at the exact center of the target. These three characters have been referenced by DC as the Trinity in comics since 1999.[8] This nomination is presented unironically, and the fact that this goes largely without comment in the culture invested in the superhero suggests how much the concept holds true for the general superhero mythology. In both 2002 and 2008 they were the subject of limited series, both using the term *trinity* as part of the title, which underscored their centrality in the DC universe. It is also significant that they are three of the most prevalent superheroes in print, all ranking in the longest running of comic book superheroes.[9] Among the three, practically all of the superhero tropes can be manifest with ease. However, to demonstrate this, we must be aware that the reading of these mythemes as applicable to any given character must recognize the entire corpus of stories that surround that member of the mythology. It is a rare story that will include in and of itself all of the tropes with any degree of success, even though we expect that they still maintain a presence in the background, the untold portions, of any given story. Thus, mythological readings cannot be too entrenched in any single narrative. As we move from the center, we will find more and more superheroes at first. However, as the circles expand, we would find stories such as Whedon's *Buffy the Vampire Slayer*, Gilgamesh, Beowulf, and even—perhaps at the very fringes—stories like Disney's live action film, *The Sorcerer's Apprentice* and the Harry Potter series.

Suggested to me by Bruce Haley, a Las Vegas building engineer,[10] Disney's *The Sorcerer's Apprentice* manifests the way the superhero mythos frequently transcends the bounds of traditional men in tights. The tropes mentioned in this example fall in line with the mythemes expanded upon and examined in this chapter. Here they are presented with minimal comment. In this reading, the heroes, Balthazar and later Dave, wear shoes and a ring that stand in for a costume. They're required for him to function adequately as a superhero and Dave's powers fail when he doesn't wear the outfit. We know nothing of his parents, effectively making him an orphan. The place where he works is an abandoned subway terminal, a place of safety and training which functions as his lair. He faces a huge threat from the central supervillain of the film, Horvath. There are several confrontations with villains, both major and minor, which always contain a strong element of violence. Because there are actually characters within the superhero mythos who claim sorcery as their superpowers—Dr. Strange is, after all, the sorcerer supreme according to Marvel mythology—it is no real stretch to discuss the hero's sorcery as a form of superpower. Dave seems to have been both born with inherent abilities with sorcery—fulfilling the born subtrope of the *powers* mytheme, but is also given a ring which enables him to use his powers—a hinting toward the thrust upon subtrope. In both cases, his otherworldly powers appear prior to puberty, but fail to truly manifest until after his teenage years. Furthermore, he has relationship troubles, both with a young woman and his mentor.

Though calling *The Sorcerer's Apprentice* an actual superhero story stretches the superhero genre to a point beyond legitimacy, our ability to read it as engaging with the mythology seems fairly apparent. In varying circles of the mythological target, stories like the SyFy series *Alphas*, ABC's short-lived series *No Ordinary Family*, and the also brief *The Cape* as well as *Heroes* all add to the complexity by pitching original characters in a way that at the least engages with the superhero mythology without an originary presence in the comics. I'm not suggesting that Harry Potter and other characters at the fringes of superhero mythology are or should be considered superheroes. To push superhero mythology that far is to minimize the validity of the mythology as its own unique force in popular culture, which is something that I cannot do. What is suggested is that there are many characters both in and out of the genre of the superhero who engage in the myth. If we fail to realize, recognize and pay attention to the outliers of the mythology, our scope becomes too narrow and we risk creating a paradigm that begins to serve no purpose in regards to cultural critique and awareness. To some extent, the structure of the mythology has to be able to support readings of characters in ways that still engage with the mythology, though not in obvious ways. At the core, certain elements are more integral to the mythology, especially in how they are expressed.

What follows is not a comprehensive list of all the tropes that can be applied to characters broadly encompassed by the superhero myth. It is a lexicon of the most universally applicable tropes, those most closely allied with the characteristics of the superhero. Though several are rarely found outside superhero mythology, some should be familiar to the broader scope of the basic heroic adventure, and some to storytelling in general—especially oral storytelling tradition. Indeed, superhero mythology owes a debt to all sorts of heroic narratives and shares many tropes in common. However, this commonality with sources outside the mythology does not change the import these mythemes have within the myth of the superhero.

Ageless

Though Superman has been wearing his trademark outfit for almost one hundred years, he still appears to be in his early thirties, the same age he was when he first leapt a building in a single bound. Apart from stories that take place in divergent *iterations*,[11] in which Superman has been presented at varying stages of age, the main continuity of the Superman myth maintains his age as a fairly constant thing. The television show *Smallville* should be considered an alternate *iteration* as far as the traditional Superman mythos is concerned. This series presents Clark Kent as a high schooler. Traditionally, Kent is somewhere in his late twenties or early thirties. However, and this is a challenge faced in new traditionality, for some people, their main exposure to Superman's mythology is through the WB show. This creates, for these individuals, a sort of alternate privileged iteration that complicates the idea of a dominant rendition. However, the scholarship of superhero mythology must be couched, at least primarily, in the privileged current form of the specific character, if one exists. At times, this is untenable as multiple iterations of the character exist with roughly equal dominance at the same time. These sorts of considerations become increasingly interesting as the mythology is introduced to different lenses of popular culture through different media.[12] Typically, film is the dominant media through which the myth is expressed in the current culture, however this has not always been, nor will it always be, the case. The proliferations of various storylines and means of access require that we be aware of the potential variety of coexisting starting points and mythological developments for popular society. Discussing this idea of elaboration of mythic developments, Doty posits, "At one moment the same mythological material may be 'heard' quite differently even by coequal members of the same society," resulting in a fragmentation of the central myth into various iterations and interpretations.[13]

This is especially true for long established characters like Batman, Superman, and the X-Men. Even the X-Men, who have gone through various team members at various ages still seems, at least in general, to have a fairly consistent age for the individual characters. Granted, to serve the purpose of individual stories within the mythology, characters can and do age. However, they nearly inevitably reset to a standard age for the character. For those who have been with the team from the beginning, a slow aging process has been manifest in a few of the *iterations*. However, considering there have been nearly twenty X-Men titles, the variation in age can be attributed to alternative continuities and divergent iterations as much as to any inconsistency in the mytheme. Generally, superheroes tend to stay within a decade of the same age. Spider-Man rarely manages to finish his post-high school education. Despite the amount of time he has been fighting crime, Batman tends to appear to remain in his early thirties. In fact, most superheroes tend to be of an age somewhere between puberty and middle age. This holds nearly constant throughout superheroes within the mythology. The passage of time has very little influence on superheroes. Certain characters do change their established age. Dick Grayson, the original Robin began his career as a consistently young teenager. He aged to his 20s when he became Nightwing, and now seems to be somewhere in his late 20s to mid-30s. For the time being, however, his aging has reached a plateau and very likely will remain there for many years.

A fascinating twist to this is the way Captain America has existed within the Marvel Universe. Because his origin became so closely tied with events of World War II, the willing suspension of disbelief by readers was more taxed, as he survived unaged and relatively unchanged throughout the decades. The term *willing suspension of disbelief* was coined in 1817 by Samuel Taylor Coleridge and can be explained as "the process whereby we consciously allow our imaginations to run free and accept as real what at first appears illogical or improbable."[14] In essence, it is that which—however briefly—allows us to accept the fictional reality of a story or mythology. This was especially relevant due to the fact that he was out of print for several years, making his relaunch into Marvel canon an important event to get right. Though he originally had contact with some of the other Marvel superheroes, because of his origin, Stan Lee and Jack Kirby felt it prudent to find a way to explain his lack of aging as well as his dormancy in the comics.[15] This need for an explanation resulted in the idea that Captain America was frozen in ice toward the end of World War II and was found and thawed out by the Avengers in 1964. Of course, since then, he has followed the standard of agelessness, remaining "to this day in the limbo of 25–30 years of age into which most adult superheroes settle."[16] "Yet Steve Rogers/Captain America has now remained 'frozen' in his late twenties for far longer than he was literally frozen in the ice. Clearly, intertextual and metatextual continuity create a subsidiary world in which the process of time can be kept under control."[17] However, the control attempted can be as much of an illusion as the superhero's apparent agelessness. Changes in convention will always occur as the story or myth necessitates adjustment.

Alter Ego

The myth of the superhero sees the superhero as the primary existence of the character. But most heroes have a secondary personality, a persona that exists outside of the primary persona that remains the focus of the mythology. When this alternate personality is kept secret from others, usually the public as a whole, it is known as a secret identity, a subtrope of the alter ego mytheme. Traditionally, the alter ego is also a secret identity, however, as the myth has evolved this has no longer become a requirement. When the hero has a secret identity, there are frequently one or more characters that feel the need to try to discover and reveal this identity and one or more characters given the responsibility of helping the hero maintain the secret. Though this has faded as a primary aspect of this mytheme, it still plays out from time to time, as demonstrated in *Spider-Man 2*, as Harry Osborne goes to great lengths to find the identity of Spider-Man.

Many characters that do not participate in a separation of the alter egos into distinctly different identities still use superhero codenames. The Fantastic Four were the original superhero team to avoid the idea of secret identities. In their first appearance, they even went without costumes. Despite the fact that they have codenames for each other, there was never any effort to hide that Reed Richards was Mr. Fantastic; Susan Storm, who later married Richards, was the Invisible Woman; Johnny Storm, Sue's brother, was the Human Torch, and Ben Grimm, the hardest to disguise, was the Thing. The most prevalent current example is most likely Tony Stark who is publicly known as Iron Man. Others include most of the X-Men: Scott Summers as Cyclops, Henry McCoy as Beast and so forth. In fact a great many Marvel characters have done away with the concept of keeping their alter ego secret. This change has gone so far that some superheroes have, within the last decade or two, become known simply by their name, dismissing any sort of superhero moniker almost completely. When Jean Grey appeared as one of the original X-Men, she was known as Marvel Girl. Though her codename status has been complicated by some retconning,[18] she was also known as Phoenix and Dark Phoenix for a time. However, recently in the X-Men films and frequently in the comics she is referred to simply as Jean Grey.

Even when the alter ego is known to the world, superheroes in general spend a fair amount of time in both their personas, depending on the needs of a specific story. However, for most superheroes there is a clear delineation between the superheroic ego and the "powered down" version of the character. In *The Avengers*, though Steve Rogers' identity is not a secret, at no point in the film does he exercise his superabilities without wearing his entire outfit, including his helmet. Furthermore, when he is not wearing the full uniform he manifests less confidence and leadership than when he is suited up. This is because, as Captain America, Rogers is a more confident individual, a battle-tested hero from World War II. Steve Rogers, however, is the man out of time, the man who is still adjusting to the strange new world. He is allowed to be less confident and on edge as he tries to adjust to his new surroundings in part because as Steve Rogers he is allowed to be more "human" than as the superhero Captain America. The difference between Rogers and Captain America is lessened quite a bit in *Captain America: The Winter Soldier*, however, he still manages to have his shield with him at any time he's acting as the Captain, and when he exposes Hydra to the agents working at SHIELD, calling them to action, he is back in his full uniform, the uniform he wore to fight Hydra in World War II. Thus, the costume, at the very least the shield, is a vital part of who he is as Captain America.

Frequently, there are physical manifestations of the difference between the personas. The most classic example is Christopher Reeve's portrayal of the dual nature of the Man of Steel and mild mannered Clark Kent in the 1978 *Superman* and its sequels. In the films, Reeve's Clark Kent slouches as he walks and speaks in a thready tone emanating largely from his nasal cavity. By contrast, Superman stands square-shouldered and has a deeper timbre to his voice that resonates more from the chest. In *Superman*, after Superman takes Lois Lane for a flight around Metropolis, he quickly swings around to her apartment door as Clark Kent. When Lane leaves the room briefly to get her coat, Reeve stops slouching, squares his shoulders, and removes his glasses. He starts talking to Lois before she enters the room, preparing to reveal his secret identity to her. At first, his voice is robust, the deeper "Superman" voice, "Lois, there's something I have to tell you. I'm really …" When she enters the room, he hesitates for a moment before changing his mind about revealing his secret. Quickly he starts slouching, returns the glasses to his face and begins stuttering through the next lines in the nasally, "Clark Kent" affectation, "Um, I-I mean, I was, uh, at first, really nervous about tonight, uh, but then I decided, well, darn it, I was gonna show you the time of your life." The obvious physical change as Reeve shifts from his portrayal of Kent to Superman is important, but this is underscored dramatically by Reeve's voice and the way he delivers his lines. He makes a clear distinction between Superman, the last survivor of Krypton, and Clark Kent from Smallville, Kansas.

The differentiation between divergent egos is exemplified as well by Christian Bale's performance in Nolan's *Batman Begins*. Bale contrasts Batman's gravelly growl and perpetual glower with an easy, devil-may-care nonchalance as Bruce Wayne. This aspect of the mytheme is perhaps more prevalent in film wherein voice and posture can be more clearly articulated, but the separation between these alter egos is pronounced in practically all formats and stories. In his discussion of the costume as part of the superhero, Richard Reynolds explains, "The authentic Iron Man requires the right man in the right armoured suit."[19] He then quotes a soliloquy from an issue of *Iron Man*:

> After all these years you'd think the whole world would've put two and two together … and pieced out my dual identity! [….] But then, why should most people even care? They've got other things on their minds … like the rising cost of living […] Why should Joe or Jane America care who … or what … is inside this metal suit … as long as Iron Man gets the job done? As long as I risk my life to bring them peace of mind?[20]

In his analysis of the artwork that accompanies Stark's words, Reynolds foregrounds the contrast between the robotic nature of the superhero and the human side of the alter ego. Significantly, the final panel of the series shows half of Stark's face, the other half obscured by the edge of the panel. Behind him, "[t]he shadowed profile is wholly sharp and robotic" in this case manifesting "the burden the heroic identity places on Stark."[21]

In *Superman II* and *Spider-Man 2*, both Clark Kent and Peter Parker find the burden of maintaining dual identities to be too much to bear. They both opt not to forgo their "normal" persona but to deny their heroic role in society in an effort to become a part of the world, attempting to excise the superheroic alter ego in an effort to find—in both cases—true love. However, as is always the case in the superhero mythology, the hero cannot be divorced long from the need he has to be two people: the normal non-powered individual and the superpowered alter ego. No matter how little a story arc may address the issue of alter egos, nearly every superhero will have and maintain at least a modicum of division between the two parts of his being.

Amazing Physique

Perhaps one of the most easily identified characteristics of the superhero is their physical appearance. Superheroes are, almost without exception, paragons of physical idealism. In fact, most characters that inhabit the superhero universe tend to be depicted in the form most ideal for the society. As much as the unique physicality is typical for both male and female superheroes, there are two distinct types of the physical ideal, almost exclusively delineated along lines of gender. For the male characters, the pectorals and biceps are well defined; generally the abdominal muscles form a classic washboard. The shoulders are wide and the waist is narrow. The legs are muscular and well defined. His hair is full and usually fairly conservatively cut. Most are clean-shaven and have a chiseled jaw. Essentially, the male superhero fits the ideal most who engage with the mythos expect in a man. In fact, the physical ideal of superheroes, both male and female, conforms to the general sense of hegemonic masculinity, that men are foremost in society and women exist in a subservient and less dominant role. For this reason, women tend to be depicted with narrow waists, large round breasts, and shapely legs. Less emphasis is generally placed on their musculature and more on their curvaceousness. In "Superheroes by Design," John Jennings explains, "The superhero is a symbol of power that is reified as the hyper-physical body, and that body then comes to be a visual representation of that power."[22]

The overt application of this exaggerated physique is manifest in Sam Raimi's *Spider-Man*. After he returns home from being bitten by the superspider, Peter Parker strips off his shirt to reveal a scrawny, pasty torso devoid of superheroic muscle mass. Shortly afterward, he crashes to the floor and falls asleep. When he wakes up, he stands before the mirror revealing a much more muscular frame. Even the skin is more toned, less pale than before.

When the superpowers develop, they almost by necessity bring with them the bulk expected of a superhero. This amazing physique has perhaps been most clearly manifest in the efforts of actors like Chris Evans, Hugh Jackman, and Chris Hemsworth. When they were preparing for their roles as Captain America, Wolverine, and Thor respectively, all three began a careful and exhausting diet and exercise regimen in order to develop a physique similar to that of the characters' appearance in comics. This has also led to all three appearing shirtless at least once in the films, a factor which will be developed in the discussion of the *androcentric* mytheme.

As much as the men in comics are an idealized presentation of fictional reality, the women are perhaps even more idealized and objectified. Female superheroes are expected to have slender waists, large breasts, well-styled hair, always wear heels[23] and still have enough strength to at least partially hold their own against much more muscular male counterparts without any real manifestation of the sort of muscle a woman would have to carry on her frame to be able to do so. This conceit is furthered by the rumors and discussion surrounding the casting of Wonder Woman in *Batman v Superman: Dawn of Justice* before Gal Gadot took the role. The women in superhero mythology also tend to be strangely adept at standing in provocative poses more suggestive of lingerie advertisements and men's magazines than for standing in heroic stances indicative of Superman and the male superhero. In truth, the physical ideal for women is vastly different than that of men. The Hawkeye Initiative tag on Tumblr[24] highlights the discrepancy between the two ideals by redrawing the Marvel character Hawkeye in the provocative poses in which women tend to be drawn in comics. There is also a recognition of this in the crossplay found at conventions where men who fail to fit standard ideals of fitness dress as various superheroines, ironically highlighting the unrealistic expectations of superheroes in general and female superheroes specifically. While the difference between the sexes is discussed more in analysis of the *androcentric* mytheme, it is necessary to delineate the two types of physical idealness postulated in superhero mythology. Again, for the man the ideal is that of a heroic, in control, powerful character. The woman is presented as an object to be gazed upon,[25] to be sexualized in an unrealistic and idealized manner. In any case, both male and female characters are expected to appear as an idealized physical being to be a part of the mythology.

Androcentric

In superhero mythology, the default position of the viewer is that of a heterosexual male. Though there has been some change over time, superheroes fairly consistently favor a male dominated worldview. *Violence*, the manifestation of the *amazing physique*, and various other tropes and story elements support the reading of the perceived viewer through the lens of the male gaze. While an effort has been made to avoid direct and overt application of theory due to the limited nature of the way this study presents these mythemes, the androcentricity of the superhero is best expressed through the development of the male gaze as postulated by Laura Mulvey in "Visual Pleasure and Narrative Cinema," first published in 1975. Her explanation posits that

> The [...] male gaze projects its fantasy onto the female figure, which is styled accordingly. In their traditional exhibitionist role women are simultaneously looked at and displayed, with their appearance coded for strong visual and erotic impact so that they can be said to connote *to-be-looked-at-ness*.[26]

She goes on to explain

> According to the principles of the ruling ideology and the psychical structures that back it up, the male figure cannot bear the burden of sexual objectification. Man is reluctant to gaze at his exhibitionist like. [....] A male movie star's glamorous characteristics are thus not those of the erotic object of the gaze, but those of the more perfect, more complete, more powerful ideal ego [....] The [male] character in the story can make things happen and control events [....] In contrast to woman as icon, [....] The male protagonist is free to command the stage, a stage of spatial illusion in which he articulates the look and creates the action.[27]

Mulvey suggests that the female is subject to the male gaze, but the male resists such objectification. The male gaze suggests that the female is there to be gazed upon whereas the male serves as wish fulfillment for the reader. While she applies this analysis exclusively to film, her critique applies equally well to superhero comics.

Especially clear in the works of some artists, the women of superhero mythology appear in the story largely to facilitate and suggest fulfillment of the desires of the masculine gaze. The early superheroine known as the Phantom Lady as well as a vast array of femme fatales from the long running *The Spirit* comics are early examples of the focus of the male gaze. The infamous Rob Liefeld was guilty of this, but his art generally defied logic in many ways. Others include Ed Benes, Frank Cho, Frank Miller, and—perhaps the king of this trope currently—J. Scott Campbell. From costume design to character design to the posing and positioning of the characters within the panels of comic books and any sort of graphic drawings, paintings and depictions, the female is the object of desire. In her FAQ regarding the male gaze on *Finally, a Feminism 101 Blog*, the author known as tekanji uses an example from the Frank Miller scripted *All Star Batman and Robin, the Boy Wonder*. In the script for the comic, Miller says, "OK, Jim, I'm shameless. Let's go with an

ASS SHOT. Panties detailed, Balloons from above. She's walking, restless as always. We can't take our eyes off her. Especially since she's got one fine ass."[28] While Miller is perhaps one of the worst in regard to sexist portrayals of female characters, consider the women in *Sin City* and *The Dark Knight Strikes Back*, his comment here exemplifies the predominance of the heterosexual male as the default viewer in superhero comics.

However, recent superhero films, namely *Captain America: The First Avenger* and *Thor*, seem to be a brief invitation to participate in a heterosexual female gaze. Though it has been suggested that this kind of invitation to look might be better typified as the gay male gaze, it is no less problematic than calling it the heterosexual female gaze. In truth, both the terms used referring to the gaze are rife with a privileging of a certain kind of viewer over others, a privileging which fails to recognize the complexity of human sexuality. The least problematic seems to be that which works in contrast with the established term, the male gaze. In any case, both these films have a scene that lingers erotically on the naked, well-muscled torsos of the hero. They are, if only briefly, presented from the perspective of the female gaze. In contrast to their hint of equality in regards to the gaze, both these films significantly reduce the proactivity of the female characters in the film. Specifically, the love interests, Peggy Carter and Jane Foster respectively, spend the majority of the films passively unengaged in the struggle between the protagonist and antagonist. Essentially, in these films that hint at a female gaze, the role of the women takes a regressive step away from allowing them proactive engagement with the central conflict of the film, ensuring masculinity remains secure for the male viewer.

Significantly, superhero films with stronger proactive superheroines such as *The Dark Knight Rises* and *The Avengers* severely downplay the potential of a "female gaze" in their films. Though Christian Bale, Chris Hemsworth, and Chris Evans all contain shots hinting at a female gaze in other films, no such shot is clearly manifest in subsequent films in which these actors portray superheroes.[29] Furthermore, both films also contain stronger female characters than were prevalent in the prior films that featured the characters portrayed by these actors. There seems to be a careful balance between allowing for stronger characters and allowing for the female gaze. If one is present, the other must not be. This fact strongly supports the androcentricity of the superhero.

Antagonistic Authority Figure

Throughout the adventures of the superhero, he frequently must engage with and work around many authority figures within his society. These authority figures can be military, political, or business leaders, but all tend to have significant influence regarding the sphere in which the superhero must function. They own the business wherein the superhero works, are a major political figure in the community wherein the superhero must function, or are part of a military organization tasked with bringing down or working with the hero. In some cases, they are an authority figure directly related to either the superhero's origin or the hero's alter ego. As opposed to the *cooperative authority figure*, the antagonist always works at odds to the efforts of the superhero. In many cases, the superhero is driven to work directly against this authority figure in order to achieve the goal of any specific story arc, sometimes even going to the point that he must take down the character opposing him in order to achieve his goal, though he is rarely completely successful.

In Sam Raimi's *Spider-Man II*, Peter Parker engages with several authority figures throughout the film. Ultimately, practically all of them work against him through one means or another. He works as a freelance photographer for J. Jonah Jamison, who has made it his life's work to discredit and eliminate Spider-Man. His professor, Curt Connors, comes down on him for lack of focus and threatens to fail him in the courses he is taking in college. Even when Connors becomes more friendly toward Parker as he begins to perform better in his school courses, those aware of Spider-Man's larger mythology know that Connors will later become another authority figure gone bad when an experiment turns him into the supervillain known as the Lizard. Connors' move from mentor to villain plays out in the more recent *The Amazing Spider-Man*. In *Spider-Man II*, Parker's friend, Harry Osborn, arranges a meeting with a visiting professor named Otto Octavius. It is significant that Octavius begins as a mentor and authority figure to Parker, working together to advance their ideas and research. They enjoy one scene together bouncing ideas back and forth regarding Octavius' research and a mutual love of science. Only after a tragic accident does Octavius become the sinister supervillain Doctor Octopus. The relationship between Parker and Octavius in the film is complicated by the relationship between Doc Ock and Spider-Man, a complication of which Parker is fully aware. Even the usher at a theater where Mary Jane Watson, Parker's romantic interest, is playing in *The Importance of Being Earnest* refuses to let him in because he arrives late. At every turn throughout the film, Parker is thwarted by those in authority around him.

The stress of trying to live his dual life, exacerbated by the antagonism that comes down from those in authority over him, is enough that Parker begins to lose his powers, manifesting the affect this mytheme can have within the mythology. Those in authority can be a great cause of conflict for the superhero in a variety of ways. Frequently, these figures exacerbate the sense of solitude, and ultimately individual strength, with which most superheroes struggle. Though the stress for Spider-Man and its resultant affect on his ability to *be* Spider-Man is more dramatic than usual in superhero mythology, the fact remains that those in authority who work at odds with the superhero's purpose will always be an issue with which the hero must contend. Frequently, the antagonistic authority figure will overtly or inadvertently work with the supervillain. In some cases, one character will perform both as the antagonistic authority figure and the supervillain. In general, there are frequent occasions when these characters are performing both mythemes in close relation to each other at the same time. However, whether the antagonistic authority figure is also the supervillain or not, this authority figure is a vital figure in the overall context of superhero mythology.

Chevron

Nearly every superhero or superhero team has a visual symbol, or chevron, by which they are represented.[30] Frequently, this symbol takes the form of a stylized letter or animal. At times, the chevron is little more than a simple image closely tied to the character. This image will almost inevitably reflect some of the personality and abilities of the superhero to which it is attached. In other cases, the image is a bit more abstract, perhaps a cluster of images, colors, tools, or associations. This type of iconic image is part of what draws readers to a character on a visual level. There tends to be a connection between the personality, the powers, and various other components of the superhero. The interrelation is an important aspect of the superhero and is detailed more fully in the final chapter of this book. However, some exploration of the chevron as it applies is worth consideration and exploration. This mytheme is less about story and more about the visual aspect of the character.

The Punisher represents himself with a white, stark image of a skull. The image reflects the fact that he is one of the few superheroes willing to kill without hesitation. This is a reflection of his personality, and even has connections to his origin. The Punisher, also known as Frank Castle, began his life in comics as a vigilante who started out by hunting down the mobsters responsible for the death of his family. Eventually he branched out and became a sort of gun for hire who has found himself working with and against nearly every member of the Marvel universe over the course of his career. The starkness of the image allows for him to be read as villain or anti-hero, but he will never be recognized as the true blue type. The symbol becomes a vital part of the superhero's individual mythos. A well-established chevron can transcend the stories of the superhero and is instantly recognized no matter the media. This level of superhero identification is frequently a part of the merchandise, the relics of the mythology, surrounding the superhero.

The clearest demonstration of superheroes that have developed the most complete level of iconicity is usually presented on t-shirts, lunch boxes, and other merchandise. Even when stylized, chevrons for characters like Batman, Superman, Captain America, Spider-Man, and even Wonder Woman are easily recognized by people who have no interest or much experience with superheroes or their stories in any fashion whatsoever.

Detailed in the entry on *costume*, in *Invincible*, the title character works with a costumer to design a suit as he embarks on his career as a superhero. The costumer insists that he come up with a codename for himself before they can design the costume. After he settles on a codename, the costumer develops a costume that includes a stylized "i" incorporated into the design that becomes an image associated with him throughout the series. In the case of Invincible, the "i" on his uniform closely parallels a similar device used by Image Comics, the company that produces Invincible. Thus, Invincible's chevron, as much as it's presented, mirrors the iconic images associated with Image Comics, the company that produces the comics wherein the character's mythology is being developed. This level of interrelativity is uncommon but does make an interesting example of the chevron in the mythology of a specific superhero. However, Invincible's chevron is in some ways similar to others' in that it is partially about "feel" and a bit less about the actual visual itself. He doesn't have the sort of image that can be lifted from his costume, like Superman does, but he has a signature look. This look may develop into an image as iconic as the S on the chest of the Man of Steel, but they iconicity of the look is further complicated by the fact that Invincible's costume has gone through several variations in a much shorter time than that of Superman. In whatever form it takes, the vast majority of the superheroes will have an iconic visual image that is integral to the way they are perceived.

The character's chevron may not be simple, complicating this particular mytheme, but even superheroes that don't use this device can still have an iconicity to them, even those of questionable relation to the myth of the superhero. Swamp Thing, for example, has a vine-like protrusion above his nose and down the sides of his mouth, giving his face a very distinct look that is instantly recognizable to those who have experience with the mythology. This iconicity is vital enough that changes to it can be problematic, even dangerous. John Constantine[31] was originally designed to be a chain-smoking occultist who looked like the singer/songwriter Sting. He was snarky and sarcastic with light blonde hair.[32] When the film version of the comic, titled *Constantine*, went into production, the title character was played by Keanu Reeves, a long faced, dark haired, morose looking actor. The original character had a sharp British accent, but Reeves played the character as an American. Though the film had other issues, one of the challenges was the break in the strong iconicity of the central character. In some ways, such a change in a character's iconicity as radical as that made by the film fragments the myth of the character creating an alternate version that doesn't always feel connected to the originary mythology.

This level of iconicity is also presented by the fact that an easily recognizable synonym for a person's weakness is kryptonite. The only people in all of fiction who are influenced by actual kryptonite are those from the planet Krypton, most notably the Man of Steel himself, Superman. However, the idea of kryptonite has infused our society to the point that nearly everyone knows what it means. While not specifically about the chevron of the superhero, the idea of the iconic imagery of the mythology is also worth consideration as a part of this visual element of the superhero. Strong superheroes nearly inevitably develop some sort of chevron, from the X-Men's X to Spider-Man's spider to the Green Lantern's stylized lines and circle lantern. A superhero can be iconic without a clearly specified chevron, but those near the center of the myth will nearly always be able to mark their position with their own iconic symbol.

Codename

While it may go without saying that any fictional character's name is important and frequently comes with symbolic significance, superheroes make this significance overt through the choice they make in the name they use when acting as a superhero. The name used by the character can be significant in terms of *spectacular origin*, *costume*, and/or the *chevron* and signifies their character usually in significant ways. Thus, both Captain America and Superman are seen as moralistic characters that believe in "truth, justice, and [sometimes] the American way."[33] Superman's codename is perhaps the most literal, tied to the Nietzschean idea of the *Ubermensch*, but most superheroes have codenames that say something specific about them to purveyors of the mythology. When Steve Rogers loses faith in the government of the United States, he relinquishes the title of Captain America, going by Nomad and at a later break with the government The Captain.

Ant-Man has shrinking abilities and can communicate with ants. Rarely, as Ant-Man, does the idea of growing to gigantic proportions become part of the conversation. This is true for Hank Pym, Scott Lang and others. When Hank Pym does use the same technology to grow larger than normal, his codename adjusts accordingly, to Giant-Man or Goliath. Thus, the codename is not inherently connected to a specific person, but it does seem to require a reflection of the character in some significant way, usually relating to the *power* of the codename's user. The codename is a necessary part of establishing the identity of the superhero.

A lesser-known superhero perhaps epitomizes the way codenames matter in the mythology of the superhero. Robbie Baldwin spent the majority of his career as a superhero going by the codename Speedball. Speedball's kinetic energy combines with a flamboyant personality to make him a vibrant part of the New Warriors in Marvel Comics. However, shortly after his involvement in the cataclysmic event that set off the Civil War storyline, Baldwin's powers and personality changed. His powers became more internalized and explosive and could only be activated when he felt pain. He adopted a new suit lined with spikes on the interior and changed his codename to Penance. The change is mirrored in his personality as well. However, over time he has reverted back to his original abilities and personality and the codename shifted once again to reflect who he is as a character.

A suit and personality shift don't always require a change in codename, but the change is usually designed to be significant in some way. The many variations on Peter Parker's Spider-Man costume tend to go without a change in his codename, including his time in the symbiote suit. However, when Parker uses the suit created for him by Tony Stark, he is frequently referred to as the Iron Spider, a sort of nickname codename that links the suit back to the creator as well as to the wearer. In the Civil War storyline, the suit and nickname become significant in Parker's relationship to the factions. When he works with Stark, he wears the Iron Spider suit. However, when he has a change of heart and breaks with Stark he has to get rid of the costume to avoid the technology Stark built into it. For most of his career in the comics, Parker has changed costumes without changing codenames. When that changes, it has significant impact on the story being told, and he shortly reverts to maintaining a consistent codename throughout, both in film and comics, despite other changes the character faces.

Different characters react with their codenames in different ways. Some go back and forth between using codenames or not. Some switch codenames with dizzying frequency. Others have consistently used a codename, or gone without for years. Regardless of the specifics of a characters association to the codename, it is a vital mytheme in the character and mythology of the superhero.

Cooperative Authority Figure

In direct contrast to the *antagonistic authority figure*, the cooperative figure is in a position of power, whether it be political, governmental, business, or military, to help the superhero in his efforts. This character, whether willingly or no, finds himself working with the superhero to bring about the goals of the hero. Of all the characters in the superhero mythos, Commissioner Gordon from Batman mythology perhaps best exemplifies this mytheme. No matter the incarnation, from the Batman television serial of the 60s, to Nolan's Batman trilogy, James Gordon always works with the Caped Crusader in his quest for justice. Though in *Batman: Year One* Gordon is less excited about working with the vigilante, he quickly learns that working with the Dark Knight is the best way to accomplish their shared goal of bringing justice to Gotham city.

Authority figures can work with superheroes in other ways. In fact, the President of the United States has made frequent appearances in comics. President Barack Obama shares a fist-bump with Spider-Man in *The Amazing Spider-Man* #583. In the 1992 death of Superman storyline, President and First Lady Clinton were part of the funeral proceedings for the Man of Steel.[34] However, this is not necessarily a recent phenomenon. Before the United States entered World War II, Franklin D. Roosevelt ordered clandestine efforts to fight the Nazis in Timely Comics.[35] These included the creation of a series of mechanical men and Project Rebirth, which resulted in the creation of Captain America.[36] The most interesting, however, may be the appearance of President John F. Kennedy. In *Action Comics* #309, JFK serves as a stand in for Clark Kent, prompting Superman to remark to the president, "I knew I wasn't risking my secret identity with you! After all, if I can't trust the President of the United States, who can I trust?" Unfortunately, the issue hit newsstands the week after the assassination, putting a very unpleasant spin on the story. By that time, there was no way to recall the story, so it remained on the shelves despite the death of the president.[37]

As much as the cameos by real authority figures are an interesting interaction of the real world with the superhero myth, the general state of the myth includes fictional authority figures working with the superhero to make his efforts run more smoothly. Again, Commissioner James Gordon from the Batman mythology is perhaps the epitome of this mytheme, so much so that tvtropes.org has named this trope after the head of Gotham's police force. It is very common for the character that fulfills this mytheme to cross over into the role of father figure for the rest of the characters involved. Professor Charles Xavier of the X-Men is a prime example of this sort of supportive, fatherly authority figure. As the lead figure and namesake for Xavier's School for Gifted Children, Professor X serves as headmaster and mentor for both the students and the team. Though Cyclops is the recognized leader of the team, Professor X has a role as the authority figure to which all of the team must eventually answer, regardless of their roles out in the field.

A scene from the 2003 *X2: X-Men United* serves to illustrate the role Xavier plays as the friendly, cooperative figure of authority. When Logan returns to the mansion, he meets with the Professor in Cerebro. As he enters, he is still smoking one of his trademark cigars. Professor X remarks, "Logan, my tolerance for your smoking in the mansion notwithstanding, continue smoking that in here and you will spend the rest of your days under the belief that you are a six year old girl." When Logan questions his sincerity, he replies, "I'd have Jean braid your hair. Welcome back."[38] The humor in the rebuke by no means lessens the Professor's need to be respected, but helps to indicate affection for even the roughest of his charges. It also underscores the way that the *cooperative authority figure* frequently also ties into the mytheme *please the father*.

Costume

Though not quite as universal as some may think, the superhero costume is an integral part of the mythos. "Costume functions as the crucial sign of super-heroism [....] The appearance of a costumed character in a story will generate a specific set of expectations—a state of affairs which the writer can work with or against, but which cannot be left wholly out of account."[39] A much more involved explanation of the costume as an integral part of the definition of the superhero is included in Coogan's *The Secret Origins of a Genre*. The costume nearly always includes the superhero's *chevron* integrated into the design. Significantly, each superhero generally has a distinct costume. Unless the superhero derives his primary identification as the member of a superhero team, as in the case of several of the X-Men, his costume will be significantly unique to him. In cases where he derives his identity from association from another character, it is possible for the costumes to bear obvious similarities to the parent costume, but the overall design will be his own. When Dick Grayson decided to become a new superhero, his first costume shows the influence of both Batman and Superman, the characters most responsible for his formation as a character. Grayson even takes his new codename from that used by Superman in Kandor.[40] It, and later costumes, consist of dark colors and the second iteration included utility pouches similar to the Dark Knight's that have remained consistent in subsequent redesigns. However, Nightwing's pouches are strapped at his calves and forearms rather than on a belt around his waist.

Emblematic of this mytheme is the origin story from *Invincible*. *Invincible* is a slightly irreverent take on the superhero genre. It deconstructs the superhero mythology while at the same time celebrating it. Because of the nature of the story, it is a good storyline for examining the superhero mythemes and breezily employs practically every mytheme involved in the structure of the mythology. After the protagonist of the story, Mark Grayson, develops superpowers, he visits a tailor who specializes in superhero costumes. During their discussion, the tailor admits,

> Everyone wants iconic costumes but no one knows what that means. Look, iconic is a little tricky to do, but [...] I'll give it a shot, but I'm going to need to know what your name is going to be, that helps [....] see if you can come up with a few good ones before you come back here. Then we'll see if I can't whip up something more iconic based on the name.[41]

Once Mark settles on Invincible, the tailor creates a blue and black suit with splashes of yellow that form an "i" on his torso and head. Mark settles on the codename based on a chance comment from his principal, but it has a strong connection to his abilities. The discussion of a superhero character construct in the final chapter presents more information regarding the interrelation of origin, powers, purpose, codename, costume and chevron within superhero mythology. The costume itself is emblematic only in the way its stylized letter represents Invincible's codename. However, the solid blocks of color that make up the costume also give the reader a hint regarding the kind of superhero mythology in which Invincible takes place. Bright yellows and blues relate closely to the simpler primary colors of the golden age, but the black elements help to modernize and give a mild sense of gravitas which collates well with the moments of severity within the work.

One of the challenges of this mytheme is determining what exactly constitutes enough of an iconic image to qualify as a costume. There is an argument that Wolverine's hair and claws have become so clearly identifiable with his image that they, in and of themselves, constitute an entire costume. However, he frequently wears the more traditional yellow and blue tights—or the black leather of the films and some iterations of the comics X-Men—that epitomize his more traditional superhero costume. The confluence of costume and chevron may be *the* determining factor in identifying the superhero as opposed to a character that simply engages in the mythology. At times Wolverine and others have moved further from the center of the mythology simply due to a more relaxed and civilian attitude in their dress.

Reynolds notes, "Non-costumed characters aren't involved in the hierarchy" of superhero powers.[42] No matter how important Commissioner Gordon may be to the Batman mythos, his prowess in superhero combat is practically speaking not only unrated but unimportant in large part for the simple fact that his tan trench coat, glasses and mustache are insufficient to qualify as a superheroic costume. Another aspect of the superhero costume is the way it ties in to the *androcentric* nature of the mythos. There is typically a fairly drastic difference between the costumes worn by male superheroes and those worn by their female counterparts. "Superheroines tend to reveal a lot more bare flesh than their male colleagues, but costume color and other details vary across the board for both sexes."[43] Nightwing and Huntress work with Batman and have some similarities in their costumes. However, Nightwing's second and subsequent costumes cover his entire body besides his head. Huntress' costume tends to frequently reveal her legs and has a panel missing from the torso, baring her midriff. There is no rationale in the comics for her revealing attire, and the difference underscores the *androcentric* mytheme of the mythology.

The superhero costume as been much derided in the past for the so-called "underwear on the outside" style. The alternating color surrounding the crotch and buttocks of the superhero is most prevalent among men and dates all the way back to Superman and his first appearance in Action Comics. Over the years this style has become less and less prevalent, so far so that Superman goes without the red briefs in *Man of Steel* and the change was met with limited resistance by the superhero community. The new 52 designs also eliminated this style for iconic characters like Superman and Batman. However, the origin of this design element is emblematic of some of the ideals behind Superman and to some extent superheroes in general. When Siegel and Shuster were designing Superman, it was during the heyday of the three-ring circus. Included in the classic elements of the circus was a strongman act, a man capable of bending steel bars, lifting horses, and other feats of nigh impossible strength. The slightly unnatural nature of the circus combined with the incredible strength of the circus strongman seems to resonate through comics to this day. The typical strongman costume was a leotard worn underneath a pair of briefs or occasionally a caveman singlet. When the duo behind the Man of Steel designed their signature character, they intentionally drew on this costume motif in the look of the costume of the original superhero, a look that has perpetuated as a part of costume design for decades.

Death Is Temporary

In the opening of his work "Save the Day," A. David Lewis references a tagline for the *Final Crisis* story arc for DC comics. He explains that *"heroes die, but legends live forever*—that is, heroes *can* die, but there is a class above the hero, that of the legendary *super*hero, whose members can bypass permanent death."[44] Though Lewis mentions later that those around the superhero can face the permanence of death, Ben Parker, and Thomas and Martha Wayne, for example, superheroes rarely, if ever, stay dead for long. Thus, mortality can threaten the superhero, but not directly.[45] The inability of superheroes to stay dead is one of the mythemes that is frequently derided. Any character that exists as a major part of the superhero mythology, no matter how he is killed or what efforts are taken to attempt to keep him dead, will eventually be brought back to life. Perhaps the most famous literary example of this trope is from a character many proclaim to be a forerunner of the superhero. Sherlock Holmes was originally killed off because Sir Arthur Conan Doyle was tired of writing about him. However, the public outcry was sufficient for Conan Doyle to be pressured into bringing back the character and continuing his adventures. Holmes' incredible detective skills are certainly part of the inspiration for Batman's own abilities and the death of Sherlock ripples through this trope and the superheroes that must deal therewith. From Superman and Batman to Captain America and Jean Grey, superheroes die and are brought back to life with a frequency that can be disturbing to the casual reader. Sometimes this resurrection can take years to come about, but so very many superheroes after tasting of death will find themselves brought back to the land of the living.

In the case of Superman, when he was killed it made national headlines. Taking place in 1992, the death of Superman was perhaps the first major character death in the superhero mythos. The event was such an event that President and First Lady Clinton were depicted at his funeral and even spoke at the memorial. In a knock down, drag out fight with the monstrous Doomsday, Superman is eventually beaten to death, killed at the same instance that he kills the alien creature. The event of his death was conceptualized with the intent of resurrecting Superman as part of the storyline. Even before the funeral is over, the body of the Man of Steel is removed from its supposed final resting place. Shortly after his body disappears, four men appear claiming to be directly or inspirationally related to Superman. Eventually, the Man of Steel returns from the dead and takes over the protection of Metropolis and the cosmos. The four who preceded his resurrection become either his partners in conflict or antagonists. Thus, his resurrection becomes a major event in the overarching mythology of the character. The death itself made headlines in the United States and was a major boost in the sales of Superman related comics and merchandise,[46] including a black armband matching that worn by the pantheon of DC's superheroes.

Superman's death and rebirth led the way for many other characters in the DC universe in their return to life after they died. It seemed to have been an inspirational moment for Marvel characters as well. Indeed, many of the major superheroes have gone through this process. Spider-Man, Bucky Barnes who was Captain America's sidekick during World War II, and Jason Todd who served as the second Robin have also come back from the dead. Captain America's death and rebirth also made headlines in the United States. As in the case with Superman, the death of a superhero can, and sometimes does, coincide with a boost in sales for that hero's titles, especially when the event comes as part of a larger overarching story line.

However, rather than being simply a cheap trick to boost sales—though it has been used specifically if not admittedly for that purpose from time to time, and that is always at least a secondary intent—the death and rebirth of the hero is one of the mythemes that figures well within the new traditionality and mythological nature of superheroes. Writing in response to the 2011 death of the Fantastic Four's Human Torch, Bob Gough explains, "all that matters for fans who have been through so many of these dramatic demises [...] is the story. Is it a good death? Do the other characters react well? [...] What are the collateral consequences [...]? How about the resurrection? Is it handled well?" Ultimately, those engaged with the myth care about these characters enough to overlook the minor inconveniences and inconsistencies of death and rebirth. As is the case with *iterations*, the logistics of making all the narratives within a specific character myth coherent and consistent are subservient to experiencing the stories surrounding that character.

Expository Narration

It still happens that there are passages, especially in the comics, where the words explain the situation more than the images. Usually designed to invoke a sense of the epic, these passages tend to be florid and either immersive or over the top. One recognized form of this mytheme rests almost entirely on the supervillain. The long, drawn out monologue in which the villain lays out his entire plan is not unique to the superhero genre, but it was practically perfected in the pages of superhero comics and radio shows. This trope is parodied in *The Incredibles*. In a stand off against Mr. Incredible, the villain known as Syndrome begins to exposit on his plans for the behemoth of a robot he has constructed. He drones on for several minutes until Mr. Incredible eventually throws a log at Syndrome, interrupting his rant. At this point, Syndrome exclaims, "You sly dog. You got me monologuing."[47] *The Incredibles* gently deconstructs and satirizes the tropes of superhero mythology and the recognition by Syndrome of this trope manifests its presence within the mythology almost single-handedly.

Perhaps the most recognized form of exposition, and the one which is an integral part in the development of the superhero myth, is the internal monologue. This trope had its beginnings early on in superhero comics. As the stories unfolded, it was incredibly common for the superhero to articulate what he was attempting to do and why as he was making the effort, a halfway breaking of the fourth wall without directly addressing the readership. Almost without fail, the why—the rationale of the superhero for his actions—had something to do with thwarting the end of the world or saving a damsel in distress. However, as with some of the other mythemes, the interior monologue has mutated into something different. It became a way for the artist to engage the reader in an epic fight scene while the writer would be able to give the reader some vital piece of character development or plot information at the same time. Not unlike the asides in Shakespeare's plays, these internal monologues are a weakening of the fourth wall so that vital information or scene development can be presented to the reader in a less stilted manner than huge blocks of text on the page.

However, the monologue can still devolve into the ridiculous, as demonstrated by Joss Whedon and John Cassaday in *Astonishing X-Men*. As Colossus leaps into battle he comments on the fact that, instead of Professor X calling the shots, he hears the voice of Cyclops in his head, but he realizes that he "really should concentrate." Beginning in the next panel, Shadowcat is shown protecting civilians from the cataclysm caused by the beast. As she does so, she reflects on her efforts to spark a relationship with Colossus, Before she too recognizes that she "should probably concentrate here." At which point she returns to focusing on the conflict at hand. Colossus' inner monologue takes place over the course of three panels. Shadow Cat's stretches across five. The next series is a four panel layout of Wolverine fighting the monster. As he fights, we are granted an insight into his inner monologue during combat. The first three panels are entirely devoid of commentary. In the final panel of the series, he thinks, "I really like beer."[48] Whedon and Cassaday intentionally create a gentle parody of the trope. Both Colossus and Shadow Cat begin to degrade the believability of the mytheme in the way it's used and Wolverine's internal monologue sells the point. It is perhaps because of this underlying ridiculous nature that this trope is rarely seen in television and film.

However, the mytheme is used to good effect in *Hawkeye: My Life as a Weapon*. Written by David Fraction and drawn by David Aja, the first collected volume of Marvel's relaunch of Clint Barton's solo series makes extensive use of expository narration as Barton thinks through the events he faces. Four of the five individual issues begin with Barton admitting, "This looks bad." His exposition then helps to explain the series of events that lead to the moment when he restates his opening comment. Again, the mytheme is used for comic effect, but there are moments where it helps to bring the reader into the events of the story. Specifically, in an apparently unimportant moment, Barton takes aim at a target. Kate Bishop, also known as Hawkeye, talks with Barton while he draws back. A series of panels depict her face as though in stop motion, her words drawn out in the gutter beneath the panels. Barton's internal monologue recites the practiced moves, "The wire tenses. Back muscles tighten and lock. Slow your breathing. Exhale—relax your hand—" The arrows fly true into his target.[49] Though it appears to be an innocuous moment, and unimportant to the story as a whole, it adds a depth to the tale.

Later, in the same issue, Barton and Bishop are in the middle of a quick and unplanned exit from a circus cum robbery, headed by the ringmaster Domitian. After jumping out of a window into a pool, Barton watches as the younger Hawkeye takes aim. "The wire tenses. Her back muscles tighten and lock. She slows her breathing ... exhales.... And just as she relaxes her hand—" Bishop says, "Suck it, Domitian." Barton's narration starts in again, "See? She's perfect." The parallel between the two events shows the connection Barton feels to his superhero namesake. The connection between the two becomes an interesting element to the stories that follow.[50] The narration, then, becomes a part of establishing key parts of the storyline for the reader.

Of all the mythemes listed here, this is perhaps the one most relegated to a single form of media. Interestingly, however, this mytheme does make a comeback in the television series *Arrow*. The series is a reimagining of the character of the Green Arrow from the DC universe. Drawing on the success of the gritty Batman framework from Christopher Nolan's *Dark Knight* trilogy, *Arrow* places Oliver Queen into a central role as a disturbed vigilante masquerading as a rich playboy. Throughout the pilot episode, Queen reveals his inner thoughts through voiceover narration very like that employed in comics in order to explain his deep-seated motivation, or at least his goals for taking down some of the major players within the city where he returns after being stranded on an island for several years. Though the series seems to be playing this mytheme sincerely, the pilot gives no overt nod to satire, its presence in the pilot episode certainly helps to tip the tone toward the melodramatic, underscoring a sense that this trope has not aged as well as others within the mythology. Expository narration is continued in the *Arrow* spinoff *The Flash*. The same introductory narrative plays out through the first season.

Helper

At some point in the history of most superheroes, almost every single one has taken on people who help him in his efforts to fight crime. Though a hero's helpers can be diverse, consider Batman's supporting cast, the sidekick is a subtrope for characters who are almost always someone in their teens and usually shares the same gender as the main hero. They frequently look to the hero as a mentor and father figure. Commonly, they are used to give contrast and color to the superhero with whom they work. With rare exceptions, the sidekick brings a lighter tone to the stories and character of the main hero. The epitome of the sidekick is the Boy Wonder who works with Batman, the acrobat/sleuth Robin. In Batman's canonical mythology, there have been four boys who have worn the red, green, and yellow of Robin and, ever so briefly, Stephanie Brown. In alternate continuities, this role plays out in various ways, including the self-appointed Robin of *The Dark Knight Returns*, Carrie Kelley. However, the helper covers a great deal more ground than just the sidekick.

In many cases, the superhero has a character in his life who serves as a confidant, a sort of best friend. This is frequently a character who doesn't necessarily know the superhero's secrets, but is someone the hero feels he can trust. This character may be the confidant, the friend, the workmate of the superhero or his alter ego, but most commonly this character is described as the pal in the superhero mythos. Very simplistically, a pal is almost always a sidekick without superpowers or a character who doesn't get involved in the superhero's heroics. In the early years of the Superman comics, Jimmy Olsen became the epitome of the pal. He has served in that role to Clark Kent for decades. Granted, the pal has waned in popularity as the myth has evolved. Originally, the pal was a non-powered confidant who has no authority, but worked with the superhero and tended to be privy to his secrets. In more modern renditions of the myth, it is not uncommon for a sidekick to fulfill the tropological role of the pal.

As the superhero myth has evolved, many characters who began as helpers or sidekicks have also evolved into superheroes in their own right. Again, Robin leads out in this regard. The original Robin, Richard Grayson, became Nightwing. The second Robin became the Red Hood, a problematic character who has been both hero and villain. The third Robin now calls himself Red Robin. In *Captain America: Winter Soldier*, Sam Wilson starts out as a helper who shortly becomes Falcon, a superhero in his own right. Others have taken similar paths to superhero status, but with less aplomb.

In times past, the sidekick was a larger part of the trope, though it is still a vital and recognizable part of the myth. It has been satirized and lampooned and still makes its presence known in traditional stories of the superhero. It was a vital development in the mythology and its resonance is still felt within the myth of the superhero. Now it is more common for the helper to share characters with the *cooperative authority figure* or assistants like Pepper Potts. The helper can also become part of the team, as is the case with Falcon or Jarvis' conversion into the Vision. Whatever the form, the helper serves as a point of support and grounding for the hero.

Ineffective Against Real World Problems

As amazing as superheroes are within their own realities, the fact still remains that they are relatively ineffective when it comes to dealing with problems outside of the supernatural challenges they face as superheroes. As advanced as Tony Stark's technology may be, he is incapable of designing a clean energy system that solves pollution and the energy crisis for the world within the stories he inhabits. Superman is also ineffective against major issues like world hunger and poverty. Storm, the X-Men weather controller, does work to the advantage of the people she rules for a time in Africa. However, during her adventures with the X-Men, her powers and the way they influence the lives of her people in Africa are rarely if ever a part of the focus of the story.

This trope is especially notable in the case of the super-geniuses like those of the Marvel Universe. Dr. Victor von Doom, Dr. Reed Richards, Dr. Bruce Banner, Tony Stark, Dr. Hank Pym, Dr. Henry McCoy, Professor Charles Xavier, all men of stunning intellect who seem incapable of finding a solution to major crises like poverty, starvation, and pollution. All have access to technology that seems to epitomize Arthur C. Clarke's famous argument, "Any sufficiently advanced technology is indistinguishable from magic." Of course, this tends to be true of superhero technology in general. Even much of Batman's gadgets, designed for a character who tends to be closer to realism than many superheroes, tend to push beyond the edges of what is considered technologically feasible. They are capable of outwitting the planet eating Galacticus, but cannot seem to bring their mighty intellects effectively to bear on the problems of the real world.

Several DC supervillains directly challenge the heroes' lack of engagement in real-world problems in *Justice* by Jim Krueger and Alex Ross. Dr. Crane, the villain known as the Scarecrow, cures paralysis. Dr. Cold creates an artificial lake in the middle of the desert. Poison Ivy brings food bearing vines to hungry populations. Another villain named the Toyman creates artificial limbs for amputees. After all these villains work to solve many real-world problems, Lex Luthor, Black Manta, and Poison Ivy appear across the globe in a speech explaining their value and the failings of the superheroes. They state that superheroes have

> never attempted to use their powers and abilities to make this world a better place. [...] Sure the Justice League may save us all from a giant alien starfish in the middle of the ocean from time to time. But they save us only to send us back to our old lives. [...] If they were really the heroes they claim to be, they'd save us from those same lives as well.[51]

In this story the villains actually step in to do what superheroes find themselves unable to do. Their actions show the potential within the powers of these superhuman beings to step in and help cure very real problems that exist in both the fictional superhero world and the real world.

Elliot Maggin, Curt Swan and Murphy Anderson approached this question through the Man of Steel in "Must There Be a Superman?" In the story, while visiting the Guardians of the Universe, Superman is told that he may be responsible for a "cultural lag" on Earth. He is shown a speech he gave on another planet he visited. He explains to the planet's denizens that "I will restore your sea's ecology ... but whatever we do can only be temporary.... You must each face your own problems—redo your thinking about how and why you pollute your planet ... even as we must do on Earth!"[52] When he returns to Earth, he realizes that by solving all the world's problems he disallows humanity to grow and learn for itself. He explains to a group of migrant workers that he will not step in and fix all their problems, explaining, "You don't need a Superman! What you need is a super-will to be guardians of your own destiny!"[53] However it is explained, superheroes, especially in comics, tend to be ineffective at resolving the kinds of problems that have real-world significance.[54]

Iterations

One narrative characteristic of superheroes is that they seem to inevitably transcend any single storyline. Of all the popular superheroes, Batman is perhaps the prime example of the way multiple tales can frequently share the same superhero. Microcosmic of this mytheme is Neil Gaiman's *Whatever Happened to the Caped Crusader*. Written to coincide with the death of Batman in the continuity mythos, the story is devoid of any sort of major conflict, but allows for multiple characters within the Batman mythology to share the story of the death of the Caped Crusader. Each story tells a different version of how Batman spent his last hours. Batman oversees this in a sort of near-death experience. He observes the disparate tellings of his death and realizes they can't all be true. After Alfred tells the tale of how he created the Joker to help a despondent Bruce Wayne work through the death of his parents, Batman says, "That's ridiculous. Do you know how much of that story is impossible? Alfred couldn't have been the Joker. I mean, I can see the Joker sitting there."[55] Later, after listening to these stories of his demise, he realizes "that it doesn't matter what the story is, some things never change. Because even when they aren't talking about me, they are. Because they're talking about Batman."[56] After seeing his life spun out over, and over, his guide through the afterlife, his mother, explains where he goes next. She says, "You don't get heaven or hell. Do you know the only reward you get for being Batman? You get to be Batman."[57] No matter how many variations on the story there may be, each story is the story of the Batman. A superhero can, and frequently does, exist in multiple ways at any given time.

Though a company may promote an "official" version of the superhero, it is no more or no less true than any version by any person who engages with the superhero and his mythology. Henry Cavill's portrayal of Superman in *Man of Steel* may be the dominant iteration of Kal-El, but for an older generation Christopher Reeve is still *the* Superman. For others, Tom Welling is the ideal man from Smallville. In reality, they are all Superman/Kal-El/Clark Kent. The multifaceted nature of the superhero allows for divergent iterations to coexist and influence each other while still remaining separate from each other. Though alternate versions are technically different than iterations, they too are a part of the divergent nature of superhero characters.

What is potentially significant and interesting about these iterations is that they sometimes cross over into each other. *Batman the Animated Series* introduced a character named Harley Quinn in September of 1992.[58] Though originally only part of the television series, and designed as a one episode character, she was shortly absorbed into other iterations and has become a vital staple of the Batman mythos, playing a key role in the Arkham series of games and seemingly a vital part of the upcoming *Suicide Squad*. Harley Quinn was an intern who worked at Arkham Asylum and fell in love with the Joker. Since that time, she has been loyal and faithful to him, helping him break out when necessary and becoming an integral part of his schemes. In some stories, and as her character developed, she became linked to Poison Ivy. The relationship between Quinn and Ivy commonly has very sexual overtones that inform the way these characters are read by those who explore them in their various iterations. Her New 52 relationship with the character Deadshot a.k.a. Flyd Lawton also seems to play a vital part in the upcoming film.

In the past, both DC and Marvel have made attempts to "clean up" the multiple continuities that eventually develop over time in the comics. The most famous of these is *Crisis on Infinite Earths* which attempted to take all of the variations on the DC superhero canon and to fuse them into one shared universe. Metaphorically and literally in the comic, the multiverse is full of Earths and each Earth has its own pantheon of superheroes. Most major superheroes have counterparts in other worlds. There are several Supermen, Batmen, Wonder Women, Green Lanterns, and so forth. In an effort to save the entirety of existence from annihilation, these worlds are brought into one. Superheroes and entire worlds cease to exist, but a supposed balance is restored. However, this canonical reality was tenuous at best. This tenuous nature is manifest in the supervillain known as the Psycho Pirate who is committed to an insane asylum at the end of the series for babbling on about multiple worlds. He knows, and so does the reader, that there was more than one storyline that existed. It didn't take long for echoes of these storylines to crop back up again.

Terrence Wandtke does a thorough reading of the efforts of DC to impose a single storyline with *Crisis* and the way it fails to succeed in the chapter "The Failed Attempt to Impose High Culture" from his book *The Meaning of Superhero Comic Books*. This work is incredibly valuable in understanding how and why the superhero myth is so nonlinear. In a final recognition of the inevitability of this fragmented reality, both Marvel and DC have launched new lines of comics purported to be devoid of the potential mess of an established continuity, the Ultimate and All-Star lines respectively. Other alternate tellings include a transportation of the Marvel universe to 1602 in a series written by Neil Gaiman and a Batman story set in a turn of the century America in *Gotham by Gaslight*. These stories make no pretense at belonging within the central continuities of the DC or Marvel Universes, but take the character types and transport them to different eras with varying degrees of success.

Another aspect of this alternate reality is the design of the superhero. Again, manifest in microcosm in *Whatever Happened to the Caped Crusader?* as several participants get up to share their stories, the costume on Batman in the coffin changes. When Commissioner Gordon stands in front of the casket, Batman is shown in a ripped and dirty costume with short ears, a blocky build and a costume in muted black, yellow and gray, reminiscent of his appearance in Frank Miller's *The Dark Knight Returns*. Ivy walks down the aisle to stand before a Batman with exaggeratedly long ears on the cowl, which stick out over the top of the casket, a more streamlined utility belt and a long cape. Azrael stands before an arguably more currently recognized Batman. His cowl has shorter ears, the costume includes shades of blue, the utility belt is functional, but more yellow than in the first image. Though costume changes are part of identifying different iterations, it is not an integral part. Sometimes costume changes do occur within continuity, as in Spider-Man's costume shift from *The Amazing Spider-Man* to its sequel, among others. Costumes can also change based on alternate realities—a different but related concept to the idea of iterations—as can be seen in a variety of DC heroes in *Kingdom Come* and in Marvel's *Earth X*. Finally, they do shift within iterations, as exemplified by the change in costume between the Schumacher Batman films and Nolan's Batman trilogy. Thus, it is indicative of the way iterations shift a character's appearance, but not an absolute manifestation of an iteration shift.

Though this discussion has focused on Batman, perhaps because he is one of the most prevalent manifestations of this mytheme, it holds true for other characters as well. A very good example of the alternate realities in costuming is the X-Men family. Their costumes, appearances, storylines and characters all twine, connect, interweave, and change depending on who it is engaging with the myth and which version a person uses to approach the reality of the X-Men. Though both Marvel and DC promote a privileged or dominant rendition of their superheroes and costumes, superhero mythology is unique in modern culture for allowing official and semi-official renditions of their characters to coexist within the same reality. *X-Men: First Class* has a slightly different story arc than the original X-Men film trilogy, which has a slightly different story arc than *X-Men Origins: Wolverine*, which is again slightly different than *The Wolverine*. Though they all exist as part of the official film manifestations of X-Men characters, they diverge enough to be difficult to reconcile into a single continuity. Granted, *X-Men: Days of Future Past* brings the trilogy and the *First Class* worlds together, but it doesn't recognize and reconcile the various small differences that exist between the two realities. The differences aren't a problem for superheroes. In fact it's a major part of why Wandtke argues they are part of a new traditional, post-oral, culture. It also manifests their role as an accessible mythology for modern society. Rather than creating new stories "ex nihilo," superhero mythology, especially in relation to specific characters, allows for writers to utilize recognized characters, tropes, and mythemes to create stories that are their own while engaging in an established social fabric.

Justice Over Law

Typically, superheroes support and uphold the law. Most try their best to work with local authority figures and within the legal system. This is why, time and time again, a superhero will turn the villain over to be tried and punished for crimes committed in a court of law. There are, however, characters who function as vigilantes, who feel justified in punishing criminals on their own. These characters are still in the minority within the mythology. However, whenever a superhero sees a conflict between the rules of the legal system and his views of justice, he will promote said justice over the legal system that holds sway in the society of the hero. Speaking of Superman, who is perhaps one of the most rigid followers of the ideals of the legal system, Richard Reynolds explains, "His loyalty and patriotism are above even his devotion to the law."[59] Further, Reynolds explains that the conflict between law and justice frequently serves the story because, "Endless story possibilities can be designed around the theme of the superhero wrestling with his conscience over which order should be followed—moral or political, temporal or divine."[60] This conflict will almost inevitably result in the superhero finding either a way to balance the conflict between justice and law or ultimately making the choice to adhere to his own code of justice. Thus, occasionally, even those who aren't vigilantes will see fit to enforce justice on their own, but even a character like Batman will resort to vigilantism less frequently than he will submit the criminal to the mores of the legal system.

Though it is usually only a question of justice versus law, there are times when it becomes a question of what the hero believes is necessary versus that which the law would require. In *The Dark Knight*, after Harvey Dent went insane and changed from Gotham's white knight to the villainous Two-Face, Batman and Commissioner Gordon recognize the difficulty in promoting the good that Dent did before his turn if his villainy is brought to light. This leaves them in a problematic situation as they try to find a way to explain the chaos and death caused by Two-Face's actions. Ultimately, Batman determines that he can become the villain, taking the blame for Dent's actions in order to maintain Dent's knightliness, the good influence he had on the city. Not only does Batman move directly against the law in taking the blame for Two-Face's actions and going on the lam, running from authorities, but he also vicariously violates his own *moral code* against killing. He feels it is what must be done for the benefit of his city, thus Batman believes in promoting what he perceives as the needs of Gotham over the laws of the metropolis. In this way, he foregrounds a value for a sort of broader definition of justice usually left unexplored in superhero tales. Nolan's vision of Batman deviates in some ways significantly with the traditional Batman mythos, a fact that allows the Dark Knight's actions to stand.

However, this large a deviation from the moral code of a character is fairly rare. Most often, a character's moral code is a large part of the sort of justice which they are likely to pursue. Different superheroes will have different relationships with the law and politics. Each of these characters still tend to attempt to work within the constructs of the law. However, their efforts will only go so far as they believe the laws are just. In the Marvel universe, the superhero community is divided over a Superhero Registration Act signed into law during the *Civil War* storyline. Several heroes, including Iron Man, support the act, working to enforce the law. However, Captain America, one of the most apparently patriotic of superheroes, vehemently opposes the act and goes underground to work against the law in an effort to establish justice as he sees it. Ultimately, the situation is resolved and the heroes opposing the law eventually find themselves pardoned, or excused. Though they may spend time in jail, ultimately the superheroes who oppose the law in some fashion always end up back out on the street and free to save the day. The demands of justice seem to have very little sway on the superheroes who violate the law. In the end, their need to serve justice at the expense of the law is viewed as the right thing to do. At times, this convergence of the two ideals leads to questions of the larger implications of the occasional difference between the rule of law and the demands of justice.

The Lair

From the Batcave to Superman's Fortress of Solitude to the Danger Room of the X-Men, most well established superheroes have a place apart from the outside world, a place where the two parts of their persona, the superhero and the *alter ego* can blend and coexist in relative comfort. This is a place of training, of learning, a place where they can let themselves be who they are. Frequently, this lair has a tie to some sort of less developed area or a place at a distance from the area wherein the superhero functions. The Batcave is established within naturally occurring caverns underneath Wayne Manor. Superman builds his Fortress of Solitude in the frozen north. Wonder Woman returns to Themyscira, the land of the Amazons, when she needs to reconnect to her origins. At times, the superhero does have to make do with his home, like Spider-Man's rundown student quality apartment, though even there the level of technology in this space surpasses that found in a typical student's place. This heightened level of technology is also incredibly common in superheroes' lairs.

The graphic novel *Hush* spends a fair amount of time with the mytheme of the lair. Of course, the fact that the subject of the story is Batman, who has perhaps the most well developed lair in all of superhero mythology, makes it almost a natural thing to include time in the Batcave. Not only is the Batcave developed in a natural cave, it is also rife with technology that is capable of things beyond even the most advanced computers in existence. The graphic novel shows several scenes which take place in the cave, including a scene wherein Ra's al Ghul breaks into the cave, planting a sword in one of the computer consoles. This act serves as a very personal message to Batman, a challenge to meet him in the desert where they had fought with swords once before. Immediately, Batman rushes into the mansion to ensure that Alfred is safe, knowing full well that any villain who knows of the lair knows of the alter ego living above it. This moment coupled with another from the story seriously underscores the intimate nature of the lair. Later in *Hush* Batman reveals his identity to Catwoman and invites her into the Batcave. After a few moments, she notices Robin lurking in the shadows. When she calls him out, Robin attacks her, exclaiming, "You shouldn't be here."[61] Batman interrupts their fight and tells Robin that she is his guest, that he allowed her into the cave. Robin argues that she can't be trusted and Batman made the wrong choice in letting her into the cave and revealing his identity to her. For him, the two are almost the same thing. The intimacy involved is no less for one than the other. Because Robin believes that Catwoman can't be trusted with their most personal secrets, she can't be trusted to come into the lair that he shares with Batman. This is true of any lair worthy of the name. The intimacy of the place is as dear as practically any in the superhero mythos.

Though this mytheme may be an older one,[62] though not necessarily original to the earliest tales of the superhero, it is still a part of the story, still a mytheme that has significant impact when used in the storyline. The convergence of Wayne Manor with the Batcave underscores the dualistic role a lair can take, and its ideal proximity. Superman's Fortress of Solitude is in the remote, frozen north and only easily accessible to people of Superman's amazing abilities.⁶³ His lair is uniquely suited to his powers and needs. It is also not uncommon for superhero teams to have their own lairs. The Teen Titans have a large, T-shaped building in which they converge for their shared missions. The Justice League has a headquarters in various places throughout their existence, including the Hall of Justice and their satellite orbiting Earth. However, the size and scope of the lair, though usually grandiose, is less significant than its existence. Tony Stark's Malibu home is his lair in the *Iron Man* series of films, as is Peter Parker's New York apartment. In any case, the lair is a part of the vast majority of superhero mythology, regardless of its form, place, or function.

Moral Code

One of the key elements to understanding the superhero and its mythology is a specific morality. While most superheroes share a basic code of supporting *justice over law* when necessary, each hero has his own specific aspects of the code. Reynolds argues that a necessary aspect of "the moral nature of the superhero" is "the 'extra effort.' No battle is ever won easily—at least, not in a properly constructed superhero narrative. [....] What the reader is generally looking for is the application of the extra effort, the moral determination to go on fighting even when apparently beaten."⁶⁴ This extra effort is frequently driven by a need to maintain the values of the hero's specific moral code. This code is also a vital part of establishing the persona of the character. The moral code comments on the kind of actions the superhero condones and opposes.

Most often, superheroes share a similar code revolving around the idea of needing to use their powers responsibly and to avoid killing, especially the innocent.⁶⁵ They use their powers for justice and to protect the innocent. They work together, come to the defense of each other even when their unique moral codes put them at odds with one another, unless one of them crosses the line and violates the superhero code. Characters like Captain America and Superman are exemplars of these virtues, frequently putting themselves on a moral level that seems incredibly strict by comparison to their colleagues. However, there are some superheroes who deviate from the classic code. Characters like Wolverine loosen the mores of the prohibition against killing. Many, like Deadpool, don't play well with other superheroes. In many cases Green Arrow's liberal politics, a development brought about by Denny O'Neil in the *Green Lantern/Green Arrow* series, put him at odds with other superheroes because he puts those values above team loyalty in many situations.

One of the best examples of the extremes to which this code can go occurs in the Marvel series known as *Civil War*. A rift has occurred between heroes and one group of heroes has reached out to the villain community to help in the conflict. When the second group, led by Captain America, is approached by two supervillains, the Punisher guns them down before they can finish making their case to join the cause. Captain America attacks the Punisher, delivering a brutal beating. No matter how hard Cap hits him, the Punisher refuses to fight back. For the Punisher, there is nothing wrong with killing villains but he will not lay a finger on Captain America because of his respect for what Cap stands for. His respect for the high moral character of Captain America makes it so that the Punisher will not strike the man, no matter what the scenario may be. At one point, Captain America says, "Fight, you coward!" The Punisher, already a battered and bloody figure, replies almost calmly, "Not against you."[66] He would rather lose teeth and be pounded senseless rather than violate his moral code, regardless of how arbitrary and off-putting it may seem to those around him.

The Punisher has a fairly extreme version of the trope. Most superheroes share a similar cluster of ideals that inform their moral code. There is a general consensus that superheroes should avoid killing, protect the innocent, make at least an effort to avoid violence, and avoid using their powers for personal gains. Some of these moral tropes are strong enough to have developed into their own mythemes. *No killing, justice over law*, and the *power and responsibility* all have a basis in the moral code trope of the mythology of the superhero, but have developed enough to be integral to the mythos in their own right. Regardless of the similarity of the superhero's moral code to that of others, every hero has a strict code to which he will adhere regardless of external factors that push for a violation of his values. Indeed, the central conflict of many stories surrounding a superhero derive to an extent from the temptation to violate his personal code of conduct.

No Killing

As cliché as this one is, it still tends to hold for almost every superhero. While some are less rigid, most superheroes go to extremes to avoid killing. In *Captain America: The First Avenger,* Captain America engages in the use of guns and weaponry that would indicate he's not trying to avoid killing—though no kills can definitively be attributed to him in the film. Also, in the first season of the television series *Arrow*, based on the DC hero Green Arrow, Oliver Queen seems to have no problem with killing those who need killing.

1. Building a Framework 61

Though he refrains from killing in later seasons, he is still willing to do so when he feels the necessity. Anti-heroes like the Punisher are an intentionally obvious exception to this mytheme.

An interesting exploration of this mytheme occurs again in "What's So Funny About Truth, Justice & the American Way." The story centers upon Superman's conflict with a group of violent, deadly superheroes known as the Elite. The premise behind the story is that the Elite represent a new way of doing things, a better way by some standards—an argument frequent in the 1990s, which saw a huge upswing in the number of superheroes who carried guns, who practiced corporal punishment, who frequently engaged in extreme and graphic violence. Superman eventually makes an agreement to meet with them and the winner would carry the day not only as the superhero for the world, but as the ideological truth to the way of superheroes. After eliminating all but the leader of the Elite, a man named Manchester Black, Superman stands before him and says,

> It frightened me. When I decided to cross the line ... do what you do.... I was terrified. Thought it would be tough—but you know what? Anger is easy. Hate is easy. Vengeance and spite are easy. Lucky for you ... and for me.... I don't like my heroes ugly and mean. Just don't believe in it.

Superman then reveals that he didn't kill any of the Elite, as Black accused him of doing, insinuating that Superman is no better than they are. At this point, as Black realizes his worldview has lost, he lashes out against Superman, exclaiming, "You're living in a bloody dream world!"

Superman replies, "Dreams save us. Dreams lift us up and transform us. And on my soul, I swear ... until my dream of a world where dignity, honor and justice becomes a reality we all share—I'll never stop fighting."[67] In essence, this story argues strongly for the fact that superheroes should not kill and attempts to justify the rationale. These heroes are our exemplars and the dreams we dream of being able to be in order to confront our own challenges in like manner. They are able to solve all their problems without resorting to terminating the life of another human being.

Even when the hero has been driven over the edge, at the center of the myth he still will not kill. In the graphic novel *Hush*, written by Jeph Loeb and drawn by Jim Lee, Batman is driven to the brink when he believes the Joker has killed his childhood friend. As he pummels the Joker, Batman reflects on all the pain caused and determines that this time, this one time, it would be a good thing to kill. However, before he can finish beating the Joker to death, both Catwoman and Jim Gordon step in and make him stop long enough to realize he cannot compromise his vow to never kill. If it weren't for this intervention, he would have crossed the line, but there will always be something to stop those at the center of the mythology from going too far.

In the animated film *Batman: Under the Red Hood*, Batman is challenged by the Red Hood, a reborn Jason Todd. In the *A Death in the Family* storyline, the Joker beats Todd to death with a crowbar. In *Under the Red Hood*, Todd is resurrected by a mystical pool known as a Lazarus Pit. With a gun to the Joker's head, the Hood asks:

> Bruce, I forgive you for not saving me. But why, why on God's earth, is he still alive? [....] If it had been you that he beat to a bloody pulp, if he had taken you from this world, I would have done nothing but search the planet for this pathetic pile of evil, death-worshipping garbage and sent him off to hell.

Batman replies, "You don't understand. I don't think you've ever understood." Todd says, "What, your moral code just won't allow for that. It's just too hard to cross that line?" Batman responds:

> No. God almighty, no. it'd be too damned easy. All I've wanted to do is kill him. A day doesn't go by when I don't think about subjecting him to every horrendous torture he dealt out to others, and then end him. [....] But if I do that, if I allow myself to go down into that place, I'll never come back. [....] I can't. I'm sorry.

As dark as he gets, the modern Batman never crosses the line into taking a life.[68] Even in *Batman Begins*, though he allows Ra's al Ghul to plummet to his death, Batman refuses to actively participate in killing his nemesis. This interpretation of the trope puts a very fine line between active killing and passive conspiracy to kill. The trope is generally more clearly delineated. In *Smallville*, Jonathan Kent cuts to the chase. Talking to a teenage Clerk Kent who is thinking of ending a threat to their family permanently by killing the man who is causing the threat. In words very similar to those spoken by the Dark Knight, Jonathan Kent tells his adopted son, "Believe me son, I know all there is to know about losing your temper. But you can't do it [....] But once you cross that line, there is no going back."[69] While this mytheme has waxed and waned during the existence of the myth, there will always be superheroes—those closest to the center of the mythological target—who will refuse to take a life, even of those who most deserve it.

One Power per Person

With the exception of the Superman type character, most superheroes get one central superpower and all their secondary powers are tangentially connected to that primary power. Thus, Storm can fly because she can manipulate winds. Rogue's power stealing abilities have allowed her to maintain some of her stolen abilities in perpetuity, especially those she gained when she drained Ms. Marvel, which include the classic Superman battery of powers, consisting of flight, strength and practical invulnerability. Thus, characters will be associated typically with a primary power, For example Invisible Girl's invisibility, even when they may have secondary powers, like her force fields which occasionally are explained as an extension of her primary power and sometimes as a secondary ability. However, there is a different type of implied secondary powers. For example, the Hulk always lifts from a place that can hold his weight as well as of the weight of whatever he may be lifting without collapsing under the combined mass. This is true for all characters with superstrength. Unless the story dictates otherwise, they always lift from a firm foundation. While this is never overtly stated as a power, this hidden secondary ability is significant enough to be worth recognizing.

When characters seem to have clusters of powers, seemingly in contrast to this mytheme, one power will still be foregrounded as the central power of the character. Wolverine has heightened senses, though his sense of smell seems to dominate his use of this ability. However, his healing factor is *the* power recognized by the majority of people, and it may play a part in his other abilities. In the 2000 *X-Men*, the film makes it clear that Wolverine's skin heals over his claws after each use. The series also reveals that the metal on his claws was possible only because of his healing abilities, connecting even his claws to this primary power.

Even for someone whose powers are as apparently disparate as Superman's can frequently be connected to a central connector. Though it's stretching to say that Superman's power is his ability to absorb and reuse the power of Earth's yellow sun, various stories make it clear that this is the source of his abilities. Ostensibly, then, he becomes a solar battery for his battery of powers. In *The Dark Knight Returns*, Batman blocks out the sun to weaken the Man of Steel causing a disturbing, albeit temporary, effect. The import of his connection to the sun has been foregrounded in *Superman #38*. In a fight with Ulysses, Superman detonates. Batman explains this new power as "a solar flare," an extension of a latent power expressed through his heat vision.[70] This new power strengthens the connection of Superman's abilities to a singular source.

Thus, though not a hard and fast rule of superhero mythology, the primacy of a single power for any character is a good indicator of a stronger connection to the mythology itself.

Tangential to this mytheme is the concept that superheroes who work together almost never share the same power. The Fantastic Four exemplify this subtrope. Even though the Fantastic Four all gained their powers in the same cataclysmic accident, the same *spectacular origin*, they all developed different powers. The fact that the same event had different results for all those engaged is a significant manifestation of this mytheme. Their powers suggest a sort of superheroic symmetry with the four elements. Johnny Storm became the Human Torch, but is the only one of the four who has any ability with fire. Reed Richards stretches and Sue Storm developed the ability to turn invisible and generate force fields, which is usually considered to be the mental projection of the cloaking ability that makes her invisible. Ben Grimm became the Thing, a nigh indestructible organic orange rock. None of the four has more than one key power and all of them are different, a factor that frequently arises in the *superteam*. In essence, this means that not only does each character only get one power, but that power is unlikely to be shared by another character with whom they would closely relate. Though not unheard of, it is extremely rare for a *superteam* to have characters with duplicate powers, or even similar powers. The vast majority of the time their skills diverge significantly from one another's.

This division manifests almost without exception throughout the mythology. Though their shared origin and unique powers are fairly unique, the *superteam* rarely shares powers between members. The exception to this seems to be that of the *pseudo-superpower*, which seems to be much more sharable between characters. Hawkeye has passed on not only his name, but his archery skills to his protégé. Batman has shared some of his skills with several Robins, Huntress, and others. However, in this case, each seems to have gained—or reinforced—different central powers from their training. An online meme separates the Robins out by their specialties: Dick Grayson as the acrobat, Jason Todd as the marksman, Tim Drake as the detective, and Damien Wayne as the "true son." This suggests that even when the training is the same, even when theoretically the same skill set exists, even in cases where a plethora of skills may apply, there is still one dominant power to each individual which is likely to set them apart from their colleagues.

Orphan

The majority of superheroes have either lost their parents or never had any that readers know of. At times, the loss of parents can play a vital part in the establishment of the superheroic identity. The most obvious example of this is the death of Thomas and Martha Wayne. Their death is the primary motivator in Bruce's efforts to become Batman. Superman's parents died in their efforts to protect him by sending him off of their doomed planet, Krypton. Spider-Man spent most of his youth living with his Uncle Ben and Aunt May. Very few of the X-Men have any sort of relationship with their parents. Even when the parents are still alive, the vast majority of superheroes live separately from their parents and siblings, making them metaphorical orphans when they're not orphans in fact. In the case of many superheroes, the fact that they are adults does justify to some extent the absence of parents. Granted, much of this is for a streamlined story; by eliminating the parents, the creators allow for fewer characters to deal with. Conversely, the loss of the parents is frequently used to some degree as a motivating force for the superhero.

In the case of the comics series *The Runaways*, which cronicles a superhero team from the Marvel universe, the team is made up completely of youth who intentionally run away from their parents whom they discover are supervillains. In their case, they choose to orphan themselves from parents that engage in incredibly criminal activities. However, they deal with many of the same sort of issues that other orphans have had to deal with, even to the point of feeling their parents have abandoned them. Though in their case it's not a physical abandonment, the moral villainy of their parents is just as alienating to the team. They have to cope with the consequences of trying to live on their own. The have to find a place to live, deal with trying to find supplies, and manage the social challenges that come when a bunch of teenagers share living accommodations.

There are a few technical deviances from this trope beyond *The Runaways*. Exemplary exceptions to this trope include, but are not limited to, the third and fourth boys to don the Robin persona. While both Dick Grayson and Jason Todd were orphans, Tim Drake originally lived with his parents until they were killed by villains. The most recent Robin, Damien Wayne, is in fact the son of Bruce Wayne, he was raised by his mother, Talia al Ghul, and her league of assassins. Though his upbringing was certainly unusual, he was raised in the presence of his mother and has developed a relationship with his father, making him one of the more interesting deviations from this mytheme. However, Damien is also symbolic of the metaphoric nature of superheroic orphaning. His upbringing was designed to turn him into a weapon and he had very little emotional connection to his mother. When Damien becomes Robin, he carries the emotional turmoil that comes with his upbringing. This turmoil leads to some dramatic confrontations with Batman and the Teen Titans.

Again, Superman is more emblematic of this trope than he may appear on the surface, more so in the recently released *Man of Steel*. Though Clark Kent was raised by Jonathan and Martha Kent, they weren't his original parents. His parents, Jor-El and Lara Lor-Van, abandoned him to Earth when Krypton was on the brink of destruction. His original parents orphaned him and he was raised by foster parents who somehow managed to legally adopt him. In *Man of Steel*, Jonathan Kent sacrifices himself during a tornado in order to keep the amazing superpowers of his son a secret from the world. Even in story lines where Pa Kent survives, Kal-El must deal with the feelings of isolation he has because of the lack of connection from his parents. The isolation felt by this abandonment, whether real or thematic in nature, is an integral part of the tropological influence of the orphan.

Outsider

The vast majority of superheroes exist at the margin of their societies. Regardless of the actual location of their home, or their place in society, superheroes are alienated in ways both temporal and social. Whether it be Superman's literal alienation or Batman's somewhat intentional psychological isolation from the citizens of Gotham City and the Justice League or the sociopolitical marginalization of the mutants in the X-Men, superheroes rarely exist at the collective center of their societies.

Some superheroes are outsiders because of their celebrity status. People celebrate their supernatural abilities. The family film *Megamind* presents the superhero Metro Man as a major celebrity in the city. Everyone loves and praises him. In fact, it is the adulation of the crowds, their constant need to see their unique savior, that drives Metro Man to fake his own death in order to make literal the metaphoric alienation he feels as the incessant savior of Metro City. Most superheroes have a more challenging relationship with society around them. In the case of Superman, he is an outsider both as Clark Kent and as Superman. Though Kent is a construct he chooses to present to society, one that is intentionally outside of the normal social order, Superman is also frequently viewed with a sense of concern and distrust, or at the least as a non-native to Earth, someone whose motives and intentions can literally be classified as alien. The outsider nature of the superhero is not necessarily one of celebrity status but frequently one of a pariah, or at least as a character with whom society has a hard time relating. Batman is exemplary of the peculiarity with which most people in the world of superheroes view these heroes. Though it's not uncommon for Bruce Wayne to be a celebrated part of Gotham's society, the Dark Knight is rarely, if ever, welcome in polite society since the 1960s television series starring Adam West went off the air. In general, superheroes are extant only on the fringes of the social order, on the outskirts. In the X-Men stories, this alienation, or Otherness,[71] is used frequently to comment on the marginalization of other social and political pariahs.

In *X2: X-Men United* a scene between Bobby Drake, known as Iceman among the X-Men, finally admits to his parents that he is a mutant. The scene plays as a metaphorical coming out many LGBT people experience as they try to broach the issue with their families. After the X mansion is attacked, a few of the mutants who escape seek temporary refuge in the family home of Bobby Drake. After the initial shock of finding strangers in the home, the family sits down with the mutants who have invaded their home. As Bobby sits with his parents, the discomfort demonstrated by the stereotypical American family echoes much of the tension surrounding homosexuality at the time. The metaphor goes so far that Drake's mother actually asks, "When did you first know you were a … a" but hesitates to say the word *mutant* and then asks, "Have you ever tried not being a mutant?" However, his status as a mutant outsider, part of the "mutant problem," is so severe that while he talks with his parents his brother uses an upstairs telephone to call the police, reporting his own brother. This leads to a violent confrontation between Drake and his fellow mutants with the police,[72] a confrontation that further alienates mutant superheroes from the normal people in society. Though the confrontations are rarely as intense as that in *X2*, the tension between the superhero and the more mundane people in the world around is a constant issue in the mythology. The characters at the center of this mythology are rarely, if ever, at the center of their civilizations.

Please the Father

Most superheroes have a father figure with whom they struggle or from whom they struggle to gain approval. They struggle both to establish themselves as unique and apart from their father figure, and to please him at the same time. In the superhero mythos it is not uncommon for this figure to be as much a figurative as a literal presence. In the case of Batman this father figure is already dead and exists in principle and ideal rather than in a physical presence. Superman seeks to please both Jor-El, his Kryptonian father, and Jonathan Kent, his Earthly foster father. The dual nature of his paternal parentage is one of many elements that link the Man of Steel to the messianic Jesus Christ whose entire life is also frequently read as a desire to please his father.[73] When Jesus was found in the temple of the Jews, he explained, "How is it that ye sought me? Wist ye not that I must be about my Father's business?"⁷⁴ He emphasizes in this moment that he is primarily interested in pleasing his non-human father rather than Joseph, his foster father. In the case of Batman, Wayne has a stand-in for his dead father in the form of Alfred who very frequently functions as a paternal stand-in. Though Thomas Wayne, his birth father, is an influence on his actions, Bruce Wayne is driven to find a way to avenge the death of his father, to please his father by making his death have meaning.

Even Wonder Woman, one of the superheroes most removed from the paternal order of things, deals with a mother figure in a very similar way as the father figure for the majority of males in the form of her mother, Hippolyta. In the pre–Crisis mythology, Hippolyta formed Wonder Woman out of clay, and imbued her with life by praying to the gods, she is the mother figure for Wonder Woman. She consistently requires of Wonder Woman an accounting for her actions and her choices. In all her actions, Diana frequently measures her actions against the standards imbued in her by her mother. However, with the relaunch of Wonder Woman that took place when DC determined to overhaul all their characters, the character discovered that her mother's story about her birth from clay was a lie and that her actual father was Zeus, the king of the gods. At other times, Ares has presented himself as her father. Diana, Wonder Woman's *alter ego*, feels a need to prove herself either worthy of their attention or at least good enough to transcend their meddling in her life. While this is a divergent reading of the trope, the need to have these figures satisfied enough with her abilities still fulfills the underlying motive behind the concept of this mytheme and the kinds of results brought about by the hero's efforts.

Regardless of the relationship status superheroes actually have with their parents, the vast majority of them spend at least one storyline focusing on making good to their father. Whether the father is still present, dead, or manifest in a surrogate, the motive to make good with the father figure is a strong underlying motivator for the actions of the superhero. Even when that figure is sometimes less than fatherly, his presence will still have a strong impact on the hero. For decades, the origin of Wolverine's non-superheroic name, Logan, was left unexplained in the Marvel Universe. In the aptly named series *Origins*, it was revealed that he was originally named James Howlett. Through the course of the story, it is revealed that James is actually the bastard son of his mother and a groundskeeper named Logan. When this is discovered, it leads to the death of his parents and he runs away, later claiming the name of his drunken father, a man he hardly knew, rather than that name under which he was raised. Furthermore, the wild nature of his life tends to be more in line with his father than with the man who raised him, becoming a laborer in a lumber yard rather than reestablishing the place he had in the society of the well-bred gentleman. While this trope is not a constantly manifest one in most tales within the mytheme, it is a vital part of the overall development of the mythology. This mytheme is a part of practically every superhero story at some point or another over the course of time.

Power and Responsibility

Perhaps most famously stated in the Spider-Man mythos as, "With great power comes great responsibility," this concept is one of the key elements that defines how a superhero can and should act. Regardless of the power, regardless of the situation or the consequences, a superhero, by the very nature of the mythology, must always act for the good. Though how the superhero determines good is frequently determined by an individual *moral code*, he must always act for the good.

This idea is emphasized in Alan Moore's *Watchmen*. Toward the end of the series, the *self-made superhero* Ozymandias explains to Rorschach and Nite Owl that he has acted to stop nuclear war, directly confronting the mytheme that superheroes are *ineffective against real world problems*. Of course, in the universe of *Watchmen*, the only superhero who isn't self-made is Dr. Jon Osterman who was accidentally subject to an experiment that significantly altered his being to the point that he has nearly god-like powers over his size, space and time, becoming the only superpowered superhero in the story, Dr. Manhattan. Everyone else has to make the best with the skills they can develop on their own. Ozymandias does have the *pseudo-superpower* of incredible intellect, which causes him to look beyond the normal expectations of superheroes and to try to solve the biggest problem threatening the alternate 1980's world wherein the story takes place, the arms race and the threat of global nuclear war. Ozymandias saw his ability as large enough that it required him to act on a global scale. Using his vast powers of reasoning, he determines that the only way to stop the danger presented by the arms race was to create a threat larger than that. Thus, he manufactured an artificial extra-terrestrial creature and delivered it to New York, knowing that it would result in the casualties and insanity of thousands of New Yorkers. As terrible as the result of his actions are, Ozymandias' plan does circumvent a global conflict as the world unites to fight against a fabricated alien menace.

Because Moore and Gibbons seek to complicate the superhero mythos in *Watchmen*, they exacerbate this trope to its breaking point. Ozymandias' vast intellect gives him a sense of superiority, leading him to feel he has a responsibility not only to preserve and save the world, but to measure up to the greatest men to ever exist on the globe. In his mind, his focus puts him beyond concepts of right and wrong normally applied to superheroes and allows him to rationalize all the collateral damage of his actions to the satisfaction of all the superheroes that confront him. Everyone in the story makes their peace with Ozymandias' plan with the exception of Rorschach who, rather than fight a fight he can't win, forces Dr. Manhattan to kill him. This is because he knows, based on his own understanding of justice, that it's the only way he can be stopped from letting the world know the role Ozymandias had in saving the world from itself. Rorschach will not let the scheme pass without trying to undo what was done. But he knows it must be left alone. Because of that, he knows he must die. It is an understanding that he shares with Dr. Manhattan, forcing the doctor to kill him.

In general, Spider-Man serves as an exemplar for this trope. In *Spider-Man*, directed by Sam Raimi, Ben Parker tells Peter Parker, "With great power comes great responsibility." Peter shortly discovers the importance of this concept. Because he uses his newfound powers in an attempt to get money in a professional wrestling match, and fails to use them to stop a thief from stealing from the same venue, Peter is unwittingly implicit in the death of Ben.[75] He fails to take responsibility for his ability and spends the rest of his life trying to *please the father* by only using his abilities for the good of society. This is the burden of those blessed with *powers* in superhero mythology. In fact, for the vast majority of superhero tales, there will always be a direct causality between a misuse of their abilities and very negative results. The long lasting results of Uncle Ben's death are rare, but the misuse of power always results in problems for the central superhero.

Powers

Of all the mythemes in this lexicon, this is perhaps the most recognized, and in some ways the most essential to the mythology.[76] The majority of a specific superhero's abilities draw from a single, particular superpower. The mytheme *one power per person* develops this concept to a greater extent. Characters usually have a central focal power or power source, though they may have several aspects connected to this central power. The power of a superhero is nearly always something supernatural, an ability that makes him superhuman in some major way. At times, this superpower is an exaggerated trait of humanity, something like superstrength. At other times, the ability is something outside the human experience, like the power of hard light wielded by members of the Green Lantern Corps. Their ability to craft solid objects out of light is limited only by their imagination and the strength of their will. Their power is completely outside of abilities accepted by humanity as even potentially within the realm of possibility. This mytheme is such a vital requirement that it can single-handedly cast doubt on Batman's claim to be a superhero. Though Batman tends to be the most prevalent example of the apparently non-powered superhero, others include Hawkeye, Green Arrow, and occasionally even crossgenre characters like Adam Strange and John Constantine. Those characters, however, who appear to be part of the mythology who have no clear superpowers do fit into the category in their own way.

Perhaps the one of the best statements on the categories of powers that exist is that "some are born great, some achieve greatness, and some have greatness thrust upon 'em."[77] In the world of the superhero, greatness is frequently synonymous with power. Thus, superheroes derive powers from birth, from their own achievements, or by having them thrust upon them.

Those Born with Powers

For these characters, the superpowers are extant within the hero from birth. However, even for these superheroes it is uncommon for them to take to the streets until they're older. This sub-trope includes the mutants who make up a large component of the Marvel's pantheon of heroes, but the most prevalent are those who belong to the X-Men. It also includes characters born to different, mythological, cultures from which they derive powers, like Wonder Woman, Hercules, and Thor. In essence, these superheroes are those born to greatness, as opposed to those who have greatness thrust upon them. They have no opportunity to avoid developing unusual abilities, they can only choose what to do with those abilities.

The most obvious member of this subtrope is Superman. Commonly, he is told by his adopted father, Jonathan Kent, that his powers need concealing. For those born, there seems to be a sense of trepidation in outing themselves as a powerful individual. In the case of the Kents, this fear is manifest for different reasons, but the danger of being different plays a factor in every case. By the time Clark Kent is older, and can understand better the portent of his powers, he finds a way to use them for the benefit of others, but it still almost always comes with a sense of being the *outsider*. In fact, those who are born into their powers seem to be most cognizant of their difference and most alienated by it.

Whatever the reaction from their society or from themselves, those born with powers have no real choice over whether they want these powers or not.

They have them and must determine what to do with them. Those who recognize the import of *power and responsibility* will almost inevitably become superheroes in terms of the mythology. There are a few outliers who seem to recognize their responsibility, like Magneto, but choose to fulfill that responsibility differently, but for the general population of the mythology the responsible person born with powers will become a superhero.

Those Who Achieved Powers

Some superheroes seem to spring ready made into their roles as saviors of the world. Some require training of their innate abilities before they dare take on the role of superhero. Others must develop abilities before they have even a chance at being any sort of superhero. A great many self-made superheroes are also the kind of heroes with some sort of pseudo-superpowers.

Emblematic of this subtrope is the path Batman takes to becoming a superhero. With little more than an overdeveloped drive for what he calls justice and others would call a vendetta, Bruce Wayne goes through mental and physical training that takes an above average man to the level that, with help from the applied use of technology, he can challenge *the* superpowered superhero, Superman. In fact, Batman has not only challenged the Man of Steel but has also taken him down. He is not the only superhero who has developed real-world skills to the point that they have become superhuman. There are many superheroes who must work out to develop their abilities, including several whose abilities fit within the bounds of an exaggerated societal norm, characters like the Punisher, Green Arrow, Nightwing, and Black Widow.

Though it can be argued that many superheroes develop their abilities, several characters in the mythology crafted themselves into a superhero in such a way that sets them apart. It is through such development exemplified in this subtrope that characters with no recognizable superpowers can become a member of the cadre of superheroes, can hold their own against those who have abilities beyond even the most unrealistic of realities.

Those Whom Powers Are Thrust Upon

In this case, the superhero's powers are gained through some sort of unusual source, quite frequently an event that is extraordinary, and for some reason irreproducible. This source may be a radioactive spider bite, a gamma bomb experiment gone wrong, a freak laboratory accident, or even an alien visitation. What tends to be true for characters who gain their powers this way is that it's rarely, if ever, reproducible. For this reason, even though Steve

Rogers chose to be a part of the Super Soldier program, he still has his powers thrust upon him. He put himself in the position to be changed by extranormal means.

Thus, though the phrase implies a lack of choice on the part of the character, this subtrope covers any superhero who is not born with powers and who doesn't achieve those powers directly through their own efforts. In essence, on their own, they wouldn't be the superhero they are in the mythology. Even if it just means being in the right place at the wrong time, like Bruce Banner, or being chosen, like Hal Jordan, these heroes are given powers that they must then figure out and use to the best of their abilities.

Perhaps the most well known example of this subtrope is Spider-Man. The bite of the spider that changed Peter Parker was an event out of his control. Typically, Parker's first thought is not to use his powers for the greater good, but for his own benefit. However, after understanding the portent of his *powers and responsibility*, he turns to more altruistic modes of expressing the powers he didn't choose but were given to him. When the powers are thrust upon a person, it comes with the need to make a choice about what to do with those powers. Those like Captain America have already made that choice before the powers come. Spider-Man, and his kind are faced more starkly with a set of abilities that force them into considering what it means to have superhuman skills.

What is noteworthy about these sub-mythemes is that even in those instances where more than one of them may play into the development of the character, one will still be clearly dominant. Indeed, one will typically be tied to the reason for the hero to become a superhero. The power is typically a turning point for the character, in the case of Batman, the character is decided before and then revealed by the gaining of power. For Spider-Man, the powers force him to explore the kind of person he wants to be. In the Sam Raimi version of his origin, Parker takes a chance as a professional wrestler to earn some extra money. It is only after his uncle is killed and he understands that great power begets great responsibility that Peter opts to wear the red and blue of Spider-Man and work for the good of humanity as a superhero. Traditionally, he makes his own costume and, more importantly, the web shooters he uses to swing through the streets of New York. Though he has the climbing, strength, and leaping abilities of a spider, the celebrated webbing is something he made himself. He made himself into the superhero he became. Thus, the power is connected to the origin of the character in some significant way.

There is a very significant subtrope to the mytheme of powers. Pseudo-superpowers are integral for the understanding and inclusion of important characters in the mythology. Most superheroes have the sorts of superpowers that extend well beyond the pale of abilities that might exist in reality. In the case of superheroes like Batman, Iron Man, and Hawkeye—essentially those who achieve their superhero status—their skills lie hypothetically within the bounds of reality. Peter Coogan states, "While [Batman] has no distinctly 'super' powers, his physical strength and mental abilities allow him to fight crime alongside his more powerful brethren."[78] One of the things that drew director Christopher Nolan to Batman was the fact that he was a character who was a normal guy who had "simply done a lot of push-ups."[79] Because of this, there are those who question the Dark Knight's validity as part of the superhero canon. This subtrope recognizes characteristics usually not considered to be superhuman abilites, but in the context of the character function in the same way as more recognized superpowers seem to. Abnormally large fortunes, excessive strength of will, pseudo-scientific gadgets all count as part of the subtrope. Accordingly, Iron Man and Batman are perhaps the most recognizable superheroes who claim no traditional superpowers.[80] Neither Tony Stark, pre–*Extremis* in the comics, and still in the films, nor Bruce Wayne have the kind of powers typically associated with superheroes. Neither is capable of unassisted flight, superstrength, or any sort of pseudo-magical abilities. Their superabilities, insofar as they have any, lie in their intense intellect and the fiscal ability to achieve the research and development necessary to make their practically impossible ideas into reality.

Those superheroes who exist without traditional powers seem to have abilities that exist in the real world, but the mythological forms of these abilities are exaggerated to an extreme. By way of example, both Marvel's Hawkeye and DC's Green Arrow are capable of impossible feats of archery. In *The Avengers*, Hawkeye is able to take down enemy combatants without even looking where he is shooting. In *Arrow*, the recent re-imagining of the Green Arrow, he is shown on several occasions shooting at bouncing tennis balls, pinning them to a concrete wall and making other ridiculously impossible shots. Though there appears to be no clear supernatural source for their abilities, their skills are beyond any sort of shooting capacity by any archers in the real world. However, in *Stan Lee's Superhumans* the producers meet Byron Ferguson, a man who is capable of shooting a small aspirin out of the air.[81] While this feat certainly borders on the supernatural, his skills are practically mundane when compared to the abilities of the archers in superhero mythology.

The sorts of characters who fall under the paradigms of this subtrope are fairly rare within the scope of the mythology. Most superheroes have demonstrable powers that exist beyond that of normal humanity. However, with the prevalence of Batman, the concept requires recognition. The self-made character trains himself to the peak of physical perfection to be effective against supervillains. These heroes also tend to have at least one aspect of their abilities that sets them apart from other characters, something that makes them unique in some way. In general, these characters tend to be darker and grittier than the typical sort of superhero. They tend to get down in the trenches and slug it out when necessary, getting bloodied and battered in ways that other heroes manage to avoid for the most part. Even so, they can be lighter in tone in some cases, significantly, Green Arrow's boxing glove arrow tends to be met with humor whenever it is brought out. Furthermore, the 1960s Batman television series reflected a deeply campy tone in the comics to the character that infected his mythos for several years. No matter the tone, characters with powers that don't quite line up with the typical superpowers can still find themselves in company with their more powerful cohorts. They can, through pseudo-superpowers, match up, and sometimes take down, superheroes of much more supernatural skill sets.

The powers mytheme, in conjunction with its subtropes, including the means by which the characters gain their powers and the pseudo-superpower, is perhaps the most integral mytheme of the superhero, the part that serves as a foundation for all the other tropes to anchor to as a point of reference. Some characters seem born to wear the cape. Some struggle to determine what to do when they find themselves in possession of extraordinary powers. What all superheroes share in common is some sort of ability that puts them on a level above the average person. Even those who have achieved their powers, ostensibly making them more like the common man, have developed abilities that are realistically beyond the scope of what is actually realistically achievable. This is the mytheme that turns these characters into the iconographic figures at the center of mythic tales.

Promotes/Maintains the Status Quo

Superheroes tend to be unwilling to push for changes both in their own society and in the society that produced them. Richard Reynolds explains, "The hero is in [a] sense passive: he is not called upon to act unless the status quo is threatened by the villain's plans."[82] Generally speaking, until the villain enacts a plan, muddying the waters as it were, the superhero does little. Characters like Batman and Daredevil may go out on patrols, but even these are passive and they only move to act when they find something which doesn't match with the ideal they seek to maintain. "The common outcome, as far as the structure of the plot is concerned, is that the villains are concerned with change and the heroes with the maintenance of the status quo."[83] The hero is reactive and the villain is proactive in the mythological understanding of the superhero.[84]

Reynolds' argument is underscored by a speech made by Lex Luthor, Black Manta, and Poison Ivy in *Justice*, written by Jim Krueger and Alex Ross. In the story, several of the major opponents of the Justice League team up to bring down the major superheroes of the DC universe. In a speech broadcast around the world, the villains explain that superheroes are

> [p]reserving the world and not daring to change it means [...] [b]owing to the status quo of human suffering. [...] the Justice League [...] save us only to send us back to our old lives. Back to our bills, back to our useless jobs, back to our suffering. If they were really the heroes they claim to be, they'd save us from those same lives as well.[85]

Luthor and his partners are condemning the superheroes for doing nothing but maintaining the lives of people they save from supernatural threats. Once the menace is over, superheroes let the citizens go back to life as it was before the threat. Thus, this story underscores the proactive nature of the supervillain. They work to change the world and leave the Justice League struggling to keep up with their efforts to change the world.

This point is underscored further in *Avengers: Age of Ultron*. After the team goes through the effort of trying to pick up Mjolnir, Thor jokingly explains, "You're all not worthy." Ultron explodes through a wall and replies, "Worthy? How could you be worthy? You're all killers. You want to protect the world, but you don't want it to change." The rest of the film rests on the conflict between Ultron's effort to change the world in a misguided effort to make it better and the Avengers efforts to stop him. Granted, the team is fighting against the extermination of humanity, a goal most would agree is valuable, but it is still at its center an effort to maintain the status quo of the world.

As important as it is to understand that the superhero is generally a passive character when it comes to the stories, this trope extends beyond the narratives themselves. It is also incredibly rare for any sort of mainstream superhero to manifest the traits of a minority or subculture until that culture has gained some level of mainstream acceptance. Almost without exception, superheroes work with the dominant social construct, the status quo of the society that produced the character. The first major black superhero wasn't created until the late 1960s. Writers have struggled with establishing strong, well-developed women within the genre. There have been some exceptions, but women in general have been relegated to secondary status in the stories. Though there have been a few gay superheroes since Northstar came out in

1992, they have always been lesser members of the team. Furthermore, it hasn't been until very recently that they have tended to be out and proud. This changed, but only slightly with the reimagining of the first Green Lantern, Alan Scott, as gay in DC's reboot of their continuity.

Alan Scott's powers are based more on a sort of magical mythos than the extraterrestrial powers of Hal Jordan's lantern ring. There have been several other Green Lanterns following in the wake of these two originary characters, but all of them follow in the tradition of Jordan rather than Scott, privileging Jordan's mythos and making Scott less of an influence and a much lesser presence in the DC universe. This is true to the point that Scott's lantern was eventually retconned to be part of the Oan powers that fueled Jordan's lantern as well. Scott's connections to other Green Lanterns in the DC universe keep him on the outskirts of the stories told about the Lanterns. He is already outside of the main Green Lantern stories, marginalized by his different origin. This makes his homosexuality of less significance to readers and those who engage with the mythos than if it had been a more prominent character.

Both within the mythos and with the way the mythology interacts with the world of the real, the superhero tends to be careful about upsetting the norm. His is a position of working to maintain the balance, even when the balance is not what many would perceive as an ideal. While this mytheme is mostly concerned with the status quo within the stories themselves, it does have application to changes outside of the narratives themselves. This is perhaps one of the deeper underlying reasons why Batman cannot kill the Joker. He is a part of the status quo of Batman's universe. To disrupt that is to change the status quo in a meaningful way, a way almost exclusively reserved for stories set in alternate realities. Mythologically speaking, proactivity on behalf of the superhero is more unwelcome than on behalf of the writers, editors, and creators, there is still a sense that certain things about individual mythoi should not be changed. While the specifics may differ from person to person, most participants in an individual mythos will demand that certain things remain constant.

Relationship Struggles

In almost every interaction between superheroes and the characters that exist around them, there tends to be a large amount of friction in practically all relationships in which they engage. Superheroes tend to develop a great many relationships over their existence; but both romantic and not, superheroes tend to have difficulty maintaining good relationships with practically all of them. Though they may be friends, or even spouses, it is incredibly rare for a superhero to have an uncomplicated relationship with anyone.[86] Making new non-superhero friends is practically unheard of and even friendships with other superheroes tend to be fraught and rife with confrontations both physical and ideological. Simplistically speaking, superheroes have a hard time keeping their relationships strong and healthy.

One of the heroes who demonstrates this most clearly is the man who stands at the center of the mythology. Lois Lane and Clark Kent are frequently in a state of relationship flux. Specifically, in the *Superman* series of films, the relationship between Lois Lane and Clark Kent is consistently strained. At first, Kent resents Lane's attraction to Superman. He would prefer that Lane be attracted to him rather than his superpowered alter ego. When Lane begins to suspect Kent's real identity in *Superman II*, it puts a huge strain on him by constantly trying to force him into outing himself as the Man of Steel. Eventually, he does reveal his dual identity to Lane. Ultimately, he gives up his powers and the persona of Superman in an effort to make their relationship work. Of course, the needs of the world eventually outweigh his own need to be with the woman he loves, and he regains his powers and becomes again the superhero, recomplicating his life with Lane. In the comics, Kent and Lane never seem to have a settled relationship. The production crew at DC Comics seems to continually move Superman and Lois Lane from uneasy secrecy to cautious flirtation to a revelation of the big secret to a resetting of the relationship back to its original state of uneasy secrecy. In the New 52 continuation of their relationship, Superman is romantically involved with Wonder Woman, demonstrating an obvious complication between Lane and Kent.

Currently, perhaps the most clear and complete example of this mytheme is the television series *Arrow*. The series didn't identify Queen as Green Arrow by name until the beginning of the fourth season, his identity in the DC mythology. However, there is no question that the two are the same superhero, even if he is rarely called by that name on television. In fact, mid way through the first season, Malcolm Merlin suggests that they call the vigilante Green Arrow, to which Oliver Queen replies that it's "lame."[87] By as early as the third season, people have begun to refer to the vigilante as the Arrow. His efforts at crime fighting put him at odds with his ex-girlfriend's father, a member of Starling City's police force. In fact, there is not one relationship Queen has that isn't strained or difficult, constantly exacerbated by his dual existence as foppish young man recently returned from the dead and as the bow wielding hero haunting the streets in order to make good the wrongs of the father.

In the series, Oliver Queen struggles to maintain healthy relationships with anyone he knows. Ex-girlfriends, mothers, stepfathers, bodyguards turned partners, sisters, former friends turned enemies, in fact practically everyone Queen meets ends up having a strained relationship with him. Felicity Smoak is emblematic of this problem. She begins as Queen's assistant at his family company but quickly gets drawn in to his efforts to clean up his city. Early on she manifests infatuation for him and her feelings seem to grow over the course of the story. Queen develops mutual feelings for her, but they come to light after she has entered into a relationship with Ray Palmer who also took over Queen's company. The twists and turns of their feelings for each other have played out over the course of three seasons and shares many of the beats of daytime soap operas.

In truth, the soap operatic nature of the relationships in *Arrow* is emblematic of the superhero mythos. In general, the way relationships work in superhero stories bear a strong resemblance to the sorts of storylines that run for years on soaps. The relationships are melodramatic, move from extreme to extreme and find their highs and lows more determined by the needs of the storyline than a more natural seeming ebbs and flows of typical relationships. The path of a superhero's relationship never does run smooth.

Spectacular Origin

It is insufficient for a superhero to simply determine to fight crime and the evils of the world just because it seems like a good thing to do. Every superhero is all but required to either have had an unusual and remarkable upbringing or to have faced a cataclysmic event that caused him to determine to fight the forces of evil. Even if they are born to a humble, seemingly normal, station in life, superheroes become superheroes through some spectacular story. Most often, this origin is also tied to the powers manifest by the character. In fact, the origin story usually explains the source of the powers the superhero possesses as well as the codename, power, and persona of the superhero. Reynolds suggests, "The cardinal moment of transformation, where the everyday world is chosen to intersect with the superhero metatext, underwrites all of a character's subsequent transformations and adventures."[88] The final chapter in this work goes into more depth on the interrelation of these tropes. The backstory is an integral part of each superhero's mythos. This is so much the case that in the media of the superhero film, the first installment of a series will nearly always include a rendition of the origin. This is true whether the superhero is less well known, as was the case with Green Lantern or Iron Man, or an American icon like Superman.

Even though there is almost nobody who watched *Man of Steel* who didn't already know the story of the Kents, Kal-El's Kryptonian origin, and the fact that Kal disguised himself as a reporter known as Clark Kent, the film took a large portion of its running time to lay out what may be the most familiar origin story of them all. Of course, there were differences in this telling of the origin. Jonathan Kent's guardedness regarding Clark's budding powers, to the point that he would rather die than allow Clark to reveal his abilities, seems to be a starkly cynical approach to the down-home, Midwestern attitude we would seem to be expecting from "Pa Kent." Perhaps this is one of the biggest reasons why the origin story is told and retold time and again. Reynolds explains that "when taking over a new assignment, a new writer/artist team will be expected to have a shot at redefining a character's origin story."[89] This concept of the retelling of the origin story plays out quite clearly with the influx of superhero films recently.[90] The basic facts may not change, but the subtleties can be part of the way we reinvent the mythology to suit the needs we have at the time we retell the story.

In the case of Spider-Man, the radioactive spider bite was sufficient to grant him his abilities, and is unusual enough in and of itself. Of course, in the more recent films, the spider is no longer radioactive, a conceit that only worked in decades past. More recent depictions of the spider have tied it to genetic manipulation, efforts to use our greater understanding of the genetic code as the "magical elixir" that grants supernatural powers. Regardless of the spider's power, it is always going to be an arachnid responsible for Peter Parker's physical change and, coupled with the traumatic death of his Uncle Ben, create the core of Spider-Man's origin story. His motivation and powers both derive from unique intense moments in his life. Batman is also motivated by the tragic death of his family. Over time, driven by growth instigated by Denny O'Neil, his back story has developed to inevitably include an element of world travel, the idea of deep focus and drive which takes him from the most mysterious of Asian monasteries to the greatest universities of Europe. The world traveler aspect of his origin is spectacular in its own right and helps form who Batman is as a character. Travel is now a constant whether it includes time in a Chinese prison, as in *Batman Begins*, or in the finest schools in Europe, as the 1980s Batman frequently claimed.

Even when this origin is left unexpressed, it is an understood part of the superhero. For decades, the X-Man known as Wolverine has lived with an unclear origin. There were stories about time spent in Japan and Canada, but nobody seemed to know why he called himself Logan, or where he was raised. So important was the character and his back story that when Marvel finally determined to let Wolverine's origin story be told, it was simply titled *Origin*.

It became one of the most important comics of the year. Though it has failed to remain as formulative in the field as *The Dark Knight Returns*, or *Watchmen*, it is a valuable study in the way an origin story, whether implied or expressed, is integral to the existence of any superhero. Done well, it strengthens their place in the mythology, but a haphazard, poorly realized origin can create a tension between the hero and the mythology. Though he can still meet all the conventions of the genre, a superhero with a poorly executed origin will resonate less with the mythology.

Strong Visual Component

No matter the media, superheroes are very much couched in a visual sort of storytelling. Superheroes naturally fit in visual media such as comics, film and television, and make much less frequent appearances in novels, short stories and other media that rely more on the printed word. Superman and the prototypical superhero The Shadow drew listeners during the heyday of the radio and other superheroes did receive broadcast time. However, this is the only real exception to this trope. Their costumes are visually vivid and more easily expressed in images than description. Their exploits and actions involve a great deal of physical manifestations, which also encourage visualizations. When presented in formats that rely largely on the word, as in novels, a great portion of the narrative is devoted to describing the physical aspects of the character and the events surrounding it.

In the 1996 book *Siege*, which takes place in the X-Men universe, the book opens with a description of Magneto aboard his orbiting space station. Magneto is described in these words:

> He was not an uncommonly large man, standing just over six feet tall and weighing just under two hundred pounds, but there was a quiet fury about him that gave even the bravest soul pause. His eyes were the blue-grey of an impending storm, his long hair an extraordinarily perfect white. Defined by his command [...] he was not given to frivolous commentary or physical expression. Still, he allowed himself a low sigh, a shake of his head, and then his hand came up to stroke his smooth chin.[91]

Shortly afterward, Magneto is joined by a character named Exodus as "[h]is robes flowed around him, reminding Magneto of a purple and black butterfly, such a contrast to the hard shell of crimson that he himself wore."[92] While the first description is not uncommon in the sort of pulp novel tradition, which was a strong influence on the development of the superhero myth, it still manifests a strong visual element while setting the character, a character already very familiar to the typical reader of this book, the second descriptor serves very little purpose in the development of the story and manifests the way visual descriptors frequently appear without any apparent narratological imperative. Tracy Hickman also spent a great deal of time with the descriptions of the technology and situations in which Batman finds himself in *Wayne of Gotham: A Novel*, a fact for which he is criticized by some reviewers of the book. Shannon Hale, more well known for her young adult fantasy, also spends significant time on description in her young adult superhero novel *Dangerous*. Brandon Sanderson, perhaps best well known for completing the *Wheel of Time* chronicles, wrote a series starting with *Steelheart* which contains cinematic descriptions of locations and events.

This is perhaps why there are so few prose works which tell superhero stories, and of those that do practically none are recognized with much acclaim.[93] It also explains why the mythology has survived so well a transition from a primacy in comics to a primacy in film. The way film can tell a strongly visual story makes it an appealing fit for expressing superhero stories. Until recently, television has been less successful despite sharing a primarily visual storytelling medium. I would argue reasons for the lack of success of the television are tied to expectations of narration and story development that differ between television and comics, though the biggest reason is most likely the financial limitations of television and the higher cost of successfully portraying superheroes on the small screen. However, there is success in series such as *Smallville*, *Arrow*, *The Flash*, and *Daredevil* which indicate that superheroic tales can exist on the small screen.

Regardless of the format, the visual design of the superhero is vitally important to the character and presentation of the superhero. The design of his costume and equipment receive special care. The hero's superpowers are designed in such a way as to always be dynamic. From Spawn's cape and chains to Wolverine's claws, from Green Arrow's boxing glove on a shaft to the solid light of Green Arrow's projections, there is always a visual characteristic in the creation of the superhero.

Superteam

Nearly every superhero who lives in a universe that includes other superheroes will team up with them at some point. Though the superteam usually includes a long term commitment to a cooperative, the shorter team ups serve some of the same mythological purposes. The team up commonly serves as an opportunity to showcase the way different superheroes approach their job and how the divergent approaches play out. This also allows for upping the ante in regards to the power of the supervillains faced. A more epic villain can sometimes only be defeated by the combining of a multitude of superheroes. Frequently, the personalities developed in superhero's individual titles influence the way the characters interact with each other. The conflict of personalities and intentions sometimes serves as the central conflict in the story, but ultimately there is a strong component of physical violence in these team-ups, whether it be within the team itself or directed toward the villain or villains that brought them together.

Nearly every superhero mythos includes reference to superhero teams of some sort. From DC's Justice League and Justice Society to Marvel's X-Men and Avengers, the superteam is a part of the fabric of the mythology. However, even outside of the team itself, superheroes do get together to fight crime in a way that shares mythological fabric with the superteam. Typically, these cooperative endeavors are known as team ups. Generally, the team up, when not a part of the story structure itself, is used as a form of spectacle, to bring some added interest and sales to a series. However, for the individual heroes who become part of a team the opportunity becomes a means for highlighting their own personalities in a way that can occasionally be sublimated in their solo adventures. Specifically, when Superman and Batman are part of a team it manifests the conflict between the ultimate Boy Scout approach of Superman and the post–O'Neil grim and gritty, antisocial methods of Batman. Though there is a strong respect between the two, their conflicts in ideals drive these stories. In many cases, this serves a sort of philosophical purpose.

While Batman generally takes on the role of the suspiciously over analytical, Superman wants to trust others, to believe in the inherent good of others. Their debates are, at times, mirror debates that we have in our own lives and society as we seek to make sense of similar challenges faced by these figures, though usually on a smaller scale. The differences in their attitudes are brought out in *Batman: Hush*. In the early rescue of Edward Lamont IV, Batman comments on the way Superman would have handled the situation. "Not just the bending steel and flying out," he says, "Clark could smile. That Boy Scout thing. And then say something homespun to put the boy at ease. But the boy doesn't have Clark. He has me. In my city. Gotham City. It is better that way." Batman, the great detective of the DC universe, recognizes the deep rift between the way the Man of Steel would handle things and the way he does. Later, when the two square off, Batman says, "If Clark wanted to, he could use his superspeed and squish me into the cement. But I know how he thinks. Even more than the Kryptonite, he's got one big weakness. Deep down, Clark is essentially a good person ... and deep down, I'm not." Superman views his kindness as an asset, something that helps him be more human, more like the kind of person who hails from Smallville, America. Batman sees his ability to do whatever is necessary, short of killing, as a greater asset. Their conflicts, ranging from the alternate universe of *Red Son* to the forward looking *The Dark Knight Returns*, tend to be about Batman's solitary pragmatism conflicting with Superman's efforts to do the most good for the most people.

Of course, there are many superheroes who exist primarily within the context of a superhero team. Almost all superteams have members who strike out on solo adventures, but there are also many characters, even in the Justice League, who exist almost exclusively as members of the team. The Martian Manhunter rarely ventures outside of the bounds of the Justice League. His primary focus is to work with the team to resolve the conflicts that threaten them, the world, and the universe. Even so, solo big hitters like Batman and Superman still venture out with their teammates and view the Manhunter as a valued and equal member of the team. Furthermore, the superheroes who form the classic iteration of the Fantastic Four rarely, though not never, venture outside of their team. Many members of the X-Men have solo adventures, especially Wolverine, Rogue and Gambit. However, Cyclops is almost exclusively defined by his connection to the team. The same can be said for Colossus and Kitty Pryde. They are depicted as distinct individuals, but almost never spend significant portions of time away from the team.

By contrast, even the most solitary of heroes will at some point feel the need to join up with members of the superhero community. Spider-Man and Batman, two characters who tend to be well known for their solo adventures, have spent time on teams. In fact, the legal issues that kept Spider-Man from being a part of the Avengers film led to satirical commentary regarding the way the business aspect of superhero films creates a strangely disjointed sense of continuity when compared with the shared universe of the comics.[94] The recent interest in creating a Batman/Superman film also underscores the tendency for superheroes to team up. Nolan's film trilogy depicts Batman as a character who has little interest in trusting anyone and only uses people as part of the mechanics by which he can achieve his goals. To go from that series to a world in which he works with Superman, even one as subdued from his previous incarnation as he was in *Man of Steel*, underscores the feeling that cooperativity between superheroes is an ideal state through which a character must pass to be a solid part of the mythology.

Supervillain

While some superheroes have less easily identifiable antagonists, all of them have villains against whom they must compete. This challenger to the efforts of the hero has become known as the supervillain. This trope includes not only the single villain but the rogues gallery as well, a large group of villains typically uniquely linked to a specific superhero. Furthermore, many supervillains serve as a negative image of the hero, casting his values and abilities into sharp relief. Some do so by being like the hero, a mirror image of sorts, some by being an opposite to the hero, like a film negative. The Joker is a prime example of the latter. His flamboyant appearance and lack of self-control sever as a funhouse mirror to Batman. The bright purple, white, and green of the Joker contrasts visually with Batman's black and grays. Furthermore, the Joker is wild and unrestrained while Batman seems incapable of letting his emotions have any sort of free expression. The interaction between a superhero and the supervillain provide the main source of conflict in most superhero stories. Those more similar to the superhero still have a significant difference from the hero, even if just in their actions or worldview. Though the cinematic Red Skull may have similar abilities to those of Captain America, including superstrength and tactical prowess, his efforts are bent on world domination as opposed to the efforts of Captain America as he attempts to create a more free and democratic world.

A classic example of the relationship between superhero and villain is presented in the leader of the X-Men, Professor X, and his arch nemesis, the human hating Magneto. Both Charles Xavier, founder of the X-Men, and Magneto are intelligent men. Both have powers beyond the scope of even most other superpowered individuals in their universe. Both understand the problematic conflict between mutants and humans is one that needs resolution. Both are very capable of leading large groups of people. The conflict arises in the way they seek to go about resolving the conflict. Professor X believes in a peaceful resolution, that human and mutant can coexist peacefully. Magneto believes that, in order for there to be peace, the mutants must rise up and suppress the humans who seek to do the same to them. Both want the best for the mutant population, they simply have very different means and ends regarding how that best will actually appear. Of course, this is based on the classic depiction and most common understanding of the relationship, much as it is presented in the Bryan Singer's first X-Men film. In the comics, since their relationship was fleshed out, both have died, Magneto became a part of the X-Men—even being the headmaster for a group of mutants at the school for a while. He was made younger, twice attempted to establish sanctuaries removed from the world political scene, and generally showed the complexity of a man who wants the best but sees it through the eyes of a survivor of the Holocaust. This certainly challenges his place as a supervillain in the mythology. At the same time, the echoes of the most classic rendition of the myth will always be a part of the story. It is likely that the mythology will never let Magneto escape his past as a supervillain, regardless of any storylines chronicling some sort of redemption or problematizing his role as a villain.

Speaking of a great many supervillains, Reynolds explains, "All are corrupted by power, and power in the particular form of knowledge" which he ties back to the serpent's promise in the Biblical Garden of Eden, "Ye shall be as gods, knowing good and evil."[95] Supervillains tend to seek for godlike power in some form, whether it be knowledge, influence, political ability. No matter their goal or how they set out to achieve it, the supervillain will always ultimately be revealed as evil before the end of the story arc. In some ways, this is the truth of the supervillains. They give us an opportunity to understand, comprehend and engage with universal and conflicting ideas of good versus evil. This is a large part of their role within the mythology. They let us see and understand the evil around us. Though some stories complicate the villain's path to malevolence, making him seem good in some way or another, ultimately the appearance of good and right is proved false and the superhero will triumph over the forces of evil.

Switching Sides

In *Avengers: Age of Ultron*, both Pietro and Wanda Maximoff, recognizable as Quicksilver and Scarlet Witch respectively, begin specifically opposing Tony Stark and by extension the Avengers in *Age of Ultron*. However, as they learn more about Ultron and his purposes, they understand that their erstwhile partner is the bigger threat to them and their nation and that Stark, despite his flaws, attempts to do good for the world. Ultimately, they join with the Avengers to take down Ultron and the threat he poses to the world. In the comics their change takes longer and is more complicated. One of the bigger complications in the comics is their relationship to their father, Magneto. Naturally, he attempted to make them a part of his villainous efforts to overthrow humanity to make room for mutant kind. Their defection is more complicated and involoved in the comics than in cinema. In the film, Ultron convinces the twins that the best way to destroy the Avengers, and specifically Tony Stark, is to side with him. Only later do they realize that he, too, wants to overthrow humanity to make room for his own kind. In both cases, the superpowered duo changes their allegiance. In both the comics and the film, the Scarlet Witch becomes a member of the Avengers. Quicksilver's storyline is slightly more complex, but the fact that they switch sides in the conflict still remains.

Though individual superheroes tend to stay true to their own individual *moral code*, they don't always agree with those around them. Sometimes, as is the case with Hal Jordan's shift from Green Lantern to Parallax, heroes become villains. Sometimes villains take on the role of heroes, perhaps best exemplified by the time that Magneto takes brief leadership of the X-Men. The Scarlet Witch and Quicksilver exemplify a list of characters who started out as antagonists to superheroes before becoming heroes in their own right.[96] Sometimes the shift is that dramatic as characters redefine their allegiances. Sometimes it's less clearly delineated.

Though Batman and Superman have spent the majority of their time together as colleagues in the fight against evil, they have occasionally shifted allegiances. In Frank Miller's pivotal *The Dark Knight Returns*, the duo square off in what first appears to be a fight to the death. This fight has resonances in the upcoming *Batman V Superman: Dawn of Justice*. Batman has had multiple experiences with this mytheme. He and Catwoman find the status of their relationship shifting from day to day and sometimes from moment to moment. Though Bane originated as an antagonist to the Dark Knight, the two have worked together on occasion. Jean-Paul Valley also started out fighting against the caped crusader until the two started working together, eventually leading to Valley's taking of the cape and cowl after Bane broke Batman's back. However, Wayne saw Valley taking the role in an unacceptable direction. This led to another shift in allegiances as Wayne took back the cowl from Valley. Eventually, the two reached an alliance.

This mytheme needs to be understood as one that plays out in both overt and subtle ways. Sometimes it makes its presence known in dramatic storylines, like Marvel's *Civil War*, and sometimes it takes place in smaller moments, as it does when Batman over-thinks Catwoman's final words in *Batman: Hush*. Though some lines are clearly delineated and rarely breached, the lines of engagement rarely stay constant in superhero mythology. Individuals may stay firm in their own sense of moral structure, but even when they do they can run into conflict with those around them, and may occasionally find themselves in situations where they feel the need to align themselves with the metaphoric (and occasionally literal) devil. And, at times, the devils fight on the side of the angels.

Traumatic Trigger

Frequently expressed in the telling of the *origin*, superheroes are driven to act or have their *powers* activated by some sort of traumatic event. This can be an event like the death of parents which drove both Bruce Wayne and Richard Greyson to become superheroes. Sometimes the trigger is built into the event that gives the characters superpowers. Shortly after the event that gave the Fantastic Four their powers, Reed Richards begins to explain how they should use them. He is interrupted by Ben Grimm, who says, "Save the speech, big shot. We get it. We gotta use this power to help mankind, right?"[97] Sometimes the traumatic is a series of events. In *Superman: Secret Origin*, Clark Kent's abilities unfold in a series of events. Lana Lang first sees Kent's amazing powers when he saves her from a thresher, surviving the blades unscathed. The second time the story shows his unearthly abilities is when, as he is talking with Lang and being confronted by the boy whose arm he broke, his x-ray vision first begins to work. Shortly afterward, when Lana kisses him, Clark's heat vision sets a banner in the school hall on fire. Each event occurs when Kent is functioning in a state of excitement.

As is the case with Kent and the kiss, superheroes frequently come into their own as such at a time near or after puberty. Sometimes directly tied to the changes that occur in normal humanity, the onrush of hormones and the changes most teenagers experience, sometimes just as a coincidence, there is something in the myth that practically requires post-pubescence for the superhero.[98] Simplistically, superheroes can't become superheroes until they have gone through puberty. In the X-Men series of films and comics this tends to be especially true. In the first X-Men film, a young woman known as Marie talks of grand post high school plans with a boy she likes. As they talk, they lean in for a kiss. In the emotional rush of that first kiss, her mutant ability activates, sending him into seizures as she pulls vitality from him. The experience is a complete shock to her and her parents. In her case, there was no prior indicator that she was anything out of the ordinary. Only later does she take on the persona of the X-Man known as Rogue, developing more fully her powers which allow her to pull abilities and energy from those whom she touches. Immediately after Marie's experience in the film, Jean Grey, in an address in Washington, D.C., says, "These mutations manifest at puberty and are often triggered by periods of heightened emotional stress."[99]

Even in the case of Superman, though he manifests his powers at an earlier age in most iterations of his origins, he doesn't engage those powers in fighting for truth, justice and the American way until after he has made it through high school and taken a job as a reporter for the Daily Planet. In fact, he spends the bulk of his juvenile existence hiding his abilities from those around him.[100] He entered into life as an adult before he engages in work as a superhero. Though it is more typical than necessary for superpowers to activate only after puberty, it is almost completely unheard of for a character to take on the role of superhero, don the tights and cape as it were, until after puberty has started. Joseph Campbell discusses the way trauma triggers these kinds of shifts when he discusses mythic rites of passage. They "are distinguished by formal, and usually very severe, exercises of severance" that set apart the person from their former life and associations. When this trauma and frequent period of subsequent isolation is over, the character "return[s] to the normal world […] as good as reborn."[101]

While Campbell is talking about the hero monomyth, this is one of the mythemes in this lexicon that crosses over between traditional hero myths and the superhero. In fact, Bruce Wayne's journey from the prepubescent boy who saw his parents gunned down in Crime Alley to the Dark Knight mirrors closely the process outlined by Campbell. Indeed, though his body may not mature at the moment his parents are killed, his psyche certainly does. Though it can be argued that the adult Wayne becomes is one with serious psychological baggage, it is still an adult who emerges from the trauma surrounding the loss of his parents. It is a young man with a mission who determines that he will spend the rest of his life seeking to symbolically right the wrong done to him and his parents.

There are some few exceptions to this mytheme within the pages of comics and cartoons. However, as a mythology, it is incredibly rare for a prepubescent to be given the kind of recognition that would exalt them into the godlike or demigodlike status the majority of superheroes achieve when they become a part of this mythology.

In the case of Invincible, he is told at a young age that he will most likely develop superpowers. Though the origin story told him by his father is a much more pleasant than the truth as it eventually comes to light, the promise hangs over Mark's head for roughly a decade before he sees a glimmer of the powers he is destined to possess. The first signal that he has powers presents itself during a trash run at the fast food restaurant where he works during high school. When he tosses the trash toward the dumpster, his nonchalant throw sends the bag hurtling toward the stratosphere. When it disappears, he looks shocked briefly but then a smile spreads across his face as what happens sinks in. It is a realization of promises made to him by his father as a toddler, that he would have superpowers of his own someday. The fact that this promise is fulfilled only after he is in high school foregrounds the prevalence of puberty as a factor in realizing the results of the trauma. However, it is his confrontation with Omni-Man, a much more traumatic event, that fully crystalizes Mark's transformation into the superhero known as Invincible.

Urban

Most superheroes are centered in urban locales. This fact is so much a part of superhero mythology that Superman's locus of operation is in Metropolis, a literal synonym for "city" or "urban." Spider-Man and a great many Marvel superheroes function out of a fictional version of New York. In *The Avengers*, Tony Stark's tower is one of the key components of an only slightly fictionalized New York skyline. By the end of the film, it becomes clear that this tower is destined to become the headquarters for the superhero team forged during the film. Furthermore, in a discussion of the city that plays host to the Dark Knight, Bill Finger succinctly points out that "Gotham is another name for New York."[102] All of them are only exemplary for the vast majority who function in cities primarily in the northeast, but also in metropolises across the United States and infrequently in densely populated areas around the world.

Talking of New York as the nexus of all superheroes, Reynolds states, "It is a city which signifies all cities, and more specifically, all modern cities, since the city itself is one of the signs of modernity."[103] Batman, Superman, Green Arrow and nearly every superhero in the DC universe live in fictional cities, or fictional versions of real cities, but all of these cities seem patterned in some way or another after a major metropolis, most frequently *the* major metropolis that is the Big Apple. Star City, Coast City, Gotham City, and Metropolis, all fictional DC cities that superheroes call home, share qualities with real cities in America.[104] The level of artificial reconstruction of the *urban* in superhero stories reached a new level in a recent superhero film. In *The Avengers*, great pains were taken to create an accurate and detailed digital map of New York through which the epic final battle raged. The entire city was digitally scanned and recreated in a computer so that the conflict would appear in a realistic rendition of the city the superheroes call home. Even when, as is the case with the Nolan take on Batman, the superhero's city is less New York it still bears the marks of major urban locales.

Of course, there are instances of small towns in comics. Specifically and perhaps most obviously, Clark Kent traditionally grew up in a small town, fittingly known as Smallville. Indeed, it is part of his apple pie, all-American upbringing to have been raised in a town almost as inherently typical of the idyllic small town as Andy Griffith's Mayberry. Granted, it is an upbringing that exists in mild irony to his unusual immigration status. As much as he spends his formative years as an unusual immigrant in a rural area, evoking the pastoral in his specific mythology, he doesn't really come into his own as Superman and put on the tights and cape until he moves to Metropolis, to the big city. Even over the course of *Smallville*, a television series centered in the titular small town, Kent's Superman costume is noticeably absent for the vast run of the show. Indeed, the run of the show is more about Clark growing into an eventual role as a superhero rather than about his actual exploits as a superhero. When Clark Kent becomes Superman, it is in a place where he has an opportunity to "leap tall buildings in a single bound."

It is not uncommon for a superhero to seek refuge from the incessant pressures of his work in rural or suburban locales. His efforts to escape drive him from the city and he only returns when it is time to become a superhero again. In *Quiver*, the series articulating the rebirth of Green Arrow, Queen comes back from the dead in the alleys of Star City. Even though he doesn't remember the events of his death and subsequent resurrection, he immediately jumps into the fray. His costume at the start of the story arc is ratty and his arrows are cobbled together out of castoffs and refuse, but it is distinctly recognizable as Green Arrow's costume. This aspect of the Green Arrow is immediately ready to engage in superheroics. However, in a strange twist, there is another aspect of Queen that is not interested in being a superhero anymore. He is found in an Elysium like field completely devoid of buildings doing nothing more than shooting arrows at a target. In this case, part of the character is a superhero and lives in the city and part is not and exists in a pastoral landscape. Furthermore, when the Avengers need to go to ground in *Age of Ultron*, they go to a secret farmhouse where Hawkeye hides his family and where they can take refuge from Ultron and regroup.

Anciently, as is the case with Gilgamesh, it was life outside of the walls of the city where danger was found. Safety was found within the bounds of civilization, though sometimes the wilds did encroach upon this safety, as Grendel did. Fairy tales abound with this sense of uncertainty accompanying trips into the woods. However, by the time Siegel and Shuster wrote Superman's adventure, the city had become something just as unsettling as the wilds were in the past. Because of this, the modern hero is frequently found in the new wild of the city. In *Bending Steel: Modernity and the American Superhero*, Aldo J. Regalado explains the shift to the city by explaining that the superhero "affirms his identity in the face of a sprawling metropolis, whose very structures and massive size threaten to render individuals insignificant."[105] The superhero "is made super by his ability to affirm his manhood in the face of urban landscapes."[106] At times, the city serves as a backdrop not only to test the superhero but to allow other mythemes their fullest expression. Spider-Man's web slinging mode of travel, both a manifestation of his *powers* and *strong visual component*, would be sharply curtailed if there were no skyscrapers to use, certainly. But in any case, the urban situation will always be an important part of the myth of the superhero.

Violence

A vital element of nearly every superhero story is violence. There are many superheroes who claim to want to solve the problems they confront with only the most non-violent method. No matter that desire, their pacifistic efforts will last only so long before they are forced into a situation that requires them to react violently. Though a hero's intelligence, virtue, wisdom, and other aspects of his personality can be tested, the vast majority of challenges usually require a great deal of physical violence to resolve. Though individual stories can center on various aspects of the superhero's persona, from virtue and intelligence to investigative skills and speed. However, the likelihood of this focus being all that is of note in the story is almost nonexistent. Most stories include at least one major physical showdown with the villains. Even when the hero seeks to avoid violence every viewer knows the big fight is lurking just around the corner.

In "What's so Funny About Truth, Justice & the American Way?," written by Joe Kelly and penciled by Doug Mahnke and Lee Bermejo in 2001, Superman confronts the superhero team known as the Elite. Their hyperviolent ways run contrary to Superman's ideals. They willingly and wantonly kill those who challenge their authority and heroic morals, frequently in a visceral and violent fashion. Ultimately he finds himself facing off against the Elite. Despite his desire to avoid a violent confrontation, he ends up taking out the four members of the team in incredibly violent ways. One appears to have been ripped limb from limb. Another's lungs collapse as Superman creates a vacuum around him, depriving him of air completely. The third is hit so hard that bits of his costume are ripped from his body and are left hanging in the air as a blue, red, and yellow streak blurs across the panel. The last, though not quite as overtly violent, is lobotomized by Superman's heat vision. True, the lobotomy is very localized, focused on the small area of the brain that controls the powers of Manchester Black, the leader of the Elite. Superman even admits the brain will heal. However, that doesn't mitigate the detail that the Man of Steel burned out a portion of a man's brain. The fact that Superman spends the majority of the story attempting to oppose the violence of the Elite makes the violence he resorts to using all the more poignant.

The violence inherent in superhero stories can be played to different effect. For example, the film *The Avengers* utilizes the violence inherent in the battle between the superheroes and the extraterrestrial invaders to underscore the value the heroes place on human life. The plan Captain America lays out for the team includes a focus on protecting the citizens of New York from the damage caused by the fight. Captain America instructs New York's finest to move citizens to areas outside of the fight zone. Iron Man works to direct the invaders, known as the Chitauri, away from populated areas. Thor is directed to keep the Chitauri from a more massive invasion by keeping them bottlenecked at the portal through which they are coming to Earth. By contrast, the fight scene between Superman and General Zod in *Man of Steel* has been much criticized for the way it handles the violence in the contest.[107] Zod and Superman go one on one through the streets of Metropolis. They crash through skyscrapers, churn through streets, and wreak mayhem and havoc throughout the city. During the fight, there is no indication that Superman has any concern for the citizens of the city. Critics have taken the filmmakers to task for showing a character known to some as the ultimate Boy Scout presenting no indication that he regards the innocents of the city as a factor in his fight with Zod. How true the reading is may be debatable, but one of the dangers of violence is the way it can lead to this kind of reading.

In comics, even those as violent as *Kick-Ass*, the violence in the book is rarely accepted without a sense that it serves a purpose in the story. It has to be a part of establishing the superhero's goodness and wellbeing. Because *Man of Steel* depicts a superhero with apparent disregard for the people he is supposed to serve and protect it runs contrary to the accepted purpose of the mythology. In fact, trailers for *Batman Vs. Superman: Dawn of Justice* indicate that Bruce Wayne's motive for opposing Superman is tied to the fact that he saw the fight in *Man of Steel* through much the same lens. No matter how violent the scene, the story has to be furthered by the violence, usually in the form of a resolution of the conflict with the antagonist to the superhero. No matter the purpose, no matter how much they try to avoid it, superheroes will almost inevitably have to resort to acts of violence in pursuit of the success of their *moral code*.[108]

The structure given in this lexicon allows the myth of the superhero enough shape to allow us to examine individual mythological characters while being flexible enough to support a myth that has characters that span television, film, comics, clothing, conventions, toys, and various other incarnations. Though the characters themselves will have to be examined in more than one iteration in order to identify all the mythemes herein described, and even then some will be absent, the inherent assumption is that the superhero will connect with the majority of the mythemes. The more closely a story connects to the lexicon, the more closely it will draw to the center of the mythos. However, the inherent flexibility of the myth itself requires that we avoid slavish adherence to the terms in the lexicon. In the chapters that follow, four separate stories will help illuminate the way this lexicon can be used to better our grasp on the existence of the superhero myth and how it engages with and informs character and story creation and reception.

2

Green Arrow as an Exemplar of the Superhero Myth Structure

Though the superhero known as Green Arrow has been around for decades, he has rarely found the same level of popularity as the A list superheroes of the DC or Marvel canons. He has worked with Superman, Batman, Wonder Woman and Green Lantern as part of the Justice League of America, a *superteam* which serves as the classic example of the trope. However, he has yet to meet with the level of popularity of many teammates. Though the CW series *Arrow* has changed the popularity of Green Arrow, the fact that he is by some standards a "B-list" superhero makes him a good character to use as an example of how superheroes conform to the mythology. It is natural to expect a character like Superman or Batman to conform to the mythology, since they are the characters through with the mythology was largely formed. Because the creators at Marvel, led by Stan Lee, began many of their characters with the idea of tweaking the already extant mythology, those characters are more problematic as far as typifying the mythology goes. They still conform to the mythology to a large extent, but most were designed with the idea of examining what happens when the myth is intentionally altered.

However, because Green Arrow is part of the DC canon, where the myth tends to be less problematic, and because of his current, if slight, increase in popularity, he is in many ways an ideal character through which to demonstrate the applicability of the mythological framework of the superhero. Though Green Arrow has been used as an exemplar for a few of the mythemes presented in the first chapter, those mythemes are further expounded upon in this chapter in a way that is worth greater articulation. This demonstration will lead to a better understanding of the lexicon and how it works for superheroes which will help in a more comprehensive exploration of the superhero myth outside of the basic constraints of the superhero.

The analysis in this chapter will focus primarily on the series *Arrow*, with discussions of a few graphic novels as they help to illustrate the mythemes. These books include *Green Arrow: Year One*, *The Longbow Hunters*, *Quiver*, and *The Archer's Quest*. *Year One* is the current template for the origin story for Green Arrow, including being marooned on a desert island and his ability with the bow. In *The Longbow Hunters*, Green Arrow is involved in a story that includes drugs, kidnapping, and coping with a more modern world than that with which he is comfortable. It is a grim and gritty story that includes levels of violence and blood that go beyond traditional comics. *Quiver* and *The Archer's Quest* are the first and second books that deal with Oliver Queen immediately after he is brought back from the dead. Though the second book is more recognized as an integral part of the important tales of the Emerald Archer, they both work together to a large extent to set the stage for the life he lives after he has come back from the dead. All four books ostensibly exist within the same universe, though they don't follow a clear chronology. On the other hand, the television series is a reinvention of the Green Arrow chronology.

Arrow is a 2012–2016 television series on CW, a channel that also aired *Smallville*—a show focusing on a young Clark Kent growing up in the titular town—and the *Arrow* spin-off *The Flash*—depicting the growth of Barry Allen into the speed-based superhero of the title. *Arrow* begins with the return of Oliver Queen to Starling City after living alone for five years on a remote island. The story explores the after effects of his return, his efforts to clean the corruption from the city in his superhero persona, define himself and his mission, and his memories of what happened to him between the time he was shipwrecked on the island and his return to Starling City. Along the way, he deals with several characters who are both familiar and foreign to those who know Green Arrow's history. This firmly establishes *Arrow*'s status as an *iteration* of the mythos of the specific character. The nickname of Oliver Queen's little sister, Thea "Speedy" Dearden Queen, coupled with the eventual introduction of a love interest for her named Roy Harper indicates the level of change made for these characters. In the comics, Oliver Queen had a sidekick known as Speedy whose real name was Roy Harper. Furthermore, when Roy graduates into his own role, eventually becoming the superhero known as Arsenal, Green Arrow gets a new female sidekick, again known as Speedy whose name is Mia Dearden. As is typical for adaptations or *iterations*, the producers of the television series make liberal adjustments between the mythos of the Emerald Archer in the comics and that which they create for the series.

This level of reinvention continues with the development of Dina Laurel

2. Green Arrow as an Exemplar of Myth Structure   97

Lance. In the majority of comic iterations of the character, she is known as Black Canary, sometimes lover and once wife to Oliver Queen. In many iterations, she has a sonic scream she can use to devastating effect along with excellent combat skills. At the beginning of *Arrow*, she works helping the needy in legal issues as a lawyer and only takes on the role to fill a void vacated by her sister. She eventually brings in the concept of the sonic scream from the comics, something her sister was lacking in the role. The early relationship between Queen and Lance is complicated in the show, underscoring the *relationship struggles* trope in ways that are less overt in the comics. When Oliver embarks on the trip that precedes his exile he brings Laurel's sister, Sarah, who dies as a result of the shipwreck that directly results in Oliver being washed up on the island. Because of this, there is a serious amount of tension between Oliver and Laurel that doesn't exist in the comics. The majority of the first season shows Laurel with Oliver's best friend, Tommy Merlyn—whose father also happens to be the *supervillain* known in the comics simply as Merlyn—further complicating the struggle between Tommy, Oliver, and Laurel.

Certainly, anyone who has watched the series would be hard pressed to offer an argument against the existence of the *amazing physique* in *Arrow*. One classic moment highlighted in the pilot is an exercise called the salmon ladder. This exercise, performed shirtless in the pilot episode by Stephen Amell, who plays Oliver Queen in the series, combines a standard pull up with a motion that lifts the bar up a rack of brackets, essentially turning the pull up into a method of climbing a set of poles. The scene in the show demonstrates Amell's physique to nice effect, including a stomach crunching motion along with the flexing of arm, chest, and back muscles as he proceeds. From the images seen throughout the series it appears that the fictional city in *Arrow*, Starling City, has managed to completely obliterate obesity and general unattractiveness. Everyone in the show seems to be both at least semi-attractive and in good shape. Of course, this is not uncommon in the world of comics, but to see it depicted so thoroughly on television seems ample evidence of the promulgation of the trope. Everyone appears capable of holding a second career as a model, including the computer geek Felicity Smoak, another name drawn from preexisting DC lore. A prime example of geek chic, Felicity is both incredibly smart, if a bit socially awkward, and amazingly attractive.

Smoak's attractiveness is emphasized by a shot which is duplicated on a few other actors throughout the series. In the episode "Dodger," Smoak is required to go undercover at a high end fundraiser with Queen. When she first walks in, the camera begins below her waist, emphasizing the short, slit skirt that barely covers her legs, and pans up to reveal that, at least for this soiree, she has removed her glasses. By beginning with the low shot, the camera invites the viewer to focus on her bare, shapely legs rather than on her technological know-how. This trend seems to continue throughout the series, however its import can be overstated due to the fact that *Arrow* seems to follow the general sense of the *androcentric* that still exists in the American society of 2013. Having said that, the comics tend to be a bit more forthright in the androcentric nature of Green Arrow. In both *The Longbow Hunters* and *Quiver*, the women are largely sidelined and with the notable exception of Shado from *The Longbow Hunters* seem to be more victim than savior. Of course, the nature of the costume worn by Black Canary, Queen's frequent love interest, in many ways exemplifies the objectification of women in comics. Though naturally dark haired, Dinah Lance wears a long blonde wig, a legless leotard and fishnet stockings when she fights as Black Canary. In *The Longbow Hunters*, she seems to have given up crime and is tortured by one of the villains of the book. During the torture, her shirt is strategically ripped to show as much of her body as possible without blurring the line between torture and fetish to the breaking point. Furthermore, at one point in the resurrection story *Quiver*, Lance blames her displeasure in her memories of Oliver Queen on the fact that she is "probably just P.M.S.-ing."[1]

Lance's costume manifests the existence of costumes within the continuity of this specific superhero myth. Oliver Queen himself is also a strong example of the *costume* mytheme. In the beginning, Green Arrow's costume took strong cues from the mythological image of Robin Hood. He was and continues to be dressed in green. Originally, he had the kind of hat made popular by the Errol Flynn personification of Robin Hood or the classic image of Peter Pan. Later, in the *Longbow Hunters*, this hat was replaced by a green hood. The hood was inspirational for the design of Oliver's outfit in both *Year One* and *Arrow*. Even though Queen is not known by the Green Arrow moniker in *Arrow*, going so far as to proclaim the name "lame" when presented by Malcolm Merlyn at a dinner party, he still maintains the very predominantly green color scheme of the comics.[2] In all the stories that deal with Oliver Queen, there are practically none that show him wearing anything but some iteration of this green costume. Perhaps the only potentially well-known example is his appearance in *The Dark Knight Returns*. In that book Oliver appears late in the storyline and only has one arm and wears a faded blue coat and jeans. There is very little to even connect this man with the Lincoln green archer of his prime.

Of course, *Batman: The Dark Knight Returns* is usually recognized as an alternate future. However, even outside that story, Queen has had an interesting and somewhat complicated relationship with the idea inherent in the *ageless* mytheme. In *Arrow*, Oliver is in his late twenties. In *The Longbow Hunters*, Queen is feeling the ticking of his biological clock and suggests to Lance that they have a child. In his first appearance in *Quiver*, Queen has a long, pale beard. In *Year One*, the beard is scraggly and unkempt but not nearly as full. In all of these instances the internal reference to his age is implied without ever being fully stated. The truth is that Queen could simply be having an early mid-life crisis in *The Longbow Hunters* brought on by the aging of Roy Parker—an aging common for the sidekick as they develop and take on their own superhero persona in superhero mythology. However, the overall sense that comes from reading the several key stories relating to Green Arrow is that he is generally older than the typical superhero age. While this does not preclude the sense of agelessness predominant in the superhero myth, it does slightly complicate Queen's adherence thereto.

Perhaps part of the reason Queen seems older than his counterparts is the traditional insistence that he sports a light blonde mustache and goatee.[3] This, along with the green hat or hood and the bow give Green Arrow a very *strong visual component*. This component is strengthened in *Arrow*, despite the absence of the goatee, by casting Oliver's superhero persona in practically exclusively green light. In his *lair* in the show—an abandoned factory owned by Queen Industries that becomes headquarters in the basement while the main floor serves for cover as a nightclub under construction throughout the first season—every light in the basement casts a green light. In *The Archer's Quest*, Green Arrow takes his partner Roy Harper, now known as Arsenal, to visit "the Arrowcave," his base of operations, a place Speedy calls "home." It is the first place that Queen visits as he seeks to gather important items left behind after his death.

As important as *the lair* is to Queen in both *Arrow* and *The Archer's Quest*, it is only tangentially linked to the overall image of Green Arrow. In *Arrow* he always manages to have a green smear of color over his eyes rather than a domino mask whenever he goes out in the archer persona, though the makeup serves a similar purpose as the mask. Despite the fact that the series has a slightly less overt connection to the need for the visual, whenever Queen picks up the bow there are several shots that serve little more than to give the hero some time in heroic visual shots. It has also developed a symbol that may serve more as the *chevron* for the Green Arrow mythos than anything from the comics. The title shot for the series always includes a solid, wedge shaped arrowhead with scalloped lower edges behind the show's name. The design of the head is fairly unique and does about as much as anything, short of the facial hair from the comics, to brand the archer with a unique, iconic image.

The fact that Queen does without the goatee in the series makes it much simpler to maintain an *alter ego*. Though there is some pretence at separating the characters of Oliver Queen and the Green Arrow in the comics, it is difficult to make the two personas believably different from one another with his unique facial hair. However, in *Arrow*, Queen goes to great lengths to keep his identity as the superheroic archer separate from his existence as Oliver Queen. In the episode "Damaged," Oliver orchestrates his home arrest and ankle monitoring. Once it has been made clear that he is unable to leave his home mansion, Oliver coerces his bodyguard and uneasy partner, John "Dig" Diggle, into taking on some arms dealers in the Glades, the slums of Starling City, as the hooded vigilante. Detective Lance, Laurel and Sara's father, had been convinced that Queen was the superhero he has been trying to bring to justice. Because of Diggle's efforts, Detective Lance becomes certain that Queen cannot be the superhero. Oliver goes through the entire charade in order to ensure that his dual identities are as distinct and separate as they can be.

Of course, those most closely linked to the secret are those who work most closely with the hero. Though Diggle—a name which seems to be an overt nod to the writer of *Green Arrow: Year One*, Andy Diggle, which also happens to be the name of John's brother who was assassinated by the villain Deadshot—mentions specifically that he is "not signing on to be a sidekick."[4] In "Vendetta," Queen stumbles before introducing Diggle as his "associate." Both Diggle and Smoak seem clearly to be linked to the mytheme of the *helper*. Throughout the series, Diggle certainly takes his cues from Queen. The first time they have a major conflict, Diggle insists that one of the Hood's targets is innocent because he worked with Dig in Afghanistan. In the end, Queen's opinion of the man is right, he is the mastermind behind a series of armored car heists.[5] Though Diggle does correct Queen's trajectory over the course of the first season, their roles are set and exemplified by the conflict over Diggle's former friend. Though the conflicts between Queen and Smoak are much less dramatic, she also serves as a helper to the vigilante. She begins helping him as he brings challenges to her at Queen Industries. When he comes to her after being seriously wounded, she is drawn into the circle of Queen's *alter ego*. She serves as the information technologies consultant for the vigilante, in the same way that the Oracle does for the Batman family. However, Queen himself makes it very clear that Smoak is not his sidekick. In "Sacrifice," Lance is interrogating Smoak when he gets a call from the vigilante. He says, "I've got your sidekick right here." Queen replies, "I don't have a sidekick. When I need help, I call you." This further complicates the mytheme of the *helper* because, at least at this point in the series, Detective Lance is still very much an *antagonistic authority figure*.

Queen's *superteam* has adjusted over time to include Roy Harper[6] and Thea "Speedy" Queen. He has also worked with Ray Palmer and Barry Allen at various times, though those classify more as team ups than the actually superteam. Roy's skills and *powers* make him the most likely candidate to be Queen's primary *helper*. As the only person who can match, if not surpass, Queen in flat out ability, he seems a natural for the role. The fact that he left the team foregrounds the occasional shifting nature of the *helper* in the superhero myth. The void he left has been filled by Laurel Lance, Thea Queen, and John Diggle, and Felicity Smoak in their various roles. In truth, over the course of the series, Queen has worked with—and against—a variety of people. Though Slade Wilson begins as Oliver's friend and teacher, he later becomes the overarching antagonist of the Arrow in season two. One of the clearest examples of *switching sides*, Wilson isn't the only one to do so. In order to save Starling City and his friends from Ra's al Ghul, Queen severs ties with his friends and becomes a member of the League of Assassins, going so far as to kidnap Diggle's wife, Lyla Michaels.[7] While this is not the only time, it may be one of the more poignant examples of the mytheme in the series.

As established in the Green Arrow mythology, Queen's superior ability with the bow was developed after the accident that left him shipwrecked on an island where he had to learn to shoot to survive. Though Queen claims he "was a natural bowman—the best," which would indicate an ability perhaps bordering on the born subtrope of *powers*, his abilities certainly manifest more as achieved in terms of mythemes.[8] Furthermore, Queen's abilities, as impressive as they are, are less in line with traditional powers, strengthening the connection to powers achieved, and more connected to the pseudo-superpower subtrope. At least in theory, Green Arrow's abilities with the bow are possible for a talented and trained human being to reproduce. Never is it acknowledged that Queen has any real uncanny or supernatural ability with a bow. It all seems to be simply some sort of blend of genetic luck and uncanny training. In the pilot episode of *Arrow*, Queen throws a half dozen tennis balls out in front of a concrete wall. In less than ten seconds, the balls have been pinned to the wall by his arrows. Whether they are the result of some sort of amazing, supernatural experience or not, Queen certainly has the skills to qualify as powered in the terms of the genre. Thea Queen has also developed abilities beyond the norm and appears to be developing into a more traditional *helper* in the vein of a sidekick than the series has hitherto seen.

The other factor connected to powers within the mythology is the *traumatic trigger*. In both *Green Arrow: Year One* and *Arrow*, it would appear that

Queen is shipwrecked at some point in his late teens or early twenties, at point when he can be expected to shoulder some responsibility, even if he does so poorly. Whatever his age, in both stories, he certainly comports himself in a very juvenile manner, appearing to be much less mature than his actual age. This all changes for Queen after his time on the island. From his Silver Age origin to the present, Green Arrow has formed the core of his superhero identity based on the trauma he had to face on the island and by events surrounding his time thereon. The idea of *one power per person* connects to his time on the island. Though the interest in archery predates his shipwreck in *Year One*, his skills are honed on the island. He has trained several sidekicks to shoot with nearly the skill he possesses. However, with the exception of his arch nemesis Merlyn, there are no other major archers in the DC pantheon. And most of them have combat skills that connect to their primary skill with the bow, accuracy. This mytheme plays out a bit more purely in *Arrow*. The only other archer of any note, besides the characters who gave Queen his early lessons, is the same villain from the comics, Malcolm Merlyn, known in the series as the Dark Archer and the father of Queen's best friend, Tommy Merlyn.

Queen's relationship with Tommy Merlyn helps foreground the *outsider* mytheme. When Queen returns from being stranded for five years, he finds out that Tommy and Laurel had developed a relationship, his sister has gotten involved with clubbing, alcohol, and drugs, and her mother has married the man who took over as the head of Queen Industries at the legal death of her former husband. As Queen attempts to reconnect with his family and friends, he finds himself consistently trying to connect with many people with whom he has very little in common. As they reach out to him, Moira Queen pulling him toward the company and Tommy Merlyn trying to draw him into the party scene, he resists. Because of the goal he has of bringing justice to Starling City, Queen has a hard time reconnecting to his family, friends, and community. He explains that he's "taking all these people that I love and putting them at arms length" in order to achieve his goals.[9] His continual focus is on the mission given to Oliver by his father before he died, to clean up his city by bringing to justice those whom his father claims have failed the people. Because his efforts focus on Starling City, *Arrow* certainly fulfills the *urban* mytheme of the superhero. The alternately named Star City is the setting for *Quiver*, and at least as the primary jumping off point for *The Archer's Quest*. Star City and Starling City are one and the same, the name change being a part of the several, if small, changes made as the mythos of Green Arrow was adapted for television. Furthermore, in *The Longbow Hunters*, Queen and Lance move to the real life city of Seattle, Washington.

2. Green Arrow as an Exemplar of Myth Structure   103

The fact that this mission is what drives Queen drastically underscores the presence of the *please the father* mytheme. What is fascinating about this mytheme is that it has little to no presence in the comics. Oliver's father fails to make an appearance in *Year One* or any of the other books that serve as paradigms in this book. However, in *Arrow*, it is his father who explains to Oliver what he needs to do upon returning to Starling City. Shown in a series of flashbacks throughout the first season, Oliver's father gives him a book which contains a list of names. These names are of individuals who, according to the father, have failed to protect and care for the citizens of their hometown. In many cases, those on the list have actively worked against the best interests of the inhabitants of Starling City to promote their own agendas. What this means is that the superheroic drive at the core of the character in this iteration of the Green Arrow mythos derives directly and specifically from the idea of allowing his father to rest in peace, knowing his son is making him proud, in essence one of the most clearly depicted manifestations of this particular mytheme. In *Arrow*, the superhero mythology is more expressed than in the Green Arrow comics. This fact is a large part of what makes this series an excellent example of the myth as expressed in a story or stories centered on an individual superhero.

The fact that Queen's father is dead makes the trope of the *orphan* half true. Early on, his mother lives on, married to the man who took over her husband's company. Because of this, Queen doesn't fully connect with the mytheme early on. However, when Moira Queen is killed at the end of the second season, the mytheme reaches complete applicability. His age at the time this happens is a bit unusual in the mythology, but allows for technical fulfillment, and his attitude about their deaths does suggest that he feels the pain in similar ways to those who more fully feel the burden of this mytheme. His relationship with his parents seems no more manifest in the comics and stories used to express the Green Arrow mythology. In fact, his parents seem not to be an issue in the stories at all. In *Arrow*, Queen's alienation from his mother might be considered a good enough connection to the mytheme; however, both make an effort to re-forge some form of a relationship. In this case, the case of Oliver Queen, the mytheme fails to manifest in nearly the way it does in many of the other superheroes with whom Green Arrow associates, especially the well-known orphans Batman and Superman.

Along with the death of Oliver Queen's parents, he has faced death himself. And, as is the case with so many superheroes, *death is temporary* for Green Arrow. Though he doesn't actually die in *Year One*, in a conversation with Hackett, his bodyguard and personal assistant, the idea of cheating death comes up. After breaking in to the compound used to manufacture opiates,

Queen is confronted his former bodyguard. Hackett confronts Queen, remarking, "That's twice now you've come back from the dead." Queen simply remarks, "I plan to make a habit of it!"[10] While in this case, the young Green Arrow and his opponent aren't talking about actual, clinical death, Oliver Queen did, in fact, die while protecting Metropolis from the devastation of a supervillain's bomb. When Oliver Queen is brought back from the dead, the ramifications run over two story arcs, the resurrection itself is covered in *Quiver*, but the settling in, the reconnecting of Queen to his superheroic family, the real resurrection of a sort, takes place in *The Archer's Quest*. In *Arrow* he is legally brought back from the dead after returning from the island. What is significant about Queen's atypical resurrection in the series is the fact that it marks a change in his character, a rebirth after being changed by his time on the island. This change is hinted at in *Year One*, but that storyline ends shortly before Queen returns home.

In *Arrow*, the young foolhardy playboy leaves on his father's yacht and the brooding vigilante returns, mirroring the events of *Year One*. Despite the efforts to ground *Arrow* in a more realistic world, in the third season episode "The Climb," Oliver is fatally stabbed by Ra's al Ghul. However, Tatsu, the wife of Queen's partner during his ARGOS training, Maseo, manages to bring him back to life. Oliver Queen's resurrection is followed by that of his sister through use of the Lazarus Pit in "The Fallen." Even though the second revival is part of Ra's al Ghul's plans to make Oliver his successor, it finalizes the existence of the *death is temporary* mytheme as a part of the series mythos.

Queen did officially and completely die in the Green Arrow comics as well. In an issue called "Run of the Arrow," Queen has his arm trapped within a bomb, grasping a dead man switch. If he lets go, the bomb, which is full of a pseudoscientific compound that will level the city of Metropolis, will detonate. The only solution is to destroy the plane while Queen is holding the switch, or to amputate his arm. Though Superman offers the second option, Queen refuses, insisting he go down with the plane. This event, yet to be collected and republished, leads to the events of both *Quiver* and *The Archer's Quest*. It is also, by nature of the way he dies, an excellent example of *violence* within the mythology of the superhero. Of course, this trope resonates throughout the stories surrounding the Green Arrow. From *Year One*'s assault on a druglord's compound, to *The Archer's Quest* and Queen's fight against Solomon Grundy, to the serial beat downs from every episode of *Arrow*, Queen is perfectly willing to use violence to achieve his goals. In fact, in the fight against Grundy, Queen admits, "Clark once warned me about fighting monsters. I don't care what Clark thinks. I don't care what *anyone* thinks. He'd say, 'That's what happens when you get too emotional.' Too bad for me....

I've *always* been emotional."[11] After shooting Grundy over a dozen times, punching him hard enough to bloody his own fist, stabbing Grundy with arrows held in his fist, and dodging thunderous strikes, Green Arrow eventually takes Grundy down by strangling him with the string from his broken bow. It's an act driven by desperation and a love for his partner whom he needs to protect. His willingness to be governed by emotion spills over into practically every iteration of the character. This emotionality drives Queen to making decisions that lead to less than peaceful resolutions. His volatility leads to greater amounts of violence.

The violence inherent in Green Arrow and his methods has led to complications with the *no killing* mytheme, specifically in the first season of the television series. This mytheme is at the core for many heroes. Unfortunately for a man who uses a bow to fire sharp arrows at others, it is practically impossible to avoid casualties. He has used the infamous boxing glove arrow in the comics, and even uses a modified form—a "knock-out arrow"—in the semi-realistic *Year One*.[12] However, in *Arrow* and at a few times within the comics he makes little-to-no effort to avoid killing those whom he confronts. In the pilot episode of the series, Queen is kidnapped along with his friend Tommy Merlyn. While Merlyn is in a stupor, Queen breaks free from his restraints and attacks his would-be attackers. Most are killed in the action, arguably as the unfortunate result of the violence of the conflict. However, one of the kidnappers manages to break loose and attempts to flee. Oliver chases him down and subdues him. While the kidnapper is subdued in a choke-hold, he pleads for his life, saying, "You don't have to do this." Queen replies coldly, "Yes, I do. Nobody can know my secret." He then snaps the man's neck.[13] It is a deliberate move, there is no heat of battle or accident of combat upon which this death can be blamed. Not only does Queen violate this mytheme, but he does so in a very cold and calculated way. Of course, the thought behind this killing underscores the vital nature of the need to keep the alter ego a complete secret for Oliver Queen.

However, there is a backlash to the way Queen handles this mytheme. When Tommy finds out that Queen is the vigilante, he calls him a "serial killer."[14] It puts a huge strain on their friendship that leads to complications throughout the remainder of the first season. When Tommy is killed during the planned cataclysmic earthquake known as the Undertaking, it drives Oliver back to the island, feeling he has failed Starling City and his friend. He doesn't feel he has a purpose anymore. He is confronted by copycat vigilantes seeking to continue his work, but "without the restraint" Queen had as the Hood.[15] When Smoak and Diggle confront him to put on the costume again, he refuses because of "the body count."[16] When Thea Queen is kidnapped by the new vigilantes, Oliver realizes that there is a need for him to still wear the hood and carry the bow. However, he determines that he will no longer be a killer. When he is confronted by former Detective Lance, who says, "Typically when I bring in guys that you've gone after they're a little more dead," Queen replies, "I'm trying another way."[17] This shift in focus causes Officer Lance to change the way he refers to Oliver Queen's alter ego. Queen himself doesn't want to be called the Hood after the death of Tommy Merlin.[18] Lance calls Queen "Arrow," saying, "it seems more appropriate than the Hood."[19]

This shift, from the Vigilante and the Hood to Arrow to Green Arrow clearly demonstrates the way the *codename* plays a factor in the television series. Clearly, Queen has and uses a codename but it goes beyond that. The three shifts in reference are accompanied by a change in *costume* and a shift in the way he conducts his efforts to clean up Star City. Green Arrow, the most recent codename comes with a more careful, perhaps more holistic, approach to fighting the corruption of the city—including a run for mayor. The Arrow was willing to kill if necessary, but went to great lengths to avoid it. The Hood, as Queen starts his efforts to clean up his city, is willing to go to whatever lengths are necessary. The codename mirrors his approach, from the political to the deadly.

It is probable that the entire body count of Green Arrow's tenure in comics fails to amount to the number of likely kills in the first season of *Arrow*, listed at 26 in one episode.[20] However, there is some rationale for the time he spends in violation of this particular mytheme. Queen's *moral code* explains, at least to some extent, why he justifies killing in some cases and makes a strong effort to avoid it in others. As he attempts to help Helena Bertinelli, the Huntress, to deal with her own vendetta, he explains his rationale for taking a life. He argues against her massive body counts. Queen explains, "I only kill people when it is absolutely necessary. It's not my opening move. And the way that you're going, you're going to get somebody hurt."[21] When he says somebody, he means innocents, those not tied to the crimes and wrongs he seeks to punish. He kills "for the good of others."[22] His efforts are designed with a specific purpose. "People [...] need to be reminded that Starling City isn't theirs for the taking."[23] Though his actions in *Arrow* are more lethal than common in comics, he is still driven by a sense of justice, a desire to protect the innocent. For Queen, justice is sending people to jail or forcing them to give their money back rather than killing them. The desire to avoid killing through his *moral code* is strengthened to the point

Queen believes that justice is his primary motivator, the key element of his moral code. However, it is only part of what drives his efforts. Part of what motivates him is Queen's belief that he deserves to pay for killing Sara Lance, the girl he took with him on the yacht trip. He further believes that he can expunge his father's sins by eliminating the power of the people whose names are in his book. Thus, he is driven to atone for both his own sins and the sins of his father. Though his urge is deep and agitates him any time he attempts to take a break from his work, the agitation is tempered. As he tries to help Bertinelli temper her own rage, he tries to teach her the bow. He explains, "To use a bow and arrow requires patience and discipline."[24] Thus, part of what drives him is a need to wait, to accept the need to do what he should when he should. His actions are governed by an understanding of the value of waiting until the right time to strike.

As much as he recognizes the value of waiting, he is driven to use his resources to bring to justice those who have failed Starling City. He has been given a specific set of skills and he has been given access to a great deal of resources due to his financial assets. Though he squanders his money before the shipwreck, he feels a need to use it to further the ability to use skills he learned on the island. He feels the *power and responsibility* mytheme keenly. There is no sense of a desire to use his skills for anything other than his pursuit of justice, of using his abilities in a responsible way, at least in a way that he views as responsible, whether those around him would agree with him or not.

Much of his responsibility is articulated through voiceover. More than any other filmed superhero story, *Arrow* follows the norms of *expository narration*. Every episode begins with narration that establishes the parameters of the series. Throughout several other episodes, especially those early in the series, Queen explains a great deal of the events directly to the viewer through fourth wall breaking voiceover. There are also occasions wherein the characters explain important plot points in a narrative style that conforms to the trope as well. Though dialogic narration is not uncommon in television and film, Queen's monological voiceover is rare. The narration as it exists serves to bring the viewer up to speed, but does little to forward the plot. In the comics, Queen's narration frequently works with the visuals to add to the sense of drama in the stories as they unfold.

One of the fascinating thing about the voiceover narration is the emphasis on the book given to Queen by his father. The list of names in the book are those of rich businesspeople, white collar men and women who took advantage of the less fortunate, the downtrodden. Part of what maintains Queen's heroism, despite some of his less than stellar activities, is that he is coming to the aid of those hurt by big business practices. However, with the exception of one instance, Queen helps thousands of faceless people, none of them are personified for the viewers, or seemingly for Queen himself. The question that stands in regards to his actions is whether or not Queen is *ineffective against real world problems*. By rescuing the pensions of the less fortunate, by protecting the financial assets of the poor of Starling City, it would seem that Queen is working against the problems of the real world. However, in *Arrow*, we see no effects of his actions. Though Queen's headquarters are in the Glades, the apparent slums of the city, the series shows the inhabitants only as background characters. The series never shows those who benefit directly from his actions. The names in the book are frequently shown with some depth. They are the focus of Queen's efforts. Whether or not he is effective is entirely dependent on circumstantial or implied evidence. In this case the mytheme is unresolved, but favors the likelihood that the trope is extant to a very large extent in Green Arrow's stories.

Queen's efforts to bring justice down on those in his father's book put him in frequent conflict with the police force in Starling City. Because of this, and for other reasons, one of the city's lead detectives is Queen's *antagonistic authority figure* of the superhero mythology. Detective Quentin Lance is the lead detective building the case against the vigilante he calls "the Hood." He is also Laurel and Sarah Lance's father. Thus, he actively pursues Queen's identity as superhero as well as having a vibrant antagonism toward Queen himself. Because of this dual antagonism, Lance makes for a practically textbook example of a person in authority who works against the alter egos of the hero and person. Lance follows every lead he can to find the Hood. He harasses Queen whenever they meet, bringing up the fact that he blames the playboy for the death of Sarah and for betraying the trust of Laurel. Eventually, he finds evidence that Queen might be the vigilante. It is this discovery which leads to the previously mentioned house arrest and Diggle's time as the vigilante.

Even before this incident, Detective Lance is careful to avoid laying too much at the feet of the Hood. In "Lone Gunmen," while the police favor the idea of blaming a fatal shooting on the vigilante, Lance opposes the idea because the evidence doesn't support it. As much as he would like to bring the Hood to justice, he refuses to follow what he sees as false leads. In this same episode, the Hood gives Lance evidence that points to the true assassin and requests that the detective help protect the next target, who will be at a stock auction later on. Lance decides to acquiesce, making it the first time that he becomes the Hood's unwillingly *cooperative authority figure*. Though it is the first time, it is not the last. Though the trust between the two never comes close to reaching the levels enjoyed by Commissioner Gordon and Batman, they do cooperate in going after larger and more immediately threatening targets.

2. Green Arrow as an Exemplar of Myth Structure 109

Much of the tenuous nature of the relationship is tied to the fact that, while both men seek justice, Detective Lance is devoted to doing so only within the law. On the other hand, Queen has no problem promoting *justice over law*, a phrase actually used by the mayor of Starling City shortly before he is gunned down by copycat vigilantes in the premiere episode of the second season.[25] Along with his willingness to kill when he believes it is necessary, he also acts against the law in several instances. In the pilot episode, Queen uses a specially made arrow with a built in program to wirelessly hack into Adam Hunt's account. Hunt is a business owner against whom Laurel Lance is bringing court proceedings for swindling "hundreds of people out of their homes and life savings." The program embedded in the arrow redistributes forty million dollars from Hunt's account into the various accounts of his victims, repaying them for the harm done by his shady business dealings. He circumvents the legal system to bring justice to people. Laurel's uncertainty in winning the legal case underscores the fact that this case of justice might have been impossible by going through the legal process. The justice Queen seeks is about reestablishing justice to Starling City, a justice that has been unbalanced by the people listed in the book, a group of people who gathered together to clean up the city. They focus this cleansing on the Glades, the poorest area of Starling City. This organization, known as the Undertaking, attempt to right the wrongs done to them by the perceived dregs of society.

By fighting against the Undertaking, Queen *promotes/maintains the status quo*. The people in Queen's book have used their powers to destabilize the status quo in the city. Their actions problematize lives of those who are already struggling to survive. Though it is completely possible to argue that his efforts destabilize things as they have become since his shipwreck, Queen's efforts are presented in a positive light in *Arrow*, a way to balance the scales unbalanced by the rich and powerful. Thus, at least for the viewer, the Hood is a man who rebalances the status quo, the way things were before the destabilizing influence of the Undertaking. To a lesser extent, *The Archer's Quest* is also about the return of the status quo. After he is resurrected, Oliver Queen goes on a road trip to retrieve items that belonged to him and were hidden before his death. The scale of the events in this tale exists on a much less public a schema than in *Arrow*. However, it is much more personal than the television series.

Though Queen is seeking to reclaim that which is his, he does move in a new direction while he still comes to grips with the past he once had, combining the old and new as he attempts to reestablish a status quo. His trip focuses on gathering four items from his life prior to his demise. The first is a diamond-tipped arrow which provides a diamond which Queen uses combined with a ring made for Green Arrow by the Flash to create an engagement ring which he ultimately opts not to use to propose to Dinah Lance. In this case, even his attempt to disrupt the status quo is ultimately thwarted as he realizes she has no interest in changing their relationship. His recovery efforts also include retrieving a power ring given to him by Hal Jordan, the first human to join the Green Lantern Corps, which he left in the truck the two of them used to travel together. The last item is hidden behind his certificate of membership to the Justice League. It is a picture of Oliver Queen with his son Connor on the day of his birth. It is the first time that Queen's knowledge of his son's birth is revealed. All of these items are a part of the reality Queen had before he died.

Green Arrow's quest is actually quite short on villains. He has a confrontation with the out of shape Cat-Man, a sometimes villain known as Shade, and the only real fight in the story with Solomon Grundy. However, in the broader scope of the stories surrounding the Emerald Archer he has confronted more than one *supervillain*. In *Arrow*, the Undertaking serves as an overarching villainous organization, but at the head of it stands Malcolm Merlyn, father to Oliver's friend Tommy. More significant in the fulfillment of this trope is Merlyn's second identity as the black-clad archer who works at odds to both Queen and the Starling City police force. Though the character has changed from his persona in the comics, the fact that the comic version of this character goes by the name Merlyn, though his true name in the DC universe is Arthur King. In either of these alternate versions of the character, he appears to be one of the most significant supervillains to face off against Oliver Queen. Another major figure in both the comics and the television series is the Japanese archer known as Shado. In *The Longbow Hunters*, Shado is an assassin who works against Green Arrow's efforts in Seattle. However, her role in *Arrow* is of a different sort. As of the end of the first season, Shado has yet to make her presence known after Queen returns to Starling City. However, she is integral to Oliver's development with the bow on the island. On the island, she is the daughter of Yao Fei, the man who gave Queen his first lessons in surviving. When Yao Fei ends up in the camp of the organization on the island, Shado takes over and instructs Queen in the use of the bow.

Shado's role in *Arrow* is more a part of the creation of the superhero than a later addition thereto, as she is in *The Longbow Hunters*. Thus, she becomes part of Queen's *spectacular origin* in the series. Shado is responsible for giving him the beginnings of his impossible archery skills. Her interaction with Queen stretches over a series of flashbacks in multiple episodes in *Arrow*. In the comics, the origin of Green Arrow is told in various forms. However,

2. Green Arrow as an Exemplar of Myth Structure 111

the generally accepted official version of his origin is *Green Arrow: Year One*, written by Andrew Diggle. Though there are significant differences, the influence of *Year One* on *Arrow* is worthy of note. In both, Queen survives being deliberately left to die on the ocean. He ends up being apparently stranded alone on an island, only to discover that he is not alone. In *Year One*, he stumbles upon an opium farm run by a villain known as China White, a drug kingpin who makes her presence known in Starling City in *Arrow*. In *Arrow*, the island is a repurposed penal colony wherein Queen is forced to undergo a refining process. In both cases, the carefree playboy who lands on the shores of the island is left on the sandy beaches and a new man is ultimately rescued and brought home. In all iterations of the story, the key elements of being stranded on the island, and learning his skills with a bow as a way to survive until he is rescued remain constant.

Though *Arrow* is a very specific take on the Green Arrow stories, it still fits within the overarching mythos of the character. Combined with the stories told within the comics, the series presents a character with deep and solid ties to the grand mythology of the superhero. The few tropes to which the story fails to conform tightly help serve to indicate the still nebulous nature of superheroes and some of the difficulty that exists in solidifying the boundaries of the mythology, or perhaps the value of having space in the structure of the mythology for experimentation and invention. Specifically, the challenge of Queen's ability to conform to the avoidance of killing shows how the myth of the superhero is still changing. At this point, the superhero still avoids killing, but the absoluteness of the trope is one of the more challenged within the lexicon. However, especially when viewing the tools Queen uses in his work, it is apparent that he goes to great lengths to avoid killing and conform to the mythology of which he is a part. While characters like Superman and the like are expected to be more tightly bound by the constraints of the superhero mythology, indeed the superhero mythology is largely based on the Man of Steel, secondary characters like Green Arrow help to establish how far reaching the tropes are even to those on the outskirts of the mythology. In what follows, characters who exist tenuously and at the farthest outskirts of the myth are discussed as conforming or not in ways that will demonstrate how integral certain mythemes are to the superhero, mythemes that are well exemplified by Oliver Queen, the archer in green.

3

Buffy Summers and the Superhero Myth

Reading a Popular Culture Icon Through a Mythological Lens

In 1997, Joss Whedon launched what was arguably one of the most ambitious popular culture phenomena in decades. Based on a poorly performing film, it combined teen drama, mystery, and elements of the sitcom with a strong confluence of horror. The result was the series *Buffy the Vampire Slayer*. The series, unlike the preceding film, has inspired fan conventions, websites, obsessions, and an ongoing and impressive level of academic discourse. Included in this discourse is the recurring question of Buffy Summers' status in regards to the superhero. More than any other popular culture character, the question of whether or not Buffy is a superhero arises again and again, with each scholar who has considered the question coming up with his or her own answer. In *Superhero: The Secret Origin of a Genre*, Peter Coogan explains,

> Superficially, Buffy could be seen as qualifying as a superhero. She has a mission [...] She has superpowers [....] Perhaps more telling is that Buffy has an origin much in line with the superhero origin, but it is not identified as such as is usually the case in superhero comics. This lack of self-identification with the genre helps to establish that Buffy is not a superhero.[1]

Though I agree with Coogan's assertion that *Buffy the Vampire Slayer* does not comfortably belong within the superhero genre—the purpose behind his work is to establish the structure of the superhero as a genre—I feel he has misread the text when he claims that the series does not refer to itself as superheroic. In the pilot episode, Buffy complains, "Having a secret identity in this town is a job of work." In "The Harvest," the second episode in the first season, Xander actually exclaims, "It's cool, Buffy's a superhero." This self-identification continues into the third season. When Buffy's mother finds

3. Buffy Summers and the Superhero Myth

out about her unique role in Sunnydale, she suggests they discuss it with the authorities. She says, "I mean, I think they would be happy to have a superhero ... is that the right term? I mean, it's not offensive, is it?"[2] Though the self-referentiality of the superhero within *Buffy* diminishes quickly to being another popular culture element within the weave of the show, the fact that in the episodes which establish the mythology of the show refers to itself in the superheroic is enough to problematize the confidence of Coogan's reading. Danny Fingeroth in *Superman on the Couch* proclaims, "Buffy the Vampire Slayer is surely a superhero (or superheroine, if you like). To be more specific, she occupies the subgenre of 'horror superhero comics.'"[3] Roz Kaveney simply states, "Buffy is a superhero; it is one of the most obvious things about her."[4] Though there are those who unabashedly proclaim her superhero status, and those who just as certainly insist she is not, there is enough space in the discussion that the series and situations becomes a prime opportunity to explore the existence of the myth of the superhero.

Of course, when it comes to Buffy and academic inquiry, we find a plethora of attitudes, ideas and approaches. From juried journals to individual blogs, Buffy has been the center of a vast shower of words, passionate arguments, and cries of adulation and revulsion from all sorts of acolytes of the "Buffyverse." A compound of the words Buffy and universe, "Buffyverse" encapsulates the entirety of all recognized Buffy publications whether they be in television, film, comics, fanfic and so forth. This term for the Buffy tales, also known as the "Slayerverse" is a sub-component of the "Whedonverse" which includes all works of the show's creator Joss Whedon, perhaps currently most popular for his film *The Avengers*. Matthew Pateman attempts to explain the difficulty in dealing with the series in scholarship this way:

> *Buffy* criticism cannot be 'real' because it is too influenced by fandom; or else it is so lacking in the required celebratory gestures of fandom that it is not 'true' to the show. In addition to this, the ongoing critical divide between scholars means that one group refuses television anything but the most banal aesthetic possibility, while the other rejects aesthetics all together.[5]

Indeed, this is a malady frequently found in studies of popular culture, including the study of superheroes. Because of this challenge, and due to the nature of this reading, what follows is largely a close reading of the *Buffy the Vampire Slayer* television series. Though informed by theoretical readings, the nature of this work seemed to naturally favor a close association to the text over any other approach to the work.

What follows is not an argument for or against including Buffy into the pantheon of superheroes. The intent, rather than to resolve the question, is to explain how and why she is constantly considered even if there are those who dismiss the question. There is no attempt herein to come up with a final resolution to Buffy's superhero status because it largely doesn't matter. From a mythological perspective, it is enough to show that Buffy engages with superhero mythology on some meaningful level. If she didn't have some connection to myth, the conversation wouldn't have continued as long as it has. Thus, the more important concern is *how* Buffy engages with superhero mythology rather than if she is, in fact, a superhero. For the purposes of the broader scope of this work, a close reading of *Buffy the Vampire Slayer* will simultaneously manifest how this lexicon structures the mythology and support the conceit that Buffy has a place within the mythology. For this reading, the primary focus will be on the first three seasons of the television series with discussion of the film, other seasons and the Buffyverse as expressed in comics as they pertain to development of the mythemes of the superhero within the Buffy myth.

From the outset, one of the most dominant features of superhero mythology is the *powers*. This is perhaps one of the strongest connectives between the Buffy mythos and superhero mythology. Buffy consistently manifests superhuman strength and agility. Her ability to fight, while augmented by training, seems to be somewhat inherent and instinctual. She has heightened resiliency and recovery when damaged. In season three's episode "Band Candy," Buffy is challenged to hit her trainer, Giles, with a ball while blindfolded. She bounces the ball off a wall and the ricochet catches Giles in the side of the head. Her senses frequently manifest in this way as being supernatural in their scope and ability. Aside from the dream abilities, Buffy's powers fit into the category of the generic superhuman physical abilities. A certain twist on the *one power per person* mytheme, the conglomerate of strength, agility, and superresiliency all fit under the single power umbrella of a sort of generic physical superprowess. This is not uncommon in superhero comics and film and fits well within the confines of both mythologies as a single, if broadly encompassing, superpower. Of course, because Buffy has genuine superpowers the mytheme of the *pseudo-superpower* doesn't apply to her. As much as the trope is a part of the superhero mythology, it exists largely to help explain how Batman and others like him can exist within the superhero mythos rather than as one deeply necessary to the superhero mythos.

Beyond her more typical superhero abilities, Buffy also seems to have some connection to mystical dreaming. Throughout the first season, she has dreams pointing to her eventual confrontation from the major *supervillain* of the season, the Master. Also, in the original film version, Buffy dreams of her past incarnations as the Slayer. Though this power seems to wax and wane, it does occasionally manifest very strongly. In the season two episode

"I Only Have Eyes for You," Buffy's dreams explain the existence of poltergeists who are possessing and taking the lives of people attending the high school. As her dreams develop, Xander exclaims, "Your dreams are getting wicked accurate." However, in most episodes, Buffy's abilities seem less pronounced in this regard. The film also establishes that Buffy qualifies under the born subtrope of *powers*. According to the opening narration for the television series, "Into every generation a slayer is born." Though Buffy is born to be the Slayer, her superheroic abilities fail to manifest until after she enters high school. However, because her latent abilities are tied to the death of her predecessor, a sort of *traumatic trigger*, there is an element of her powers being thrust upon her. In fact, in the film, Buffy has a sort of extrasensory ability to recognize when vampires are near that manifests itself in the form of menstrual-like cramps, the kind of powers that would feel more like a burden than a blessing. This manifestation, cut from the series, is an example of the way the film took a much less nuanced and intelligent approach to the character and motifs of the mythology than Whedon managed to bring to the television series. However, the events of the first film, from her confrontations with Merrick to the burning down of her high school, certainly qualify as a *traumatic trigger* to her start as a Slayer.

The film version, of course, is a somewhat different mythology than the television series, a deviation that is perpetuated in further stories told in the later comics extensions of the mythos. Buffy Summers has existed in *iterations* practically from the beginning. However, this shift in mythos is both a part of and contrary to the nature of the mytheme. Not unlike the arc of Batman mythology, which has moved from original noir sensibilities through the camp of the 1960s to the new grit of the Christopher Nolan films, the Buffyverse has shifted its mythology over the years—to a less extreme extent. This less intentional permutation of the trope, though extremely important in the mythology of the superhero, is a variation on the original sense of *iterations*. The divergence between the original film and the TV series fills the specificities of the mytheme. However, where the Buffyverse may just barely qualify at an iterative mythos, it excels in typifying a related trope that is not uncommon in superhero mythology. The intended permutations of the mythos, the retelling of the myth within the confines of the myth, manifest the way the characters and concepts of the arc engage with the external world.

In *Buffy*, multiple episodes deal with the idea of alternate realities, temporary breaks with the dominant reality of the series rather than completely divergent iterations of the mythos. In fact, in a moment that hints at a recognition of the fourth wall, Spike recognizes that Buffy may be experiencing "alternative realities" during one such episode.[6] Various episodes include demons that twist the reality of Sunnydale to suit their own purposes. Most notably, the Emmy nominated episode "Hush" creates a semi-alternate reality all the people in Sunnydale are divested of their voices by a group of demonic ghouls called "the Gentlemen." In this new reality, nobody can speak, and the characters are required to communicate via hand gestures and writing. However, this reality is a part of the reality which everyone who lives in Sunnydale experiences. In some way, this and other episodes like it—wherein the changes are brought wholesale, ostensibly to the whole of the world—are perverse twists on the singular, central reality. Generally, alternate realities don't maintain a sense of continuity outside of the episode in the same way that iterations do. Though these twists on reality are temporary, they do function to create brief divergences from the originary mythology.[7]

In "The Wish," a play on the *It's a Wonderful Life* storyline, Cordelia wishes Buffy out of Sunnydale, creating a parallel universe wherein the vampires have taken control of the environs. In this alternate reality, Giles admits, "I have to believe in a better world," promoting the idea of realities outside of the one to which he belongs. As much as Anya, the demon who created the world, claims, "This is the real world now. This is the world we made."[8] Ultimately, the dominant reality is restored and things are returned to the original reality. However, this doesn't happen until after Buffy dies in the alternate reality. In the restoration of the original reality, Anya loses her powers. Later, Anya attempts to recover her power. In the process, she inadvertently manages to call the vampiric version of Willow from the alternate reality into the primary universe. The fact that this is even possible suggests that, despite appearances to the contrary, all these alternate realities seem to have some sort of continuation outside of what we might perceive in the television and comics series.

One of the most interesting of these alternate realities plays out in the season six episode "Normal Again." This episode opens the series up to the potential that perhaps everything we as viewers have seen in *Buffy* has played out in the mind of Buffy who lives in an asylum as doctors try to cure her of her psychotic belief that "she's the central figure in a fantastic world beyond imagination" populated with, as Xander puts it, "vampires and demons and ex-vengeance demons and [a] sister that used to be a big ball of universe destroying energy."[9] The episode ends without resolving which world is real and which is the fiction. In fact, Joss Whedon intended for the episode to allow for that ambiguity. As the entire series was coming to a close, Whedon explained that the framing narrative for the show was up to the interpretation of the viewer and if "they decide that the entire thing is all playing out in some crazy person's head, well the joke of the thing to us was it is, and that crazy person is me."[10] This sense of continuous alternate realities does promote a connection to the *iteration* mytheme in the superhero mythology, but it still plays out differently.

Alternate personas in other realities support the possibility of *alter egos* in the mythos. Though Buffy doesn't have an alter ego in the traditional sense within superhero mythology, the concept of the secret identity might be the most clearly articulated of the superhero mythemes within the Buffyverse. In the first episode of the series, Buffy actually exclaims, "Having a secret identity in this town is a job of work."[11] Both Giles and another slayer chastise Buffy for not being careful enough with her secret identity. The alter ego is underscored in "Surprise" when Buffy asks Giles what she can do while he studies up on developments and how they will affect demonic activity in Sunnydale. He suggests that she go to class, do her homework and eat dinner. She replies, "Right, be *that* Buffy," underscoring the fact that there is a difference between the Buffy who fights the forces of evil and the Buffy who participates in normal teenage activities.[12]

The conversation from "Surprise" takes place in the Sunnydale High School library. This is a place where Buffy meets with Xander, Willow, Giles and those who work with her. It's a place where she trains. It's also a place where a great deal of down time between major fights takes place.[13] Buffy and her friends spend more time there than is considered normal for high schoolers. It's a staging area and contains an unusual amount of books on the demonic as well as a seemingly inexhaustible supply of demon-fighting weaponry. In some ways, it is as safe a haven as there is in the Buffyverse; even though it is invaded from time to time, it rarely seems to receive much in the way of lasting damage throughout the first three seasons. Though it doesn't have the flair of the Fortress of Solitude or the impressive attributes of the Batcave, it serves a great deal of the mythological purposes of the superhero's *lair*. It's also worth noting that, with only one or two rare exceptions, for the three years that the series takes place at the high school no student in the entire school seems to have any need of the library. Only the supporting team is allowed to spend any time in the library. This is so much the case that, in the season two episode "Passion," when two students wander in to the library, Xander belligerently challenges their right to be there. When they say they're there to get some books, he responds, "What do you think this is, a Barnes and Noble?"[14]

Sunnydale High itself, as part of the city of Sunnydale, seems to exist in a sort of California *urban*. There are indications that Sunnydale is more metropolis, including the existence of a club known as the Bronze where high schoolers go to hang out and listen to live band music. However, most shots of homes seem to indicate a more suburban environment. Though *Buffy* most likely fits the mytheme of the *urban* environment, there is sufficient room to play with the potential ramifications of the way this particular mytheme might impact our reading of Buffy as a superhero. Of course, there are other aspects which resolve more happily with the superhero lexicon.

Xander and the rest of Buffy's supporting team functions to touch on several of the mythemes of the superhero. Though, as is the case with some of the tropes in the Buffyverse, the connection isn't as solid as would make the familiarity to the superhero mythos as strong as some would like, the "Scooby gang" connects *Buffy the Vampire Slayer* to the myth.[15] Primarily comprised of Xander, Willow and Giles—though to a lesser extent in regards to these mythemes—joined later by Oz and Cordelia, the gang serves in the roles of sidekick and occasionally a *superteam*. As early as the third episode in the season, Xander says, "We're a team" in reference to the trio of Buffy, Willow and Xander.[16] In "Innocence," the gang begins to approach something closer to *superteam* status as they take on the combined threat of the newly evil Angelus and the apocalypse-bringing Judge.[17] Also, in "Killed by Death," Xander, Willow, and Cordelia attack the demonic Angelus after he gets the upper hand on Buffy. They even manage in that event to force him to retreat.[18] However, until Willow develops her ability as a witch, the team stretches to reach any sort of real superstatus on their own. However, this mytheme is one that supports reading *Buffy* as something other than a superhero. The show supports this mytheme only tenuously.

Of course, Rupert Giles serves a much more interesting role in the series. As Buffy's Watcher, he is the most influential authority figure in her life. The Watchers are an organization with the purpose of identifying, training and supporting the Slayer in all her incarnations. Each incarnation of the Slayer has a Watcher assigned specifically to her to help her in preparing for her duties and supporting her as she performs them. Giles serves as Buffy's Watcher within the series, with only a brief moment when another takes over. Giles constantly pushes her to practice, train and focus on her duties as the Slayer. His single-mindedness may seem to make him an *antagonistic authority figure*, but as the series progresses his devotion to her well-being manifests that he is, in fact, a *cooperative authority figure*. He consistently goes out if his way to ensure she is well in ways that extend beyond just her physical health. This is so much the case that he also serves as a father figure for Buffy, making him the character through which Buffy manifests her efforts to *please the father*. Throughout the first three seasons, the relationship between Buffy and Giles is obviously and overtly related to that between a daughter and father. In season two, a pair of episodes revolves around Buffy the vampire slayer and Angel the good vampire having sex. By granting Angel a moment of pure bliss, this deprives him of the soul that kept his vampiric demon in check, turning him back into the evil Angelus. Near the end of the second episode, "Innocence," after Buffy has revealed her actions and their role in creating Angelus, she gets a ride home with Giles. Before she gets out of his car, she fearfully says, "You must be so disappointed in me," a two-part statement referring both to the demonizing of Angel and the act of sex itself. Her query and Giles' response manifest the kind of relationship they have and even a partial success in her efforts to please her father figure. He says,

> No, no I'm not. [...] Do you want me to wag my finger at you and tell you you acted irrationally? You did and I can. But I know that you loved him and he has proven more than once that he loved you. You couldn't have known what would happen. [...] If it's guilt you're looking for, Buffy, I'm not your man. All you will get from me is my support and my respect.[19]

For Buffy, this helps her resolve a concern that is rarely, if ever, resolved for most superheroes. She gains some peace and strength from knowing that Giles is not, in fact, disappointed in her in any way. Their relationship is underscored in season three's "Helpless" when an official from the Watcher organization states that Giles "has a father's love for the child."[20]

Of course, he is not the only authority figure with whom Buffy must cope. During the first season, the principal at Sunnydale High is killed by a bunch of hyena-possessed students. His replacement makes no effort to hide his distaste for his pupils and takes great joy in forcing Buffy to conform to his demands. Though most of these demands are relatively minor, they do reveal the depth of his antagonism. At moments when her identity as the Slayer requires her absolute attention, Principal Snyder forces her to participate in the school talent show, take a group of elementary schoolers trick-or-treating, and take part in the school job fair. His antagonism extends up to, and includes, the graduation ceremony attended by the entirety of the Scooby gang, a ceremony that results in absolute chaos and yet another attempt by the forces of evil to open the gates of hell that exist in Sunnydale. Throughout the whole of his tenure as principal, Snyder has been working for other mysterious authority figures. Ultimately, it is revealed that he is unwittingly taking direction from those who report to Richard Wilkins, the mayor of Sunnydale. It is eventually revealed that Wilkins has been mayor for over one hundred years, making his position as an antagonistic authority figure firmly established in the superhero myth. After his introduction, the mayor quickly takes over as the antagonist in authority for the remainder of the third season. His actions are integral in turning Faith, onetime friend of Buffy, against her. This is not the only time, but one of the most vital, when *switching sides* makes an appearance in the series. At various times, Willow, Xander, Riley, and Spike have worked with and against Buffy. Buffy herself has even abandoned her Scooby Gang, marking the mytheme's presence strongly in Sunnydale. In the process of Faith's move from friend to foe, she and the mayor develop a sort of perverse *please the father* relationship that presents a perverse reflection of the relationship between Giles and Buffy. The fact that the principal and the mayor both turn out to be demonic only exacerbates the fact that they fit very well as the *antagonistic authority figure*.

The mayor may be the best example of the *supervillain* in the first three seasons. He begins as a minor, background character, an invisible force pulling the strings. The more he manifests himself in the series, the more interesting he becomes. Early in the third season, he becomes impervious to harm, healing from a literal split head. He is fascinating as a character. Though he is seeking to open the gates of hell, making deals with demons as he makes his plan to ascend to a higher plane of existence, he also loves miniature golf, claims to have a home life, and is severely uncomfortable with the idea of germs. The mayor is the one responsible for the path a second Slayer, Faith, takes from quasi-anti-hero to full on villain status. In some ways, he might be one of the strongest carryovers into the superhero mythology. However, his demonic power source is a bit of a contrast to typical sources of power for the villain. Before the mayor arrives on the scene, the more straightforward villain from the first season, the Master, maintains the status of *supervillain* for the show. From the pilot episode, there has always been a superpowered villain scheming and working to take down Buffy the Slayer.

The authority figures aren't the only characters within the series who create *relationship struggles* for Buffy. Xander develops an infatuation for Buffy early on in the first season which impacts the way they interact, which is further complicated by the fact that Willow has strong feelings for Xander. When Cordelia, the queen bee of the popular girls, develops a relationship with Xander it further complicates the interactions between the people involved. Buffy constantly has to find a way to work with her mother, trying to keep her protected from the villainy that surrounds her. Even when the truth about Buffy's role as the Slayer finally comes out, the relationship is still complicated and difficult as they try to resolve the changed dynamic of their relationship. In later seasons, Buffy has a boyfriend named Riley who works for a government agency that hunts and studies demons. Their relationship has some unique complications that inform these later seasons, as does her later relationship with Spike, the bad vampire turned good. However, all these challenges are minor when compared to the biggest, and most convoluted relationship in the early seasons of the Buffyverse. Specifically, Buffy develops a relationship with the "good" vampire Angel. Their relationship is complicated simply by the fact that she is the vampire slayer and he is a vampire. The fact that his soul is restored to him, giving him angst and a desire to work toward redemption is what allows them to have a relationship at all.

However, at the moment when they finally consummate their relationship, giving Angel a moment of pure, unsullied bliss, he loses his soul. He goes from good to evil in a few moments and creates one of the most complicated of any romantic relationships in popular culture. Now, the man whom she loved and slept with has become one of the most fearsome vampires to ever live in Sunnydale. Her duties as the Slayer are clear: he is a threat to be eliminated, but at the same time she is a high school girl who is struggling to reconcile the loss of her first love. At the same time she prepares to confront and kill the new evil boyfriend, the Scooby gang is working on a spell which would restore Angel's soul to him again, essentially returning him to his former state. At the moment when the gate to hell is opened, Angel's soul is restored to him. The only way to close the portal is through the death of Angel. The conflict between her chance to save her boyfriend, potentially returning to a life with him, and her duty as a Slayer and protector of the world from the literal forces of hell reaches a climax when she has to choose between his salvation and saving the world. She has a moment when she can have her boyfriend back or she can kill him and stop the rising of a world-destroying demon. The first stage of the complicated relationship she has with her boyfriend culminates when she kills the man she loved and lost and found again. The second stage pushes the complication into more interesting directions. Of course, Angel manages to find a way to return from the hell to which he has been banished, because not only is death temporary but it seems that eternal damnation is as well. By the fourth episode of season three, Angel has returned—though a much different Angel than the one who left. The relationship between the two of them is complicated further by his return, what he did before he died, and the general sense of melodrama belonging to teen romances. Of all the aspects of the Buffyverse, the relationships in which Buffy finds herself are certainly the most soap operatic of them all.

The relationship between "good" Angel and the evil Angelus—Angel's other name—underscores the *moral code* at work in the Buffy mythology. There is very rarely much in the way of gray area in the stories. Things are either evil or good. Evil things need to be killed or banished. Good things need to be protected and preserved. In the Buffyverse, evil things are always demons, vampires, or those who intentionally and willfully work with the forces of hell. Humans, on the other hand, are where all the good is in the world. Though individual humans might ally themselves with the evils of the world, with only one or two exceptions all the demons and almost exclusively the demons are the bad guys in the Buffyverse. Buffy's morality rests on this concept. Humans need to be preserved; demons need to be destroyed. This morality is strong enough that in "Ted," when Buffy believes she has killed the man who was dating her mother she has a minor breakdown. She believes she inadvertently violated her moral code and killed the innocent. She is equal parts relieved and revolted when she discovers that her mother's "perfect" boyfriend is a robot built by a mad genius scientist before he died.[21] Though Ted is not strictly speaking a demon, he is both non-human and a threat to Buffy and her mother. Therefore, he is evil and deserves the destruction Buffy visits upon him. This morality by which Buffy functions is rarely challenged in any complicated or meaningful way throughout the early seasons.

This morality also underscored a slightly complicated take on the mytheme *no killing*. While Buffy has no problem killing vampires, those who have died once already, and demons, who apparently aren't alive in the traditional sense, the series is much more careful about killing off humanity. Those who die tend to be the innocents killed by evil or those who serve to perpetuate the evil. Further, when a human is killed, Buffy is never the one to actually end a life. In "Gingerbread," Buffy even asks hypothetically for an exemption to the rule that she not kill humans to go after a group of humans she believes were responsible for killing two small children.[22] The human villains who are killed are removed either through their own evil or through the accidental fate wrought in a form of cosmic justice. The importance of this aspect of the moral code is underscored by the death of Deputy Mayor Allan Finch of Sunnydale. Faith, the second Slayer to come to work with Buffy, manifests a recklessness that results in failing to identify Finch as a human before she stakes him through the heart in season three's "Bad Girls."[23] The tension and ramifications of this event stretch throughout the remainder of the season. Ultimately, this act pushes Faith to ally herself with the evil, demonic mayor against Buffy and the Scooby Gang. The killing of a single human is enough to turn Faith from rough-around-the-edges Slayer to full on villain. Her change in loyalty extends to the point that Buffy ultimately stabs her in an attempt to save the vampire-turned-good-guy Angel.

Of course, the methods Buffy uses to dispatch these villains is emblematic of another mytheme. No matter what the themes and emotions of any given episode in *Buffy the Vampire Slayer*, she is first and foremost a Slayer.

Because of this fact, her very existence is framed in the concept of violence. Episode after episode, no matter the conflict, Buffy ends up being involved in a physical conflict that results in both direct damage and collateral damage to the villain, Buffy and the surrounding environs. Every time Buffy has to face off against a vampire, the slaying is never as simple as just a stake to the heart. Every slaying involves a significant amount of martial art style violence.

Buffy's *spectacular origins* are distinctly tied to the violence that surrounds her. The event which brought her to Sunnydale resulted in the immolation of her previous school's gymnasium due to her efforts to destroy a band of vampires that attacked at a high school dance. However, Buffy's origin as the Slayer is complicated. The Slayer, according to early mythology, is a reincarnative avatar of the previous Slayers, accessing the memories and emotions of her predecessors—which means that her origins stretch back to prehistoric time when the first Slayer was bound with a demon to make her more capable to face off against the demon/human hybrids known as vampires. Conversely, Buffy was drawn from the most popular of the popular at her first high school. Whedon intentionally created in Buffy the antithesis of the strong, self-controlled superhero. Her development from valley girl to vampire slayer was a transformation Whedon was interested in developing. His intent was to challenge one of the most accepted stereotypes of the late 1980s to early 90s, to explore the bleach blonde valley girl as superhero. The fact that she is called the Slayer by multiple people throughout the run of the show is a strong indication of the existence of the *codename* mytheme in the Buffyverse. Though she shares the moniker with later Slayers, it fulfills the tropological requirements.

As the story progresses, so does Buffy. Her origin, and the events of the film in the context of the TV series,[24] takes place during her freshman year of high school. The television series starts during her sophomore year. Each season of *Buffy the Vampire Slayer* takes place in a subsequent year in the life of the characters. In this regard, Buffy disconnects with the *ageless* superhero mytheme. The series ostensibly takes place through the course of seven years in the life of Buffy and the other characters. The timeline seems to slow down in the comics, but it avoids the sense of timelessness that accompanies the majority of superheroes. This assertion can be challenged, however, because the Buffy mythos hasn't existed for more than two decades. The fact that Buffy still exists, at least in the pages of comics, manifests a potential agelessness. However, at this point in the Buffyverse, the sense of agelessness is less developed than is generally expected in superhero mythology.

In other regards, *Buffy the Vampire Slayer* misses a few superhero mythemes. Some of these seem intentional, but others demonstrate the way Buffy and company fail to conform to the more strict definitions of the superhero mythology. Though the actors have become iconically identified with the roles they played, within the Buffyverse, none of them have a truly iconic element—neither symbol, color scheme, or anything else. Typically, the superhero *chevron* is a stylized animal or letter. Occasionally, it might represent a device or tool used by the hero. By way of example, in Whedon's parodic web series *Dr. Horrible's Sing-Along Blog*, which views events within the superhero mythos from the perspective of the villain, the superhero, Captain Hammer, has a hammer in a yellow circle on his chest as his chevron. In the case of Buffy, there is no distinct *chevron* that would be used in the same way as a visual stand-in for the Slayer. To a large extent, the same holds true for any sort of superhero *costume*. Obviously, Buffy doesn't wear a traditional costume of the spandex variety and the script for the first episode contains no evidence of intentional costume change. Nor does she have the sort of limited wardrobe or an iconic outfit that other characters who participate in superhero mythology have. However, in early episodes Buffy does alter her costume by adding a leather jacket practically every time she goes out slaying. It seems that every time she prepares to change from Buffy the high schooler to Buffy the Slayer, she tends to signal this shift through a minor change of wardrobe. Because this change frequently includes leather, there is a partial connection to protection and armor, but the connection between this costume change and the superheroic costume is strained.

The *expository narration* mytheme also exists in the Buffyverse only in a strained form as well. For the first two seasons, most episodes begin with a brief voiceover by the Watcher, Giles, which explains the purpose and meaning of the Slayer. In most episodes, there is also expository dialogue wherein one of the cast—most frequently either Giles, Willow, or Buffy—takes the time to explain the demon of the episode to the rest of the Scooby Gang and the viewer as well. As true as this is, and as much as it superficially resembles the trope, it functions on a seemingly more practical narratological level than is typical of this trope in comics. As discussed in Chapter 1, this type of narration tends to be less important to the overarching narrative and have more to do with side stories or to narrate events being depicted as the narration unfolds. Though still prevalent in comics—as much in late Buffy comics as in superhero comics—this mytheme is rare, though not unheard of in film and television. In order to conform to the conventions that come with a shift in media, the voiceover and exposition tend to be sublimated if not outright removed from the stories entirely.

On the contrary, the superhero mytheme that presents a *strong visual component* is certainly in evidence throughout the film, television series, and subsequent comics. The fact that Joss Whedon moved from writing *Buffy the Vampire Slayer* to *Toy Story* to writing comics indicates a strong visual writing style. Whedon has written exclusively for visual media. In fact, Whedon's work with visual storytelling in *Serenity* was recognized by AMC by listing his opening tracking shot from the film among the ten best long tracking shots ever committed to film.[25]

By the time Buffy walks down the halls of Sunnydale High, it becomes apparent that she is going to be, in every way, the *outsider*. Not only do her duties as Slayer ostracize her from her schoolmates, but she finds herself quickly identifying with the slacker, the brain and the librarian. She spurns the interests of the popular girl, Cordelia, as she defends the geeks and freaks—as long as they're not demonic. In the first season episode "Witch," Buffy attempts to reintegrate herself into the mainstream popularity by trying out for the cheerleading squad. However, due to the efforts of a witch who is also seeking to live in the limelight, Buffy is forced off the team and the overall attempt pushes her further out of the mainstream clique in the high school.[26] Though her outsider status is perpetuated throughout the first three seasons, she is recognized in "The Prom" for being the one person who seems to always be there to stop evil and to allow the graduating class of 1999 the distinction of having the lowest mortality rate of any in recent history.[27] Despite this brief moment of recognition, however, Buffy is most frequently found on the outside—even among her own colleagues and her mother, Joyce Summers, at times. Indeed, until Buffy's mother finds out that she is the slayer, their relationship is incredibly tense and strained. Buffy frequently finds herself feeling alienated from her mother. Though things improve once Buffy is able to explain to her mother what she does, her status as Slayer frequently adds tension to their relationship.

On the other hand, to call Buffy an *orphan* is severely disingenuous to Mrs. Summers. Even before she finds herself dealing with a daughter destined to slay all the evil that arises in Sunnydale, Joyce struggles to do her best as a single parent to a teenager. Whedon and the other writers for the show ensure that she never devolves into cliché and gives respect to the struggles of Mrs. Summers. However, Buffy does struggle to identify with a father figure, especially early on. Though Rupert Giles eventually does seem to fill that role, in several episodes it is apparent that she yearns for a good connection to her biological father. In "Nightmares," when everyone at Sunnydale High is forced to face their worst nightmares, Buffy is confronted by her father who finally tells her he wants nothing to do with her and that she is a disappointment and a nuisance to him.[28] Significantly, this is the second to last time he makes a physical appearance in the series. He shares a conversation with Buffy's mother in the season two premier, "When She Was Bad," wherein he mentions a distance between the two of them.[29] All his other appearances are in alternate realities or dreams. Though this may be worth further inquiry, it would be possible to argue that Buffy is some sort of half-orphan. Her relationship with her father does manifest the mythological properties of the mytheme. The presence of Joyce within the series—at least until her death in season five's "The Body"[30]—make it difficult to fully commit this mytheme to the hero of the Buffyverse.

What is not difficult is recognizing the fact that Buffy struggles with the *power and responsibility* mytheme. Beginning with the film and extending throughout the series and into the comics, Buffy struggles with reconciling her own desires with her responsibilities as the Slayer. The aforementioned efforts she makes to join the cheerleading squad go directly against the wishes of her Watcher, the super-ego to her id. Rupert Giles, and later Wesley Windham Price, constantly remind Buffy of her responsibility to guard the citizens of Sunnydale, and by extension the world, from the dangers emanating from the hellmouth lying underneath the town. Though she only deviates from this responsibility for rare short periods, she constantly yearns for a more typical teenage lifestyle. Her relationship with the much older Angel perhaps exemplifies the tension that she, as well as others in the superhero mythos, constantly feel. By the most technical of standards, Buffy's duty would be to stake Angel through the heart. He is a vampire and, practically by definition, he is the evil that she was born to destroy. But Angel also has a soul and he works with her against other vampires. This bad boy gone good—along with his understanding of her dual roles as savior and student—make him an appealing romantic lead for Buffy. Their relationship leads to a point in the season two finale "Becoming Pt. 2" when Buffy has to make a choice between her high school desires to save her boyfriend and her duty as Slayer to save the world from literal hell on earth. Though she hated doing it, Buffy chose to take responsibility for her role as the Slayer over teen desire and stabbed Angel, closing the portal and sending him to hell.

Though she frequently saves the world from demons, Buffy rarely confronts real world problems, making her—as with most superheroes—*ineffective against real world problems*. However, though she never deals with global hunger, global warming, or other problems of the real world, she does manage to stop a suicide attempt in season three's "Earshot." The episode begins with Buffy fighting two mouthless demons. During the conflict, she gets some of their blood on her hand. This blood gives her an "aspect of the demon," which in this case means the ability to hear the thoughts of others. In the crowded cafeteria, she overhears someone thinking of killing everyone in the school. She and the Scooby Gang work frantically to find the source of the threat. Ultimately, their search leads Buffy to confront a student named Jonathan in the school's clock tower where he has a rifle and appears to be preparing to go on a shooting spree. As she talks to him, Buffy realizes that Jonathan was only there to kill himself.[31] Whedon admits that the similarities to the Columbine shooting resulted in delaying the broadcast of the episode, even though the boy with the gun was not going to shoot at others. She talks him out of his attempt, and in a sentimentally satisfying moment, it is Jonathan who presents Buffy with the award "Class Protector" in the later episode "The Prom." Despite this moment when she does react to and prevent a real world problem for many teenagers, her efforts to confront problems of the real world are almost nonexistent and tend to be severely sublimated by her confrontations with the world of the supernatural.

By the same token, Buffy's efforts to stop the forces of hell tend to put her on ground unfamiliar to law enforcement. She has very few run-ins with the police of Sunnydale. When she does, as in the episode "Bad Girls," she almost never finds herself supporting *justice over law* though she doesn't support the law, per se, either. In "Bad Girls," she follows the lead of Faith in escaping from officers who arrested them for stealing from a store that specializes in weaponry of the less traditional variety. Neither was motivated solely by an effort to promote justice. Though Faith does argue that to kill vampires they need to be free from incarceration this is only a poorly disguised rationale for their actions, not a true primary motivator. Essentially, *Buffy the Vampire Slayer* seems to exist in a reality somewhat out of sync with law enforcement. Though the police have a presence in the series, and there is an implied legal system in Sunnydale, this all seems to serve less as a part of the storytelling of the universe and more a simple background element of the series.

However, much like the police which do exist in *Buffy*, the Slayer spends most of her time in efforts that *promote/maintain the status quo*. From her beginnings in the first film throughout the series, Buffy is only called to action when the denizens of hell seek to pay a visit to her environs. In both the film and the series, Buffy is frequently shown waiting in a graveyard for a newly created vampire to find its way out of the final resting place and into the world of the not-so-living. More than perhaps any other image, this epitomizes just how much Buffy is only interested in maintaining rather than improving the status quo. She must constantly wait for the change to occur before she can kill the vampire. When there is no hellish threat to Sunnydale, Buffy feels no real need to train, or shore up her defenses or do anything outside the typical teenage life in high school. Granted, that in and of itself is less than status quo material. The upheavals of high school, including dating, peer pressure, drugs and sports, are frequently metaphorized in *Buffy* through the demonic powers which Buffy must face. On the other hand, Jonathan, the character Buffy rescued from suicide in "Earshot," underscores Buffy's adherence to this trope. The character, unnamed until the scene with Buffy in the clocktower, appears in several episodes, starting as early as the fourth episode of season two—and even credited with an appearance in the unaired pilot episode, but never really registers on Buffy's Slayer radar until she perceives him as a threat to the status quo of the school. Even Buffy's relationship strengthens this mytheme. It is only when Buffy actively changes the status quo of her relationship with Angel that he goes from angsty hero to full-fledged villain.

It is interesting to note that, though Angel is the villain perhaps most closely linked to Buffy, he never manages to kill her. That distinction arguably belongs only to the Master, a supervillain from the first season who chokes Buffy to death in the season finale. This is one of two times in which Buffy actually loses her life. The second occurs at the end of season five. In both cases, she manages to return from the dead and rejoin the fight against evil. For Buffy, as well as for other characters in various ways, *death is temporary*. However, Buffy's first death in "Prophecy Girl" is thwarted through a very familiar method. Xander is able to bring her back through CPR.[32] Her death is absolutely confirmed by the fact that a new Slayer is activated. The original mythology of the series was that there was only one Slayer at a time, each one being called at the death of the previous incarnation. Kendra, the newly called replacement, visits Buffy during season two and is replaced when Kendra dies by the bad girl slayer, Faith. Angel's "death" wherein he is condemned to hell in order to save Sunnydale is also a temporary state of being. Before the midpoint of the third season, he has managed to escape hell itself in order to return to life in Sunnydale. Buffy's second death, after Angel has left the show to pursue his own interests, is much more impressive than both his and Buffy's previous brushes with the grim reaper. Buffy's return from death is also vastly more involved than Xander's pseudo-CPR, but is still effective nonetheless.

In "The Gift," a god called Glorificus, shortened to Glory for the bulk of the series, manages to open a portal which will eventually lead to hell on earth if not closed. Buffy's sister, Dawn, was the key to opening the portal and the blood of her death is required to close it. However, because Dawn was made from Buffy's essence, her blood, Buffy realizes her blood will do just as well.[33] Dawn was a new character introduced in the fourth season with no lead-in. The idea was that, in order to protect the Key which Glory sought, a group of monks sent it to the Slayer and gave it human form to protect it. In doing so, they gave everyone who knew Buffy false memories of her having a younger sister. Thus, Buffy's younger sister, Dawn, was literally created from Buffy, and retconned into the Buffyverse more than three years after the story began. Buffy throws herself into the portal, saving both Dawn and the world at the cost of her own life. In the opening of the next season, the Scooby Gang performs a spell with the expectation that it will bring Buffy back from the dead. Willow explains that she fears Buffy has been relegated to some sort of place of torment and pain, a place from which they must try to rescue her.[34] They believe the spell fails and leaves Buffy in her grave at the end of the first episode. However, Buffy, in a manner similar to her vampiric foes, is shown bursting out of her grave and eventually rejoining with her friends. Before she adapts to being alive again, she asks her sister Dawn, "Is this hell?"[35] This second death and traumatic return to life are very obviously and overtly a connection to the conceit that *death is temporary* for Buffy. In the subsequent episode, after telling the gang that they had saved her from hell and thanking them, she admits to Spike, the resident outcast of the group, that she was pulled from a place of happiness and peace—what she calls "heaven"—by the spell, denying her rest and leading her to again proclaim, "This is hell."[36]

Even though there are some strong psychological consequences to both of Buffy's deaths, neither seems to have any real effect on Buffy's physique, though Buffy doesn't measure up to the typical meaning of the *amazing physique* mytheme. Buffy is a high schooler and has a physique that fits her status. However, just being a high schooler isn't enough to rescue Supergirl from the unnatural application of this trope. Despite her supposed youth, Supergirl shows a ridiculous level of physical maturity and appearance. Since the 1970s, her breasts are never drawn at anything less than a C cup coupled with an abnormally thin waist and ridiculously long legs.[37] Of course, Supergirl is a cartoon and Buffy, due to the nature of the medium, must be portrayed by a living human. This requires a certain level of realism not applicable to most comics characters. Having said that, it would have been possible to cast a person who more typifies the mytheme. Even Charisma Carpenter, who plays Cordelia in the series, draws closer to the physical constraints of the mytheme. Buffy isn't nearly as pneumatic as most superheroes. Also, because Sarah Michelle Gellar is shorter than Carpenter, her legs don't have nearly the length to which Carpenter and female superheroes reach. To be clear, this is not to say that Gellar is not an unattractive actor who is incapable of manifesting a strong attractiveness and sexuality. However, the extreme physiques, especially in regards to chest size, is not something to which she can measure up.

This may have been an intentional part of the mythology on the part of Joss Whedon, who had a great deal of oversight into the formation of the show and its presentation. Though sometimes vehemently contested, Whedon has developed a strong reputation as one of the most effective and well-known of feminist authors and producers working in popular culture. The manifestation of gender and its roles within the Buffyverse is incredibly complicated and a matter of a great deal of debate. What does go without saying is that he created in *Buffy the Vampire Slayer* a unique look at the female hero. He has admitted that he intentionally chose Buffy's name because of its completely innocuous overtones. "It was the name that I could think of that I took the least seriously," he said in 2003, "There is no way you could hear the name Buffy and think, 'This is an important person.'"[38] His intent was to turn as many conventions as he could on their heads while still telling an engaging story. From the outset, Whedon intended to confront the *androcentric* nature of not just superhero mythology but also horror and action mythology as well. Indeed, in a 2006 speech at Equity Now, Whedon expresses part of what he was attempting to do in creating Buffy. He said, "When I created Buffy, I wanted to create a female icon but I also wanted to [...] surround her with men who not only had no problem with the idea of a female leader but were in fact engaged and even attracted to the idea." It was in this same speech wherein Whedon uttered the much repeated phrase, "Why do you write such strong female characters? Because you're still asking that question."

Making the determination regarding whether or not Whedon's place within the feminist movement is well deserved is outside of the scope of this work. It is also a question which may be irresolvable with any degree of empiricism. Furthermore, there have been many readings that complicate the gendered identity of several characters and the series as a whole. Queer readings, readings promoting the possibility of a feminine gaze, and readings of sexuality and gender in other forms make up a strong component of the scholarship surrounding the Buffyverse. What is certain is that the presentation of gender and sex roles in *Buffy* complicates a positively *androcentric* reading of the universe. However, the complications relating to this mytheme seem to all be intentional on the part of the writers, producers, and creators within the Buffyverse.

Ultimately, Buffy Summers' relation to the superhero mythos remains complicated. Though she connects well to several of the mythemes, there are enough to which she is more tenuously positioned. Some of the latter are of the most central tropes to the superhero myth. Because of this, Buffy's place in the mythos is less certain. Perhaps the best example of this complication and a reiteration of the importance of certain mythemes is the way the *costume* mytheme influences Buffy's inclusion. Because she lacks a clear, specific costume, the Slayer moves further from the center of the central superhero types. Though she is not unique among superheroes in the mythos, her place is further complicated by the kinds of villains she faces. Peter Coogan suggests that because Buffy faces off against demons and creatures of hell almost exclusively she is part of a different kind of hero, a very familiar hero type made familiar by Dr. Van Helsing, the vampire hunter.[39] Of course, this is reflected in the show's title, but it fails to recognize the vast quantity of time Buffy spends facing off against the denizens of hell which bear little to no similarity to the blood sucking vampire. Granted, the exclusivity in villain type does seem to indicate that *Buffy the Vampire Slayer* is more strongly connected to the horror genre than to superhero mythology. The truth is that Buffy is not a superhero in the traditional sense. The argument that she belongs in the same circle of myth as Superman, Wonder Woman, and the X-Men seems without sufficient support. On the other hand, there is enough connectivity between Buffy Summers and the superhero mythos to deny her participation in the myth. Indeed, this reading of *Buffy* manifests the need for the mythological approach to the superhero. This approach allows for those parts of the Buffyverse which correlate with superhero mythology to coexist with the mythemes which would disqualify Buffy as part of the superhero genre. Being able to do so allows for us to read into the tales and see the workings of the mythology both within and without more recognized parameters.

4

Finding the Superhero
Reading SyFy's Alphas *Through the Mythological Lexicon*

In 2011, the SyFy channel debuted a new, if short lived, television series. Based on the exploits of people with extraordinary powers, *Alphas* was SyFy's most watched premier in two years with approximately 2.5 million viewers. Though its viewership has ebbed and waned, the show was popular enough to warrant a second and final season. The show follows a group of gifted individuals, known as Alphas. Led by psychiatrist and neurologist Dr. Lee Rosen, played by David Strathairn, the group works both with and against the government in order to find and collaborate with or incarcerate other Alphas. Though the special abilities in the show are very similar to those found in superhero mythology, an aspect that will be central to what follows, there are very few—if any—specific and direct connections to superhero mythology. The effort of this particular reading is to show the way superhero mythology influences stories that seem to intentionally avoid overt connections to the myth but engage with major mythemes regardless.

Though the series was cancelled before the shows mythology was fully developed, there is sufficient evidence to support this claim from the episodes which aired. It is significant to note that there was nothing in the advertisement for the show, nor within the show itself, that makes any intentional connection to superheroes. It is also worth noting that the online discussions of the show connect it to *Heroes*, *Misfits*, and other overtly superhero-themed shows. Further, these discussions talk openly and candidly about *Alphas* as if it were a part of the superhero mythology regardless of the efforts made by producers and advertisers to avoid intentional comparisons. Also, because of the newness of the show and the general—if sometimes undeserved—lack of respect for SyFy as a station, there has been little to no scholarship and certainly no scholarship of note on the series. Thus, this chapter will by necessity include some lengthier discussions of the show and its story.

Of all the superhero themed shows to have played on television, *Alphas* may not be an obvious choice. *No Ordinary Family, The Cape,* and *Heroes* were all overtly more concerned with superhero mythology. *Smallville* and the newly minted *Arrow* both deal with well-established superheroes, as do the myriad animated shows from both Marvel and DC canon. These animated shows include, but are not limited to, several incarnations of Batman, the X-Men and the Avengers, as well as Spider-Man, Iron Man, and a short-lived Spawn series. However, the live action *Alphas* earns some distinction for lasting more than one season, a feat not matched by the first two programs on the list. It also seems to have maintained a consistency which *Heroes* lacked. Further, because it deals with new characters, it disallows the preclusion into the mythology that would come from being tied to a previously established superhero, as *Smallville* was to Superman. Furthermore, in "Alphaville," Skylar, a technology Alpha, makes a shout out to the team's apparent superhero roots. Noticing that Nina, a member of the core group of Alphas, is feeling tension in the company of the rest of the team, she remarks, "Trouble in the Justice League?" creating an overt reference to perhaps the most established superhero team in the mythology.[1] However, by focusing more on story than on mytheme, the series manages to maintain a consistent quality that was apparently lacking from other forays into putting the superhero myth onto television.

Perhaps the most clear way in which *Alphas* connects with the superhero mythology is the special skills most of the team use, their *powers*. All members of the original team have their abilities clearly spelled out in a pseudo-scientific way in the pilot episode. Nina Theroux has "hyper induction" which means she "overrides willpower in others," a sort of mind control. Bill Harken has "enhanced strength" based on activating his adrenal glands. Rachel Pirzad has a bizarre form of "synesthesia" wherein she is "able to enhance [her] senses" to superhuman levels. Gary Bell experiences "transduction" which means he is "able to see all electromagnetic wavelengths." He is capable of viewing any broadcast electronic impulse. They are joined by Cameron Hicks who has "hyperkinesis" or "perfect synchrony between thought and action."[2] All of them are born with their individual abilities, fitting them in as the born rather than the thrust upon or achieved type of *powers*. Because the powers manifest in the show are obviously of the more traditional type, there is practically no room for *pseudo-superpowers*. Having said that, Dr. Rosen's intellectual prowess borders on fulfilling this mytheme. However, based on the events of the second season finale, "God's Eye," Dr. Rosen's *pseudo-superpow-*

ered status will, by necessity, shift.[3] Either he will develop legitimate and real powers, or he will have to die, based on the rules set up by the last several episodes of season two. In the second season, the team expands, but it practically goes without saying that they do band together to form a *superteam*.

Even from the above brief descriptions, it is also apparent that *Alphas* follows the *one power per person* mytheme. Though both Harken and Hicks use their abilities in similar ways in a fight, they draw from uniquely different skill sets. They all have one power and none of their powers duplicate each other. If, as the series claims, these Alphas are an evolutionary step, it would stand to reason that there would be a strong similarity in powers and skills manifest. However, because *Alphas* is closely tied to the superhero myth, the skills they manifest are very different. Even those that appear similar in nature have unique properties. These "similar but different" abilities are spelled out in the second episode of the series.[4] Another Alpha, Marcus Ayers, one of Dr. Rosen's first patients, has abilities not unlike those manifested by Hicks. Ayers can predict and control cause and effect. They both are able to see the kinetic interaction in events in a way that makes it possible to both understand what will happen and what did happen. Ayers is viewed as a serious threat to others and is housed in the combination prison and treatment facility known as Binghamton. When Hicks realizes this, he makes the connection between himself and Ayers and worries that Rosen and others will see the connection and place him in Binghamton. Dr. Rosen clarifies to Hicks that their abilities, and—of course—their intent and drives, are very different. He explains they are "similar but not the same."

Further, underscoring the *strong visual component*, the way Hicks' and Ayers' powers are displayed is very different. When Hicks retraces an event Ayers causes, the camerawork and special effects highlight the integral parts of the event in such a way that it leads him to uncover what he calls "the first domino."[5] The way it is presented gives the appearance that Hicks manifests his ability in a very instinctual way. He works in the way a well-trained athlete might, letting instinct take over in the moment to guide the unfolding of his actions. By contrast, when Ayers' ability is presented it includes formulas and calculations, showing angles, measurements, and data. Where Hicks' ability seems organic, Ayers' ability is presented as calculated and careful, like a game of chess. Though, in this case, the visualization of abilities is used to underscore the difference, at least in kind, between the abilities of two Alphas, it manifests nearly every time an Alpha activates his or her abilities. When Harken amps up, the camera rushes through his veins, showing the blood cells leading to his heart. When we reach the heart, it begins to beat more rapidly, indicating the onset of his adrenalin rush and stronger abilities.

Of course, Harken's ability is brought in to play only shortly before any sort of *violence*, especially inflicted on another Alpha, comes in to play. Since he amps up at least once an episode, the viewer can expect at least one violent confrontation within each forty-five minute show. Though the majority of the violence takes place in physical combat situations, there are also scenes of torture, shootings, and sonic disturbances which cause damage and pain to various characters. Emblematic of the violence of the series is a scene in "If Memory Serves." In the episode, Hicks and Kat—whose ability allows her instant recall in short term memory at the cost of all her memories approximately a month old or older—square off against an Alpha who can heal from any injury. A side effect of his ability is that he becomes extremely dense as his bones regenerate. Kat uses this factor to eliminate him by driving him deep into a lake using a large tractor truck. His dense skeleton makes him sink to the bottom of the lake and he is apparently unable to pull himself out before he drowns.[6]

This incident is an obvious violation of the *no killing* mytheme. Furthermore, it is not the only time lethal force is used by the heroes. Throughout the two seasons, the protagonists both directly and indirectly cause the death of opponents and the occasional innocent victim. However, there is a strong effort to avoid killing in favor of the more typical hand-to-hand beat-down. Emblematic of the effort to avoid killing is a scene in "Alphaville." While Hicks is trying to rescue the Alpha daughter of Skylar—an Alpha with an amazing technological ability—he confronts one of the kidnappers. He vaults over a balcony, takes one shot at her as he spins down to her level. Rather than targeting her, Hicks takes aim at her gun, his single bullet sending the gun spinning out of her grasp. They then engage in a brutal fight to submission.[7] Furthermore, in nearly every instance in which a death takes place, it is treated as a significant event. After Kat kills the Alpha in "If Memory Serves," she has to deal with the consequences. As she tries to come to grips with the situation, she says, "I don't know if I have the stomach for this [...] that guy, I killed him and I don't like how it feels." Though she has the ability to forget anything that happens, she chooses to commit this memory to a video diary she has been keeping. She records herself saying, "I killed a man today and I don't ever want to forget how that feels."[8] Though it is unclear how she expects to retain the memory of the pain she experiences, what is clear is that her pain and anguish over the death of another person is not something she wants to let pass. Rachel, Nina, and Dr. Rosen all have similar reactions to death and pain throughout the series.

Their reaction to death is indicative of the larger sense of mortality in the *Alphas* universe. Death seems to be a fairly permanent occurrence in

Alphas. With the exception of Stanton Parish, there really is not much of an indication that *death is temporary*. Most people who die stay dead. However, Stanton Parish has managed to come back from death for decades, since his Alpha ability first shows up after he was shot in the head during the Civil War. As previously mentioned, "God's Eye" introduces a wrinkle into the presence of this trope. The buildup to this penultimate episode of season two introduces a pulse device which augments the abilities of Alphas and kills normal human beings. Though the team manages to minimize the effect of the pulses, Dr. Rosen is exposed. Coupled with the fact that, in "God's Eye," he is suffering from major blood loss due to a gunshot, this pulse should have killed Dr. Rosen outright. However, his ultimate fate is left unresolved due to the cancellation of the show. Having said that, it is likely that Rosen would have survived and his survival would have lent credence to the existence of the *death is temporary* trope within the *Alphas* universe.

The trope is further problematized by the tenuous existence of another trope. It is uncertain whether the *ageless* mytheme is present in the series or not. Of course, the long-lived Stanton Parish, along with immortality, remains at the same apparent age as when he first realized he had an Alpha ability. However, he is the exception rather than the rule. After two years, the actors haven't obviously aged in any way. The only real change in appearance is Dr. Rosen's facial hair. He wears a beard in the pilot episode, but in several episodes of season one he appears clean shaven. However, in season two his beard reappears and remains consistent throughout. Though there are ups and downs in individual character arcs, generally the characters remain relatively unchanged for the course of the series. There may be no indication of aging, but a careful viewing of the series fails to reveal any concrete sense of the passage of time and its effect on the characters. Though, over the course of the two seasons, Gary Bell has to deal with an expanding sense of reality through the lens of his autism, the fundamental nature of his character seems relatively unchanged. This is also true of Nina Theroux and her struggles with the ramifications of her abilities to manipulate the minds of others. The characters have momentary story arcs which indicate a sense of learning over the course of the arc, the learning is usually sublimated back into the main storyline with minimal impact.

One of the changes to the team that does have some permanence is when Gary moves into the office space inhabited by the team. This is a direct result of an experience he had when his close friend and Alpha, Anna, is killed during a government raid on the apparent headquarters of the terrorist organization known as Red Flag. This is a physical change for Gary, and it stems from a change in his morning routine, but this change shows no sign of an actual aging effect on Gary. In an effort to cope with the trauma of Anna's death, Gary screams for ten seconds every morning. This disturbs his mother enough that she approaches Dr. Rosen to help Gary change. As a result of a conversation among the three of them, Gary opts to move into the office, much to his mother's chagrin. However, his move into the office does underscore the role of the team's space as *the lair* in the series. When they move in, each person takes the time to ensure that his or her space mirrors the occupant's identity. Rachel needs to deep-clean, Gary insists there is a hum that needs to be changed, Nina hangs an original Van Gogh on her office wall. However, what truly underscores the lair-like nature of the office space is Harken's security protocols. When he meets the real estate agent for the offices, he immediately asks, "How about the keypad entry system and the lobby surveillance cameras?"[9] Later, the office is shown to have a holding room designed to neutralize any Alpha ability with emergency shutdown protocols.[10] The additions to the office space push it beyond typical space and into a science fiction realm recognizable in superhero stories.

In every episode, the team spends time in the office space. It is a space of security and home-ness for the team, especially after Gary takes residence.[11] It is a known locale wherein they can let down their guard to an extent, to be themselves. Here, Rachel can allow her extreme sensitivity to germs, scents, and other external stimuli to have free reign as she maintains a strong degree of sanitation in her own office space. Here, they can also allow their Alpha abilities free reign. Harken carries a soda machine in to the office, lifting it by himself and placing it where he wants it. Hicks bounces pencils off his office door handle to ricochet them into the tiles of his office ceiling. It is largely a place of safety and belonging. When it is invaded, they react more extremely than in conflicts external to their lair.

Significantly, the office is rarely invaded. Practically every invasion which does take place is tied to a move by the acting *supervillain* in the current storyline. For the bulk of the first season, Red Flag acts as a sort of nebulous supervillain. In the finale, when it seems that Red Flag has been decimated, Stanton Parish rises to fill the supervillain void. The conflict between Stanton Parish and the team is clearly similar to the most recognizable relationship between Magneto and the X-Men. Magneto is the revolutionary, advocating a strong reaction to humanity and their reaction to mutants whereas Professor X, as de facto mentor for the X-Men advocates working for an integrative approach to Alpha/human relationships. Parish is branded a terrorist by government agencies and generally by the team as well. He believes that a violent response, involving actions which will kill myriad innocent humans, is the proper response to the rise of Alphas in the population. Dr. Rosen, in contrast, believes that the unique abilities of the Alphas can and should be part of a symbiotic relationship, viewing the Alphas as a part of humanity rather than as something outside of the human condition.

Dr. Rosen's pacifistic approach aligns him strongly with the mytheme of the *cooperative authority figure*. He is constantly and consistently aware of the needs and struggles of the Alpha team. He serves as both advisor and counselor. In the case of Kat, he is the one who suggests she begin to record her memories in an effort to aid her in developing a more lasting memory than she exhibits when she joins the team.[12] Though, as of the finale for season two, Dr. Rosen is presented with no Alpha ability, he does strongly identify with the Alphas and their condition. After his daughter Danielle, also called Dani, dies, he does begin to display a more selfish and very antagonistic personality but until that moment he is devoted to the long-term well-being of the team. This paternal positioning is reciprocated by most of the team and places Dr. Rosen in the position of being the one the team idealizes in their attempts to *please the father*. After Dani's death, in "Need to Know," Rosen has triggered the ability of an Alpha who can burn people with his touch while his hand is chained to his own chest. Rachel witnesses this and opposes his actions. She brings the rest of the team in to stop the torture. When Rosen and the others who side with them find out, Rachel admits that she didn't want to get her hands "this dirty," while looking pleadingly at Dr. Rosen for understanding. He replies, "It's all right, Rachel," and proceeds to vacate the building, giving Rachel a measure of peace in her apparent act of betrayal against the father figure.[13]

This attitude of desire to please the paternal figure is manifest strongly in "When Push Comes to Shove." In the episode, Nina allows her abilities to take over her life. Her Alpha power, called pushing, allows her to bend the will of those whom she pushes into doing whatever she tells them to do. In a series of flashbacks, the viewer is shown Nina's first use of her powers. In her preteen years, she pushes her father to keep him from abandoning her and her mother, forcing him to stay and making it impossible to leave the house except to go to work. Unfortunately, the push is so debilitating to him that he eventually kills himself to be free of his restriction. She knows she failed her father and carries this feeling throughout the series.

In "When Push Comes to Shove," she uses her ability more and more to take advantage of others, forcing them to commit crimes and facilitate her own illicit and selfish pursuits. She goes so far that the government feels the need to take action. Eventually, she realizes what she has been doing. In a confrontation with Dr. Rosen, she realizes how badly she has behaved and has done things that he views as unacceptable. This realization drives her into attempting suicide herself, though her effort is thwarted by intervention from Hicks. The government agent overseeing the team, Clay, works out a deal to release her into Rosen's custody. Afterward Dr. Rosen approaches a restrained and blindfolded Nina. The blindfold keeps her from being able to push others because her ability requires visual connection. As Rosen approaches Nina, he apologizes for the restraints. She says, "It's okay, I'm dangerous." When she feels Rosen unwrapping the blindfold, Nina tries to get him to stop, exclaiming, "You can't trust me." She fears that she won't be able to control herself, resulting in pushing the man whom she cares about the most. As a demonstration of his concern for Nina and her well-being, he finishes unwrapping her bandage. Once her face is exposed, she looks away. He says, "Look at me." When she finally does and they make eye contact, he simply says, "Hi."[14] In that moment, we see both Nina's realization that she has not completely displaced her father figure and the strength of Rosen's dedication to the team and their well-being.

In an apparent direct contrast to Dr. Rosen's concern for the welfare of the team, Nathan Clay and, ever so briefly, Don Wilson serve as both the domineering government entity and the *antagonistic authority figure*. Specifically, Clay manifests a severe discomfort with the powers of the Alphas and seems very willing to simply consign them to Binghamton, a combination therapy center and prison for Alphas deemed either too dangerous to or incapable of functioning among the general population. Within Binghamton is the sinister Building Seven. Alphas sent there are imbedded with a microchip that not only renders their abilities non-functional but their higher-order thinking abilities as well. In "Cause and Effect," Doctor Vijaj Singh oversees the treatment of Marcus Ayers. Ayers sees Singh as an antagonist, and there is some evidence that he is less engaged in the more pacifistic methods Rosen espouses, admitting that he was sending Ayers offsite for a surgical solution to "suppress his ability."[15] Rosen opposes such a radical solution and this tension is emblematic of the larger conflict between Rosen and Clay. Clay is interested in national security even if it comes at the cost of Alpha freedoms.

Intriguingly, after Rosen's daughter, Dani, is killed in a terrorist bombing by Stanton Parish, this balance shifts. In a way that challenges the reality of a set Antagonist/Cooperative dichotomy in authority figures, the death of Dani in "The Devil Will Drag You Under" causes Rosen to adopt more guerrilla style tactics in pursuing Parish.[16] As he drifts into a morally gray area, Rosen begins to force his formerly closely knit team into determining whether they will follow him in his actions or move to align themselves with Clay and the government agents who seem now to occupy the moral high ground. Prior to her death, Dani most clearly demonstrates the way *switching sides* works in *Alphas*. Throughout the second season, the team comes to realize that someone is leaking secrets to Stanton Parish. Rosen realizes his daughter is the mole and confronts her. Ultimately, they agree that she will switch sides, spying on Parish for the sake of the team. Her switch, and the danger it entails, drives Hicks to break with Rosen and start working for Parish. Gary highlights the way this mytheme works. He explains, "Hicks was my friend and, and Dani's Dr. Rosen's daughter, but now that they're breaking the law, they're hurting people, I don't like either of them."[17] When Dani dies, Rosen determines that he needs to do what is necessary to take down the man who killed his daughter. It is this determination that leads to the conflict he has with Rachel. While Rosen never overtly and intentionally becomes the *antagonistic authority figure*, the actions taken by Rosen, and Clay's response, complicate the typical black and white nature of the authority figure mythemes, though it does help fulfill that of *switching sides*.

Along with Nina, Dani is one of the only characters for whom we have a sense of their origin. Nina's abilities are tied to a *traumatic trigger* in her late childhood, but the details of this development are unclear. With Dani, we get a more clear sense of when her Alpha ability becomes apparent. Dani is capable of receiving and delivering emotional states from others, known as "empathic contagion."[18] When she was younger, Dr. Rosen asked Dani to bring tea to her mother when he had upset her. Dani's ability helped keep the family together by pacifying her mother. Though Dr. Rosen claims he was unaware of the direct manipulation, Dani insists that she performed this duty until she was twelve and that Dr. Rosen "knew what [she] could do when [she] was nine."[19] Given this frame of reference, it would seem that Alphas are not necessarily beholden to a traumatic onset. This is further substantiated by the Alpha Zoe's ability to compute complex mathematic equations though she appears to be approximately four years old.[20]

Having established that Alpha abilities appear to be unrelated to trauma in some cases, the universe still seems to cling to this trope for other characters. Because we never see much backstory for any member of the team besides Nina, we have no real frame of reference for the circumstances under which their powers activate. Indeed, the earliest demonstration of Cameron Hicks' ability in the show is that of a video from his days as a high school pitcher. In the video, he throws a baseball from the pitcher's mound, bouncing it around the runner headed to first base. The ball ricochets off of the ground and directly into the first baseman's mitt, getting the final out to end the game.[21] In Hicks' case, the evidence certainly supports a trigger based on excitement, but not necessarily trauma. He admits as much in "Catch and Release" when he says, "I didn't notice anything special until high school."

Regardless of age or ability, the Alphas in the series do seem *Ineffective Against Real World Problems*. From the mathematical genius of Zoe to Gary's ability to read electronic signals, the abilities seen in the series are not turned toward solving the kinds of problems facing the real world. Though Rosen and his team do attempt to disband Red Flag, classified as a terrorist organization by the government within the show, they are relatively incapable of stopping the terrorist acts. Furthermore, they have no discernable connection to real-world terrorist organizations. *Alphas* fails to pit the characters against real world problems, ignoring any reality which has no specific connection to Alphas and their activities. This is also a manifestation of the fact that the team *promotes/maintains the status quo*, at least generally. The team is introduced as they are called to investigate a killing only because it was accomplished by an impossible shot. If it had been a typical sniping, the team would never have been called in. Until the death of Dani, the team rarely moves unless they are called upon to investigate action which is impossible to achieve without the use of an Alpha ability, without something that works outside the bounds of the typical, real world, status quo.

Though the Alphas may seem to have very little connection to the real world, despite some efforts to make them seem more aligned to our reality than other superhero tales, they do have a familiarity with a recognizable trope. The Alphas, especially later in to season two, seem to have little problem with promoting Alpha *justice over law*. In "Cause and Effect," Dr. Rosen follows clues left by Marcus Ayers to meet with him. He is severely reprimanded by Clay because Rosen failed to inform the agents of his intent to meet with Ayers. In the pilot for season two, Harken and Hicks find Gary locked up in Building Seven of Binghamton with a "pacifier chip" in place.[22] When they discover Gary there, they go against the government agents in order to attempt to free Gary from his confinement. However, the largest divergence between the team's efforts and the governmental organization occurs after the death of Dani. Clay and his agents arrive at the team's office headquarters and collect all the evidence amassed regarding Parish and his associates. When Hicks pushes back against their invasion, Clay tells him that they were invited into the investigation by Dr. Rosen.[23] Eventually, they extend this into taking over the office space, *the lair* of the team. As they move in, Rosen, Hicks, and—to a lesser extent—Nina and Rachel, begin to pull out of the team dynamic.

While Gary, Harken, and Kat work with Clay, the others work at odds with the government agency. Their plotting begins when Hicks says, "You know that if Clay catches Parish, he'll put him in prison. He doesn't deserve to go to prison." And Rosen responds, "No, no he doesn't. I'm going to need your help."[24] Immediately, the two begin working at odds with the government team, attempting to visit their own kind of justice on Parish. They recruit Kat to investigate a farmstead which results in the finding of another Alpha, Mitchell, which serves as a major blow to Parish. Though it takes time for Hicks and Rosen to fully develop the separation, it comes to a breaking point when the government stages an operation to move Mitchell to a specific location. When Parish's Alphas attempt to recapture Mitchell, Rosen's team uses it as an opportunity to capture one of Parish's agents, knowingly jeopardizing the efforts of Clay's team. However, though this seems to be a fulfillment of *justice over law*, it must be admitted that over the course of the remaining episodes that Rosen and Hicks' actions drift dangerously close to becoming terrorist in nature as well. The series leaves the justice of Rosen's actions hanging through the end of the second season. Certainly, he and Hicks believe they seek justice, and Parish's longevity create a problem for traditional legal solutions, but *Alphas* disallows a comfortable resolution of this particular mytheme as the show progresses.

The unstable appearance of this trope in the series is tied with another trope tenuously present within the series. Few of the characters in the show establish any sort of *amazing physique*. Early on, Hicks grows toward a more superheroic character than he is at the start of the show. In fact, his depiction in the show comes as close as *Alphas* gets to satisfying this mytheme, though even then it's not in a way typical within superhero mythology. In the pilot, when the team first finds Cameron Hicks, he works at a grocery store. When she sees him, Nina remarks that he's a "hot, deadly assassin [....] I like the blue-collar look and the bad-boy thing."[25] In a later episode, Kat comments on his attractiveness as well. So does Skylar, an Alpha who helps the team with her technological ability, when she remarks, "So pretty and so useless."[26] However, none of the team really measure up to the incredible physical appearance of the superheroes in the comics. Nor do they manage to stack up to most actors who play superheroes in recent film adaptations: Hugh Jackman as Wolverine, Chris Hemsworth in *Thor*, Ryan Reynolds in *Green Lantern*, Chris Evans in *Captain America*, Christian Bale in the Batman trilogy, and Henry Cavill in *Man of Steel*. Granted, Robert Downey, Jr.'s Iron Man is less physically spectacular, but the recent trend is toward much more impressive physiques even in live action fare for both men and women. This is a trend less prevalent in *Alphas*. In season two, Kat takes on the role of superhero in training as Hicks seems to reach a level of competence at which he is comfortable, peaking in "When Push Comes to Shove" when he rescues Nina from attempted suicide. As she jumps off a building, he shoots loose a construction hook, leaps through the air in a fairly heroic pose, catches

4. Finding the Superhero   143

Nina's hand and the hook and swings her to safety. Of the team, Kat seems the only one intent on improving herself toward some sort of superheroic level.

Kat is also emblematic of another key superhero mytheme. She, and several others on the team, fulfill the qualities of the *orphan*. One of the side effects of Kat's ability is a lack of long-term memory. This means that she has no memory of any event older than a month. At one point, Nina pushes Kat in an effort to help her remember. She recalls a fragmentary image of a woman she believes to be her mother.[27] She holds to that idea until Mitchell helps her pull that memory out fully, only to reveal it is nothing more than a commercial for cleaning supplies.[28] Kat, Hicks, and Harkin all appear to have no family outside of the Alpha team. Dr. Rosen has no obvious parents. As previously mentioned, Nina had parents at one point. She drove one to suicide, and her mother disappears from the narrative after only one short scene. Gary has a mother who dotes and practically smothers him. Though their relationship seems difficult and unwieldy, his concern for her is manifest after she is in a car accident. His autism makes it difficult for him to communicate his feelings in recognizable ways, but he remains at her bedside, tries to use his status as a government agent to force the staff to take better care of her and when she is communicative, he tells her, "I'm gonna stay here with you, take care of you [....] I'm glad that you didn't die, Mom."[29] Though he doesn't express their connection in traditional means, it's very apparent that he does not fit the mytheme of the *orphan*. Of the entire team, only Rachel has two parents, both very concerned with making sure she has a happy existence—despite what they see as the debilitating defect of her Alpha ability.[30]

The fact that Rachel's parents judge her ability as a weakness does give her a sense of being an *outsider* even in her own family. This mytheme echoes throughout the series in multiple ways. Harkin begins the first season trying to work toward reinstatement into the FBI, though he doesn't feel comfortable with the agents he encounters. Nina feels like an outsider after misusing her abilities on members of the team. Hicks feels like an outsider during the pilot episode due to the fact that he met the team after being coerced by an Alpha to shoot someone. Alphas as a whole remain in hiding throughout the first season, until Dr. Rosen reveals their existence in "Original Sin." Throughout the second season, they are viewed with suspicion and doubt by the population and the team is even ostracized from an isolated Alpha commune in "Alphaville." However, the most overt and continuous expression of this trope within the series comes from the theme song. The final lines of the song reiterate the sense of being on the outside by proclaiming, "People don't understand people like me." The song, written for the opening credits of the series, underscores the sense of alienation evident in the Alpha community because they are misunderstood by those who are unlike them.

Hicks' alienation, his sense of otherness, ties directly into the concept of the *spectacular origin*. Thus far the series has delved very little into the past lives of the team. Hicks is a special case because he is not a member of the team at the beginning of the pilot episode. As he is introduced to the team, the viewer shares in the opportunity to look into his origin, making him one of the only members of the team who has had some of his origin revealed. Though Nina's origin, also spectacular in its own way, is told in flashbacks in "When Push Comes to Shove," it lacks a certain level of completeness when compared to that of Hicks. The pilot opens with Hicks stocking the produce section at a grocery store. He gets a phone call that includes an address and begins to hear everyone he meets say, "It's time to kill" and "Pull the trigger." The phrases are repeated over and over by people, on billboards and newspaper headlines. He wanders away from work and finds himself on the rooftop of the building given to him via his phone. He uses a rifle found on the roof to kill a man being held by the government for questioning. When the team investigates, they discover that the shot required him to shoot through a vent and bounce the bullet off a vent cover in order to ricochet the shot into the head of the target. The team's research reveals that Hicks was "the highest rated marksman in the history of the [Marine] Corps."[31] They also discover the aforementioned video of a baseball game wherein Hicks bounces the ball around a runner in order to get the ball to the baseman for the game-winning out. Before he joins the team, Rosen drives Hicks into tossing coins across the room into a soda machine. The way he is introduced to the team and the fact that his ability naturally cues in to a very visual presentation makes the story of his origin with the team as spectacular as many superheroes. Though there is more to his origin that we are given in the pilot, there is enough to ensure that he does fulfill the requirements of this mytheme.

The aforementioned episode, "Alphaville," gives perhaps one of the best examples of another trope which tenuously exists in *Alphas* and connects it to superhero mythology: *iterations*. The main characters who form the team all function in a metropolitan area—serving to underscore the *urban* mytheme. They work primarily in cities and urban locales. They engage frequently with government agencies. All of the homes we see of team members are either in the city itself or in what appear to be local suburbs. Scenes set in less populous areas are infrequent and serve to underscore how often the team is centrally located to urban and suburban areas. In "Alphaville," the team travels into the deep woods. It's far enough out that Gary has a hard time because he is completely incapable of finding any sort of electronic signal at all, rendering his abilities completely ineffective. The community bears some resemblance to a paramilitary compound and some to communes designed to disconnect with bureaucracy and issues of larger civilization. This level of disconnect and its value are typified to some extent as Gary develops an enlightened ability to "read" the electronic communications of nature, the aurora borealis and the impulses of stars. He says, "Even the trees have signals, and the rocks have signals."[32] In a way, the reality Gary encounters in "Alphaville" is very divergent from the one to which he is accustomed.

In "A Short Time in Paradise," several of the team find themselves in the thrall of an Alpha who is capable of giving subjects an artificial sense of euphoria. The Alpha, Jonas, creates a cult-like commune populated with people who are devoted to Jonas' peaceful all-encompassing dogma. The commune creates a sense of serenity for these people. Specifically, Harken, Hicks, and Nina all get pulled in by Jonas' ability. Nina's serenity within the commune is significant because of her frequent lack of comfort in the outside world, specifically within the team. Dr. Rosen realizes that Jonas' powers have a side effect that eventually causes death in those who experience prolonged exposure to his ability. Eventually, there is a stand-off between Jonas and Rosen which results in Rosen defying his own pacifistic tendencies by shooting Jonas to save his team and the others subject to Jonas' ability.[33]

Nina's constant discomfort and alienation, part of what makes her so susceptible to Jonas' peace-making powers, stems from her struggles with the *power and responsibility* mytheme. Of all the abilities on the Alpha team, Nina's is that which is most easily abused. She is introduced in the series when she pushes an officer into eating a traffic ticket which he was about to issue to her. Most clearly manifest in the aforementioned "When Push Comes to Shove," Nina pushes a former boyfriend into acting as her lover. She also pushes Rachel into kissing her, an act which she knows will be more intense because of Rachel's heightened senses. In a preceding episode, Rachel kisses a boyfriend and is immediately and intensely overcome by the stimulation, insinuating that the single kiss was enough to induce orgasm. It is insinuated that Nina knew about this experience and intentionally drives Rachel to encounter the stimulation again. She pushes Hicks into pulling a gun on other members of the team in order to facilitate her escape from the team. Throughout the episode, Nina allows herself to use her powers more and more. Eventually, she realizes that she has crossed the line, using her powers incredibly irresponsibly. It is this realization which drives her to make the suicide effort which results in Hicks' heroic rescue. It is also this realization which drives her to attempt to avoid having her bandages removed by Rosen.

She realizes she is not worthy of trust because of her irresponsibility. Through the rest of the season, she attempts to redeem herself, but only after she has reached an awareness of the necessity to be responsible for her great powers.

Of course, she still manages to hold on to some of the gains of her powers, but only that which she can maintain using the money she earns working as part of the team as well as some of what she had prior to her crisis of conscience. This means that she continues to dress in the designer clothing she was able to accrue by pushing shopkeepers into giving them to her. As much as the trope exists in the series, her clothing serves as a signifier of her *costume*. In the same way, the fact that Harken almost exclusively wears suits, Gary in long-sleeved collarless shirts, Hicks in a semi-grunge look, Rachel in more conservative wear, and Rosen in button-up shirts and slacks, all serve to indicate what little presence the mytheme has within the series.[34] These looks fail to really connect with the complete expression of the trope, but do signify their personas in a way that does at least tenuously engage with the mytheme. However much the costume might tentatively exist in *Alphas*, neither *chevron* nor *codename* make clear and ready appearances within the show. The team does use nicknames for each other on occasion, but there is no established continuity in renaming the characters that would indicate a codename, nor do they have any sort of symbol that serves to represent them as a team or as individuals. Nor does the series demonstrate any significant *expository narration* besides the pilot's discussion of the protagonists' individual abilities.

The presence of the *helper* is complicated in the series as well; however there is strong argument that this mytheme manifests to some extent. Rosen is certainly a benevolent figure to the team early on, and they do work together, but the relationships seem to be more of co-equals than of helpers, and Rosen's actions are not always in the best interest of the team. However, one episode does present a fairly traditional example of this mytheme. In "Bill and Gary's Excellent Adventure," Bill Harken coerces Gary to accompany him on a non-sanctioned mission. This mission is driven by Harken's efforts early on in season one to be reinstated in to the FBI. Harken uses Gary's ability to read frequencies to track down a kidnapping victim. Throughout the episode, Gary serves as assistant to Harken, not unlike the sidekick in traditional superhero myth. Harken is in control of events, though he needs Gary to help him accomplish his task.[35] Following "Bill and Gary's Excellent Adventure," the duo develops a buddy-like relationship. Harken consistently teases Gary. Though it annoys Gary, after this episode, he is aware that Harken only does what he does out of a good-natured effort to demonstrate his friendship in acceptably masculine ways.

Harken's willingness to use Gary in an effort to reinstate himself, while potentially problematic, is a part of his *moral code*. He believes, rightly or not, that Gary's ability can and should be used—just this once—for his own personal gain. He takes advantage of Gary. As is the case with more modern superhero mythology, the *moral code* in *Alphas* is more complicated and nuanced than Golden Age superheroes. Dr. Rosen is driven by a pacifistic approach underscored by a desire to do what is best for his team and the other Alphas with whom he comes in contact. In "A Short Time in Paradise," Rosen faces a conflict between his pacifistic desire to avoid violence and his desire to preserve life. At the climactic moment, Rosen holds a gun on Jonas, begging him to stop using his power on the people at the religious commune. When Jonas refuses, Rosen pulls the trigger, killing the Alpha and saving the acolytes from suffering the negative side effects of Jonas' ability. Rosen is perhaps the most obviously moralistic, at least until his daughter dies. The moral code for most of the rest of the team rarely comes to the fore in the series, with the exception of Nina. For Nina, her moral code seems to shift over the course of the series. Her introduction in the series, pushing an officer to get out of a traffic ticket, shows that she is willing to circumvent the law for her own personal gain. "When Push Comes to Shove" shows Nina willing to push anyone at any time simply in an attempt to satisfy the desires of the moment. However, the episode shows Nina staring at her reflection in a car window, trying to push herself, saying, "Be happy." Despite her efforts at gratification, she finds herself unsatisfied, indicating at least a tenuous moral code for the series, if not for the individuals. The moral code is not nearly as pronounced as it is in many superhero myths.

Though it is much less pronounced in the series, Harken does present the best example of the *alter ego* in *Alphas*. The varying roles Harken plays presents different facets of his being, types of alternate egos. He begins the series very intent on rejoining the FBI. His posture, mannerisms, and dress all indicate a man who is uninterested in being a part of the Alphas team. There is a bitterness to this Harken, whose major drive is to move on to somewhere else. When he is at home, Harken's presence suggests a strong relationship with his wife. Though they talk about his desires to rejoin the FBI, he is comfortable and happy in her presence. However, when she broaches the subject of children, he does balk. In fact, Harken's performativity at home is stereotypical of the devoted, masculine husband. Stemming from Judith Butler's work in *Gender Trouble*, in this work the term performativity is used to denote that aspect of gender which derives almost exclusively on the way a person acts based on his or her perception of the appropriate behaviors for his or her gender or sexuality or sex. The concept of performativity, while linked to biological gender and sexuality, is very much a construct by the individual whether he or she is cognizant of it or not. In "Alpha Dogs," Harken spends some time undercover in an underground fight club for Alphas. After the assignment is over, Harken goes back to the club to fight some more. At times, Harken is a loving husband, at times the by-the-book agent—the only one of the team with serious experience in government work. Finally, Harken is also a member of an underground fight club. Though the overlap in Harken's egos is more than we usually find in superheroes, overlap is not unheard of.

In and of himself, Harken is a strong example of the *androcentric* mytheme. *Alphas* itself still has a much stronger masculine presence, though there are some efforts at a more nuanced presentation. Even at the surface, the team is predominantly male. Rosen, Harken, Hicks, and Gary contrast with Nina, Rachel, and—at the beginning of season two—Kat. Though Skylar helps balance out the gender equation, her occasional presence is also offset by the visits of Clay. Furthermore, though androcentrism does not necessitate a heteronormative mythology, the fact that the entire team is clearly heterosexual furthers a more narrow androcentristic mythology. There is the potential of reading Gary as asexual or homosexual. However his relationship with Anna and reaction to her death strongly support the heteronormativity of the series. The powers and abilities of the team further underscores the way *Alphas* connects with this superhero mytheme. Harken and Hicks are the two in the first, establishing, series who have aggressive, masculine type powers. Rosen, as previously discussed, serves in a paternal role. This underscores his part in maintaining the mytheme. The women in the series all tend to have more passive, non-physical based Alpha abilities. Kat does use her ability to improve her abilities physically, but the sense of memory, loss, and the fact that the only memory she thought she had was of her mother still keeps her connected to her feminine role. Furthering the way this trope continues within the series is Nina's ability. In several episodes, the power of her ability to manipulate the thoughts of others is viewed as practically the most frightening of Alpha abilities. It is easy to see the potential inherent misogyny in the way the show deals with Nina's ability. She alone can make anyone, especially the men in the series, do anything she wants them to do, frequently against their will.

This is furthered by the fact that Nina fits the *relationship struggles* mytheme more than anyone else. The social implications of Gary's autism causes strain in his relationships with practically everyone with whom he comes in contact. Though Hicks is divorced, has a relationship with Nina for a time and later a relationship with Dani—which strains his relationship with

Rosen as well, Hicks' struggles are a bit more straightforward than Nina's. Harken has to deal with balancing relationships with members of the team and others do as well. However, Nina's problems go to a whole different level. Much of what plays into this has already been discussed in this chapter. When she uses her ability against Rachel, it severely strains their relationship. When she inadvertently pushes Hicks, it's the cause of their breakup. Though Nina is the exemplar of this trope, there is not a character in the series who doesn't struggle to form and maintain good relationships with others, whether they be romantic or platonic in nature.

Ultimately, *Alphas* does measure up to the majority of the key superhero tropes. However, the show measures up in a way that is less satisfying and relatively complicated. The connections are there, but in less than traditional ways. In this way it seems to fit with the current trend in superhero comics. The mythemes have been complicated and twisted over the decades in a way that has complicated a simple application of the tropes. For established superheroes this is less problematic than for characters newly introduced into the mythology. At this point, the purest application of the superhero mythemes to storytelling seems to be in film. Because *Alphas* exists outside of the main art forms used to tell superhero stories, its lack of adherence to the mythemes is not unremarkable. Though television is frequently less connected to superhero mythology, a recent addition does tie much more directly to superheroes. *Smallville* played around the edges of Superman stories, but the current series *Arrow* directly and intentionally engages with superhero mythology. In fact, *Arrow*'s connection to superhero myths through the tropes is perhaps more direct than nearly all other formats and storylines currently in production. Furthermore, *Alphas* nearly never presents itself in connection with central superhero myth. The tenuous connection to the mytheme is partly a result of the changes in presentations of the myth in other formats and partly a result of the series' effort to maintain some distance from the mythology. However, there is an obvious connection between the mythology and *Alphas*, a show which seems to have followed in the tradition of most superhero television series. Though there are other tales and media that engage in superhero mythology, television will most likely always deal to some extent with the superhero, at least until the myth ceases to have any value in popular culture.

5

The Superhero Before the Superhero
Finding Superhero Mythology in the Old English Beowulf

There have been several studies that compare early world literature to popular culture and superheroes. Don LoCicero's *Superheroes and Gods: A Comparative Study from Babylonia to Batman* makes specific comparison between ancient texts and superheroes. However, there is not a study that makes a thorough comparison between the Anglo-Saxon hero Beowulf and superhero mythology. In Roger B. Rollin's "Beowulf to Batman: The Epic Hero and Pop Culture" Beowulf is used as a framework to discuss the solitary heroes of western films. Though appropriate for his study, it leaves Beowulf underdeveloped as a part of the larger popular culture mythos. As one of the earliest English epic heroes his place in the tradition of the hero deserves further analysis. Using the mythological lexicon, this chapter will directly examine Beowulf's connection to superheroes. Originally, *Beowulf* was studied only for its historical significance in Anglo-Saxon and north east European civilizations. It wasn't until J. R. R. Tolkien published "*Beowulf*: The Monsters and the Critics" in 1936 that this attitude shifted. Tolkien argues that "*Beowulf* is in fact so interesting as poetry, in places so powerful, that this quite overshadows the historical content [....] The illusion of historical truth and perspective [...] is largely a product of art."[1] Since that time, there has been a great deal of literary analysis of *Beowulf*. This chapter joins in the tradition of examining the mythological and folkloric underpinnings of this ancient epic. This analysis will also explain the problematic nature of attempting to retroactively examine the existence of superheroes in ancient literature. However, this will receive further explanation of this portion of the analysis at the end of the chapter.

5. The Superhero Before the Superhero   151

One of the strongest correlations between *Beowulf* and the superhero mythos is the manifestation of a super*power*. Beowulf's superpower is linked to one of the most common of the powers: superhuman strength. Though the power is obvious, we have no indication regarding *how* Beowulf got his powers. We are completely unable to ascertain whether he developed his powers due to outside intervention, through his own efforts, or whether he was born with superhuman strength, making the source of his *powers* impossible to ascertain. Whether it is true that we have no real evidence of the source of Beowulf's powers, most other superhuman characters in Nordic tales appear to be born with their unnatural abilities. Because of this, it is most likely that we are to accept that Beowulf himself was also born with his superhuman strength. While the source is unclear, his use of his powers is straightforward. In order to kill Grendel's mother, Beowulf was required to use an unusual weapon, a sword which "was greater than any other man might even bear into the play of battle."[2] After using a sword no other man could use to slay Grendel's mother, Beowulf carried back the head of Grendel. Upon returning to his men, Beowulf handed the head over to his men to transport back to Heorot. "[F]our of them had to bear, with some strain, on a battle-pole Grendel's head to the gold-hall."[3] It took four men to carry the head Beowulf managed to carry on his own.

Of course, the most famous demonstration of his strength is when Beowulf single-handedly rips off the arm of the monster Grendel. His physical abilities most likely manifest an *amazing physique*, but not necessarily in the traditional sense. There are no mentions of Beowulf's handsomeness, nor of his musculature. He is strong, and this strength appears to be based on his physical attributes, but there is no necessary indication that he fits the ideal of the washboard abdominals and rippling pectorals requisite in the superhero mytheme. Furthermore, depending on the source of Beowulf's superpowers, he may or may not be a hero who achieves his *powers* with pseudo-superpowers, though his strength and unusual abilities in the water certainly seems impressive enough to push beyond only a seeming. The challenge is the unanswerable question regarding the source of Beowulf's abilities. Because we cannot know the source, we cannot determine exactly how he qualifies exactly within the framework of powers in the superhero mythology.

However, the most consistent demonstration of Beowulf's abilities rests on his prowess on the water. When Unferth challenges Beowulf's boast that he is as good as he claims by bringing up the swimming race he lost to Breca. Beowulf immediately responds:

> I had greater strength on the sea,
> more ordeals on the waves than any other man. [....]

> We two were together on the sea
> for five nights, until the flood drove us apart,
> surging waves, coldest of weathers,
> darkening night, and a northern wind,
> knife-sharp, pushed against us. The seas were choppy;
> [....] Down to the ocean floor
> a grisly foe dragged me, gripped me fast
> in his grim grasp, yet it was given to me
> to stab that monster with the point of my sword,
> my war-blade; the storm of battle took away
> that mighty sea-beast, through my own hand.
> Time again those terrible enemies
> sorely threatened me. I served them well
> with my dear sword, as they deserved. [....]
> And so it came about that I was able to kill
> nine of these sea-monsters. I have never heard
> of a harder night-battle under heaven's vault[4]

Assuming Beowulf's version of events is accurate, he was able to engage with nine hostile sea-beasts after having swum on the ocean for almost a week. When he goes to Grendel's Mere to face off against the monster's otherworldly mother, he has to swim down to the entrance to the lair. There are various readings of the line *ða wæs hwil dæges ær he þone grundwong ongytan mehte*, but a traditional and most accepted translation is that "it was the space of a day before he [Beowulf] could see the bottom" of the mere.[5] The other common translation is that "it was daylight" before he could see the bottom of the mere, insinuating less how long Beowulf was swimming and more the time of day during which he made his attempt to enter the lair.

The place where Beowulf faces off against the mother of Grendel is about as close to *the lair* as the poem allows, but it certainly doesn't fulfill the needs of the mytheme. Certainly, the *supervillain* can—and frequently does—have a lair, the mytheme is specific to the superhero's sanctuary. Tentatively, Hrothgar's mead hall, Heorot, could be the lair of the tale, but, again, it's not home to Beowulf. Because of that, in reality the mead hall doesn't work either. In truth, Beowulf has no lair to call his own. However, the mead hall and Beowulf's kingdom actually do, to a small extent, fulfill the *urban* mytheme, at least in the context of the times. Though there were larger locales, like Rome, at the time Beowulf did his deeds, a location like Heorot was one of the more metropolitan areas in Scandinavian Europe. Especially when we consider that the poet calls Heorot "a great mead-hall meant to be a wonder of the world forever" and "the hall of halls,"[6] there is a tentative argument that Beowulf takes place in as *urban* a locale as 6th century north Europe had to offer. However, this certainly doesn't compare to the locales wherein most superheroes work.

After Beowulf returns to his homeland, when he and a band of Geats face off against the Frisians, the battle turns for the worst and "Beowulf escaped from there through his own strength, took a long swim; he had in his arms the battle-armor of thirty men, when he climbed to the cliffs."[7] Again, Beowulf's abilities on the water are coupled with an amazing feat of strength. Not only does he swim carrying thirty full suits of armor, but he also climbs the cliffs carrying the same gear. He has an ability which extends beyond any normal man. Beowulf's superpower is underscored in the way he and the dragon are buried. The dragon should not be considered a supervillain, coinciding with the conceit that we should read the dragon as a force of nature rather than a force of evil. However, the mirror-like quality of the dragon lends credence to Beowulf's association with water. The dragon is constantly and consistently described in terms of fire. When it comes time to bury the remains of the two combatants, Beowulf "chose the fire, the hot surging flames."[8] "They also pushed the dragon, the worm over the cliff-wall, let the waves take him, the flood embrace the guard of that finery."[9] In this way, the dragon is consigned to the element that was Beowulf's strength and Beowulf is consumed by the source of the dragon's power.

Also, because all of his power is centered on unnatural strength, his supernatural ability qualifies under the *one power per person* mytheme. However, any evidence of a *traumatic trigger* mytheme is circumstantial. We know that Beowulf eventually takes over the Geatish kingdom and "held it well for fifty winters."[10] After Beowulf kills Grendel and his mother, he lives at least fifty years before he faces off against the dragon. For most readers, this indicates that Beowulf faces the first two challenges at a fairly young age, but there seems to be no other indication to support an age at which his powers developed. Furthermore, the fact that he ages fifty years during the course of the poem, and that his body appears to manifest the effects of that aging, also belies the existence of the *ageless* mytheme.

Though there is no evidence of a *superteam* in *Beowulf*, the Anglo-Saxon hero does engage with a larger group of mythic supermen. There is an ancient tradition of poetic eddas from northern Europe. These tales are populated by hard drinking, hard fighting, articulate men who are capable of supernatural feats of strength and cunning. There are strong connections between these men and the Danish hero from the Old English epic *Beowulf*. Several of the Scandanavian poetic *eddas* and many Nordic sagas detail amazing acts of physical strength perpetuated by heroes while still in their youth and into their advanced old age. Many were gifted poets as well. Along with the northeastern European folkloric connections to *Beowulf* there have been several modern adaptations. We cannot know for certain about any *iterations* created at the time of the original epic, but since then it has been re-imagined in many different ways. In literature, there have been several novelized retellings of the story, notably Michael Creighton's *Eaters of the Dead*. There have been several films, including *The 13th Warrior* starring Antonio Banderas and inspired by Creighton's novel, Robert Zemeckis' *Beowulf*, and at least two science fiction adaptations on film. There have also been several graphic novel versions of the epic, but most notably—at least for this study—is the DC character Beowulf the Dragon Slayer who had his own series for ten months and has later made sporadic appearances in the DC universe. Matt Wagner has also created a deep and abiding mythos surrounding Hunter Rose who called himself Grendel. In different incarnations, the Grendel of Wagner's mythos has faced off against Batman, further linking *Beowulf* mythology to the DC universe. Though it took decades, Beowulf has ultimately developed several variations on his original mythos. This is not to mention the variety of ways that *Beowulf* has influenced the landscape of popular adventure fantasy, especially the heavy debt owed by J. R. R. Tolkien to this Old English epic.

Interestingly, most of these iterations still maintain a quasi-historical framework for the tale. Beowulf tends generally to be dressed in Hollywood renditions of medieval Norse clothing and armor. Significantly, however, Beowulf has less of an obvious *costume* than is traditionally associated with the superhero mythos. Before each of the major conflicts described in *Beowulf*, the hero spends some time on what he will wear in the coming struggle. The most famous of his "costumes" is presented when he removes his armor to fight Grendel:

> Surely the Geatish prince greatly trusted
> his mighty strength, the Maker's favor,
> when he took off his iron byrnie, [a long chain mail short]
> undid his helmet, and gave his decorated iron,
> best of swords, to his servant
> and bid him hold his battle-gear.[11]

In this conflict, Beowulf's costume is most notable for not being there at all. When Beowulf prepares to dive into Grendel's mere to confront the monster's mother, the poet spends significant time describing Beowulf's armor, a trope in hero mythology which begins with epic poetry and persists into modern storytelling with the action film's "suiting up" scenes:

> Beowulf geared up
> in his warrior's clothing, cared not for his life.
> The broad war-shirt, woven by hand,
> cunningly made, had to test the mere—
> it knew well how to protect his bone-house

> so that a battle grip might not hurt his breast
> nor an angry malicious clutch touch his life.
> The shining helmet protected his head, [...]
> encircled with a splendid band, as a weapon-smith
> in days of old had crafted it with wonders,
> set boar-images, so that afterwards
> no blade or battle-sword might ever bite it.
> Not the smallest of powerful supports was that
> which Hrothgar's spokesman lent him at need;
> the hilted sword was named Hrunting,
> unique among ancient treasures—
> its edge was iron, etched with poison-stripes,
> hardened with the blood of war; it had never failed
> any man who grasped it in his hands in battle[12]

Fifty years later, when Beowulf squares off against the dragon, again we see him recognizing the need for arming himself appropriately for the conflict. He proclaims,

> I would not bear a sword
> or weapon to this serpent, if I knew any other way
> I could grapple with this great beast
> after my boast, as I once did with Grendel;
> but I expect the heat of battle-flames there,
> steam and venom; therefore shield and byrnie will I have on me. [....]
> Then that brave challenger stood up by his shield,
> stern under his helmet, bore his battle-shirt[13]

The armor is described in detail, another connection between Beowulf and classic epic poetry, in part due to the importance of the gear in the narrative. Having said that, in every fight the armor differs. While the use of the variety of armor in Beowulf seems to work against the concept of the costume as understood in the superhero mythos, its presence in the text does lend itself to another element of the superhero. Because of the crossover between superheroic and action mythologies in film, and the way both draw from epic traditions, it is very common to see this scene in superhero films. Especially notable are the suiting up scenes in nearly every Batman film and in the Iron Man series.

Though *Beowulf* was originally composed without any sort of visual accompaniment of which we are aware, the descriptive nature of the narrative gives it a sense of having a *strong visual component*. Each time Beowulf prepares for a fight, as demonstrated, we are given a description of the event as it unfolds. Furthermore, when he prepares to face off against Grendel's mother, we are given a carefully crafted description not only of the armor he is wearing but the detail and history thereof, creating for the reader an image of what it is we are reading. This description extends to Heorot's appearance after Grendel is defeated:

> Then it was quickly commanded that Heorot be adorned [...]
> Gold-dyed tapestries
> shone on the walls, many wonderful sights
> to any man who might look on them.
> That shining building was nearly shattered
> inside, entirely, fast in its iron bands,
> its hinges sprung; the roof alone survived
> unharmed, when that horrible creature,
> stained with foul deeds, turned in his flight[14]

The beauty of the trappings contrasts with the damage done during the fight in the hall. The celebration is tinged with the memory of the damage caused as Beowulf and the monster Grendel squared off in the hall. The shining tapestries and timbers contrast with the broken walls and doors even as the foully festooned monster fled the scene. However, one of the most vivid descriptions comes at one of the most memorable moments of the poem. As Beowulf pulls on Grendel's arm, "a gaping wound opened in his shoulder-joint, his sinews sprang apart, his joints burst asunder."[15]

The graphic description of Grendel's wound evidences the visual nature of many of the descriptions as well as the *violence* inherent in the epic. Not only are the fights with Grendel, his mother, and the dragon the central moments of the epic but they are all three described in vivid detail. Each of the three monsters' initial attacks is described as well as their fight with Beowulf. Along with these conflicts, Beowulf's fight with monsters both in the swimming contest with Breca and while swimming down to Grendel's mere are described. The Finnsburh episode also centers upon the violent conflict between Finn's band and those who followed Hnæf. Beowulf's rise to the Geatish throne comes after more than one conflict. In fact, apropos to the worldview of the Anglo-Saxons, the society of the poem is steeped in conflict and celebrations of that conflict.

The Anglo-Saxon worldview also influences the lack of the *death is temporary* mytheme in *Beowulf*. Obviously, though he later developed a life outside the epic, Beowulf fails to survive his own adventure. As vital as this mytheme is to the superhero myth, for the Anglo-Saxons, there was a more vital concept which demands the death of Beowulf. Tolkien presents this idea by suggesting the following is the essence of the way they view the world, "*lif is læne: eal scæceþ leoht and lif somod*. So deadly and ineluctable is the underlying thought that those who [...] are absorbed in work or talk [...] either do not regard it or recoil."[16] Daniel Donoghue translates Tolkien's Old English as "Life is transitory: all light and life departs together."[17] Though they have come to symbolize many scholars' concept of how Anglo-Saxons viewed the world, the phrase itself is Tolkien's own creation. Translating *læne* as transitory is adequate but fails to recognize the nuances of the word. Other potential meanings of the word include inconstant, perishable, frail, poor, and weak. The sense of the phrase, *lif is læne* usually infers a sense of negativity and difficulty in life, closely related to the sense of the perishable. Essentially, the Anglo-Saxon attitude is not unlike the colloquial sentiment "life is hard and then you die." According to Tolkien, the Anglo-Saxon view of life was such that the idea of an ultimately conquering hero, one who saved the day and lived to fight more glorious battles in the future, was nearly impossible. This is consistent with the most famous declaration of the Old English perception of life. For the Anglo-Saxon, life was hard. It was full of violence and trials. For the transcribers of *Beowulf*, the only consolation in life was the hope of heaven after death, but even that was denied Beowulf according to Medieval Christianity because he died while a heathen. We cannot be certain regarding the theology of the pre–Christian Anglo-Saxons, however if we assume that they shared a similar theology with the Norse, the consolation resides in living and dying a glorious, violent life and death in hopes of attaining a seat in Valhalla.

Though the Old English thought world is inconsistent when compared with the superhero mytheme that death is temporary, it does work well with another of the more prevalent superhero mythemes. *Beowulf* is an absolutely *androcentric* poem. There are literally only six women in the epic: a brief mention of Hygd, Hygelac's wife; Hrothgar's wife, Wealhtheow; Hrothgar's unnamed sister; Hildeburh, the sister of Finn from the aside in the epic; a brief reference to the shrewish Modthryth; and, of course, the monstrous mother of Grendel. Of those six, only Wealhtheow and Grendel's mother play a real role in the tale. Hildeburh and Modthryth both serve as cautionary tales. Hygd and Hrothgar's sister have no real impact on the storyline. In the case of Modthryth, her story speaks largely for itself:

> She considered Thryth's pride,
> famous folk-queen, and her terrible crimes;
> no man so bold among her own retainers
> dared to approach her, except as her prince,
> or dared to look into her eyes by day;
> for he knew that deadly bonds, [....]
> That is no queenly custom
> for a lady to perform—no matter how lovely—
> that a peace-weaver should deprive of life
> a friendly man after a pretended affront.
> The kinsman of Hemming put a halt to that: [...]
> she caused less calamity to the people,
> less malicious evil, after she was
> given gold-adorned to the young champion,
> fair to the nobleman, [...]

> where she afterwards
> on the throne, famous for good things,
> used well her life while she had it[18]

Though Lolordo translates *Modthryth* as "Thryth's pride," most often, the term is translated as the name Modthryth. Accordingly, this paper will follow with the standard practice of translating the term as a proper name. Typically, the story of Modthryth is read as celebrating the taming nature of marriage, a warning to those who might allow a woman to live unattached. Marriage seems to be the ideal state for a woman, at least to the transcribers of *Beowulf*. Though there is no evidence to make a solid connection, the similarity between the story of Modthryth and Shakespeare's *Taming of the Shrew* makes for an interesting correlation.

Hildeburh, a "peace-weaver," was sister to Hnaef and wife to Finn, leaders of warring bands. There is a tradition in Medieval Norse society of marrying the daughter of one tribal leader to a man in the leadership of another in an effort to weave peace between two warring groups. Related to the passage from *Beowulf*, the *Finnsburh Fragment* details a skirmish between Hnæf, Hildeburh's brother, and several of Finn's warriors. In the fight, Hnæf is killed as well as Hileburh's unnamed son. "Guiltless, she was deprived of her dear ones in that shieldplay, her sons and brothers [...] she was a sad lady!"[19] She "commanded at Hnæf's pyre that her own son be consigned to the flames [...] placed on the pyre at his uncle's shoulder; the lady sang a sad lament."[20] Hildeburh presents a very different warning. In a way, her tale serves to underscore one of the weaknesses of the old Nordic society. While the writers of *Beowulf* seemed to celebrate the heroics in the poem, they were also very aware of the fragility inherent in the makeup of the society it celebrates. The constant violence and feuding led to unstable peace at the best of times. Though peace-weaving attempted to address this and cement more lasting bonds, it rarely lasts if the Norse stories are any indication. Hildeburh would have been of special significance to Wealhtheow. The majority of scholars suggest that Wealhtheow was a peace-weaver, making Hildeburh's plight especially meaningful to Hrothgar's wife.

One of the challenges with *Beowulf* is the lack of correlating information. No other document includes references to most of the characters in the poem, including Beowulf and Wealhtheow.[21] Consequently, much of the work on the poem is an effort to better understand the characters. One likely reading of Wealhtheow's name comes from dissecting her name as a combination of two words, *wealh* and *theow*. Assuming these words form a descriptive kenning, this would result in reading her name as foreign-slave or stranger-servant. A kenning is an Anglo-Saxon and Nordic poetic trope which frequently uses two words to form a descriptive phrase. A very common example is the phrase whale-road as a descriptive for the ocean or heather-stepper for deer. Very likely, this indicates that the author was identifying Wealhtheow to the audience of the poem as the exact kind of peace-bride as Hildeburh. If the reading is correct, this means that Wealhtheow is almost as much a stranger to Heorot as Beowulf, Grendel and his mother. Her efforts to maintain peace in Hrothgar's hall seem to be relatively effective. The only violence which comes to Heorot is perpetrated by something beyond that which she would be expected to handle. Even at the celebration, Wealhtheow maintains an awareness of the needs of her household. After Beowulf defeats Grendel, Hrothgar

> gave to Beowulf the blade of Healfdene,
> a golden war-standard as a reward for victory,
> the bright banner, a helmet and byrnie,
> a great treasure-sword [...]
> never have I heard tell of four treasures
> given more graciously, gold-adorned, [...]
> The protector of earls ordered eight horses
> with ornamented bridles led into the building,
> in under the eaves; on one sat
> a saddle, skillfully tooled, set with gemstones;
> that was the warseat of the high-king [...]
> Then the lord of earls, to each of those
> on the meadbenches who had made with Beowulf
> a sea-journey, gave jeweled treasures,
> antique heirlooms[22]

After the elaborate gift giving and the telling of Hildeburh's tragedy, Wealhtheow has her say. Among the words she spoke, she says to her husband

> I have been told that you would take this warrior [Beowulf]
> for your son. Heorot is cleansed,
> the bright ring-hall—use our many rewards
> while you can, and leave to your kinsmen
> the folk and kingdom[23]

She pleads with Hrothgar to remember that he has children of his own who still need an inheritance. Compared to the pomp of the gift-giving, her speech is simple and to the point, without belaboring the issue. She seems to be, for the Anglo-Saxons, an image of the ideal woman.

By contrast, Grendel's mother is an abomination. When describing Grendel, the Beowulf poet explains

> this miserable man
> lived for a time in the land of giants,
> after the Creator had condemned him
> among Cain's race [....]
> the Maker forced him

> far from mankind for his foul crime.
> From thence arose all misbegotten things,
> Trolls and elves and the living dead,
> And also the giants who strove against God[24]

Though it is specifically Grendel who is linked to the posterity of the biblical Cain—"From him awoke many a fateful spirit—Grendel among them"—we must assume that his mother is either one of these monsters as well or at least a woman willing to consort with descendants of the first murderer or perhaps the man himself.[25] Of course, for the Christian monks who recorded the tale, either of the two would be equally reprehensible. Later on, she is described simply as "Grendel's mother, monster-woman [...] who dwelt in those dreadful waters, the cold streams, ever since Cain killed with his blade his only brother."[26] What is further problematic is the mother's role in the story. Nordic society was based on the concept of the comitatus. As it applies to understanding the monstrosity of Grendel's mother, the key aspect of comitatus structure is the requirement of a man to avenge the death of any of the fellow men of his clan. This is what motivates Grendel's mother to make the trip from her cave. She "wanted to go on her sorrowful journey to avenge her son's death."[27] Though the Danes seem less concerned with maintaining strict gender roles, by the time the Anglo-Saxons recorded *Beowulf*, the way Grendel's mother usurps traditional gender roles marks her as monstrous over again. However, the story of two women named Hervor illustrates a sense that the Vikings at least were more interested in masculinity than in gender. The first Hervor earns fame by going into the underworld to reclaim the heirloom sword her father took with him when he died, taking control of his ship and men in the process. The second, granddaughter to the first, was part of the society known as the shieldmaidens, women who chose to take up arms and armor to fight alongside and against the male warriors. Both were celebrated in the *Herverar saga* and the poetic eddas.

Of all the characters in the poem, it is perhaps Grendel's mother who conforms most to the mytheme of the *supervillain*. Arguably, Grendel works within the bounds of the trope as well; however his motivation is never made completely clear in the poem. The most we get of his motive is that he "wretchedly suffered all the while, for every day he heard the joyful din loud in the hall, with the harp's sound, the clear song of the scop" (87–90). In the Anglo-Saxon society, the scop is a combination storyteller/historian/poet/singer. Why the sounds of the mead hall cause Grendel suffering is never made clear in the tale.[28] On the other hand, Grendel's mother seems to make a targeted attack, taking only one man, "the dearest of heroes to Hrothgar among his comrades [...] his chief thane."[29] It seems apparent that her attack was motivated by a desire to enact the vengeance required by the needs of the *comitatus*. Though vengeance is not uncommon in Nordic ideals, in fact it was an ideal they valued, by the standards of the superhero mythos it belongs almost exclusively in the realm of the villain. For the Anglo-Saxons the fact that she is a female only adds to the sense of wrong which accompanies her as a character.

Indeed, the tale of Beowulf seems to celebrate the idea that it is a man's world, an idea still popular in the superhero mythology. Of course, the sort of hyper masculinity present in *Beowulf* pushes the *no killing* mytheme completely out of the picture. Though Beowulf doesn't kill Grendel in their first engagement, the value placed on preserving the monsters against which he fights is simply nonexistent. There are other mythemes which connect Beowulf to the myth, but others are completely lacking. Though the poem begins with the spectacular origin of Scyld, Beowulf appears in the poem fully ready to engage with the monsters. We get no clear evidence of any sort of *spectacular origin* for the protagonist, and the greatest candidate for inclusion in superhero mythology within this poem. We have no evidence of a *lair* for Beowulf. Of course, each of the villains against which he fights has a lair. Grendel and his mother share the underwater cavern and the dragon has his treasure hoard. While this does not satisfy the demands of the mytheme, it is a fascinating factor in discussing the interaction of superhero mythology with literature on the edges thereof. Furthermore, Beowulf shows no sign of having any sort of *alter ego*. In fact, he goes to great lengths to ensure that everyone knows who he is and what his successes have been. No mild-mannered mask for Beowulf. Of course, much of what Beowulf does is intentionally designed to bring him honor and glory. He speaks at length on several occasions regarding his triumphs. Between his efforts, the speeches of the scop, and the narrator's part of the tale, it seems very clear that *Beowulf* is rife with *expository narration*. Granted, a great deal of this is due to the genre at work. Of necessity, epics are narrative. However, the long speeches given by Beowulf and others provide further exposition which rounds out the demands of the mytheme nicely.

Beowulf also fills out the demands of the mytheme of the *outsider* well. Not only is Beowulf alien to the court of Hrothgar and the Danes, introducing himself and his band no less than three times, but he seems to be an outsider to his own people. The narrator explains,

> He had been long despised,
> as the sons of the Geats considered him no good,
> nor did the lord of the Weders wish to bestow
> many good things upon him on the meadbenches,

> for they assumed that he was slothful,
> a cowardly nobleman. Reversal came
> to the glorious man for all his griefs[30]

Seamus Heaney is even more scathing in his translation of the Anglo-Saxon *swyðe wendon þæt he sleac wære, æðeling unfrom*, which Lolordo translates as "they assumed that he was slothful,/ a cowardly nobleman." His translation reads, "They firmly believed that he lacked force, that the prince was a weakling." Perhaps what is the most interesting factor in fulfilling this mytheme is the fact that Beowulf is very much alien to the Anglo-Saxons. Beowulf is a Geat whose most famous exploits are in the realm of the Danes. According to extant tales of his exploits, he never sets foot on the British Isles, nor does he have any interaction with recognized heroes of the Anglo-Saxons. Though the kind of character he is, the fearsome warrior, is not without Old English parallels, Beowulf specifically, the most famous of Old English characters, is not English in any way, shape, or form. In some ways, he is even more alien to the Anglo-Saxon monks who recorded his story than Superman is to us today. There is certainly more about the Man of Steel in our society than the man who kills Grendel in the monastery's purported society.

Beowulf's relative ostracism plays in to three other tropes as well. Relatively speaking, the hero is a practical *orphan*. Hrothgar knows Beowulf's father, having settled the *wergild* owed for the man Ecgtheow killed. The *wergild* was a price levied on a killer that he would pay rather than being killed by kinsmen of the man he slew. Literally, it translates as "man-price" or "man-gold." However, it would seem that Ecgtheow never completely redeemed his debt. Hrothgar says that "For past favors [...] and for old deeds, [Beowulf has] sought" his court.[31] He reminds Beowulf that his father "swore oaths to" Hrothgar and insinuates that Beowulf now must fulfill them.[32] Thus, to a certain extent, Beowulf's fights in Heorot are partially about his effort to *please the father* as well as underscoring the fact that he no longer has a father who can repay his own debts. This is also evidence of Beowulf's *relationship struggles*. Along with his efforts to please an absent father, and the apparent negative attitudes expressed by Geats at previous times, we can very easily read Beowulf's efforts to fight alone against the dragon as an unwillingness to trust his thanes in such a pivotal conflict. The fact that the only soldier to come to his aid is the completely untested Wiglaf would support this reading. Furthermore, when Beowulf dies, he passes his kingdom to Wiglaf rather than any offspring of his own. In fact, there is no indication that Beowulf ever took a wife. Though the lack of any woman tied to Beowulf is not unremarkable in such an androcentric tale, the complete failure to make any mention of children is potentially significant, enough so to support the fact as evidentiary of the existence of the mytheme.

5. The Superhero Before the Superhero

There is one character who seems to have a strong connection to Beowulf. Of the thirteen men who accompany Beowulf when he faces the dragon, only one disobeys his order to stay out of the fight and comes to his aid. The twelve that leave seem to make the strongest case for *switching sides*, but it's tenuous at best. In truth, this is another mytheme that demonstrates *Beowulf*'s status on the outskirts rather than the core of the mythology. The thane that stays, Wiglaf, in his first fight, helps Beowulf slay the dragon. His willingness and commitment to his king and the kingdom result in Beowulf granting reign of the Geats to this relatively untried soldier. Furthermore, as much as anyone, Wiglaf fulfills both the *helper* trope and the *sidekick* subtrope. As Beowulf slowly dies, he and Wiglaf converse over what to do with the dragon's treasure and the bequeathing of the throne. They have no clear ongoing relationship, but his aid in the fight against the dragon is instrumental to Beowulf's success. As nearly as we can tell, he is as close to Beowulf as anyone in the poem.

Though Beowulf might be an outsider on many levels, he does manifest a clear *moral code* which does have some commonalities with superheroes. The poem fails to make a clear delineation of the laws by which the story is governed, which makes identification of the mytheme *justice over law* difficult to identify. However, Beowulf's code of conduct can be clearly delineated through one scene specifically. The aforementioned moment wherein Beowulf prepares to fight against Grendel marks the first clear moment wherein Beowulf articulates a portion of his code of morality. As he removes his armor, Beowulf explains,

> I consider myself no poorer in strength
> and battle-deeds than Grendel does himself;
> and so I will not kill him with a sword, [...]
> he knows no arts of war, no way to strike back,
> [...] though he be brave
> in his wicked deeds; but tonight we two will
> forego our swords, if he dare to seek out
> a war without weapons—and then let the wise Lord
> grant the judgment of glory, the holy God,
> to whichever had seems proper to Him.[33]

Beowulf's refusal to fight Grendel with arms and armor is partially based on his need to prove himself and partially on his desire to make sure he faces the monster on even terms.

Having said that, we have no clear sense of how well Beowulf does in real-world situations. The *ineffective against real world problems* mytheme must be left in some sense unresolved in the poem. Beowulf's greatest feats recorded in the tale are single battles against obviously antagonistic monsters, the kinds of conflicts generally familiar to the superhero myth, but it is unclear what he did as a ruler and whether or not he managed to be successful in the daily tasks of feeding, clothing, and caring for his people. The text does explain that Beowulf ruled for fifty years, which would indicate some success in mitigating real world issues, but we are left with no indication of how he managed his kingdom. It is also unclear how much he felt the *power and responsibility*. Though he does travel to the kingdom of the Danes to fight against Grendel, proclaiming when first challenged, "With a friendly heart have we come seeking your lord [...] guardian of his people [...] We have a great mission to that famous man, ruler of the Danes."[34] When he talks with Hrothgar, Beowulf proclaims

> This business with Grendel
> was made known to me on my native soil;
> [...] Then my own people advised me,
> the best warriors and wisest men,
> that I should, Lord Hrothgar, seek you out,
> because they knew the might of my strength;
> [....] and now with Grendel,
> the monstrous beast, I shall myself have
> a word or two with that giant. From you now I wish, [...]
> protector of the Scyldings, a single favor [...]
> that I might alone, o my own band of earls
> and this hardy troop, cleanse Heorot.[35]

The challenge is that Beowulf seems to be doing as much to promote himself as he is to doing the right thing for others. Again, this is a valued trait in the culture, but it doesn't show that he is motivated by responsibility. Later, in preparing to face the dragon, he says, "I have survived many battles in my youth; I will yet seek out, an old folk-guardian, a feud and do a glorious deed."[36] Determining whether Beowulf sees the use of his powers as a responsibility or an opportunity for self-aggrandizement is difficult, but the evidence within the text would suggest that he is not acting solely out of a sense of duty or responsibility. While his actions and motives, including the self-promotion, are appropriate for the time and culture, they are a bit different than the typically more purely motivated superheroes of the mythology.[37]

On the other hand, the actions Beowulf take are indicative of at least an unintentional fulfillment of another mytheme, what he does consistently *promotes/maintains the status quo*. In the three fights of the poem, Beowulf's actions are consistently about returning society to an ideal equilibrium. If Grendel had never disturbed the status quo of the mead-hall, if his mother had avoided seeking vengeance, if the dragon had never left its warren, Beowulf would not be recognized as the hero he is in the tradition of English lore. Especially significant is that Beowulf ensures the return to a status quo before he moves on. Arguably, this is in part why he remains at Heorot after Grendel is defeated, because the status quo has yet to be settled completely until after the monster's mother has been dispatched. He dies only after he has assured himself that the dragon has been dealt with and that his subjects have a king to reign in his stead. Significantly, Wiglaf waits until after Beowulf has died, satisfied he has brought the Geats back into balance, to enumerate the woes that await them at Beowulf's demise

> Now this folk may expect
> a time of trouble, when this is manifest
> to the Franks and the Frisians, and the fall of our king
> becomes widespread news. The strife was begun
> hard with the Hugas, after Hygelac came
> traveling with his ship to the shores of Frisia,
> where the Hetware attacked him in war,
> [....] Even after that
> the Merovingians have not shown mercy to us.
> Nor do I expect any peace or truce
> from the Swedish nation [....]
> Thus that brave speaker [Wiglaf] was speaking
> a most unloved truth; he did not lie much
> in words or facts.[38]

Whether Beowulf was cognizant of the danger that awaited at his death or not is again unclear in the poem. In any case, at the moment of his death, a status quo had been established for the Geats. What happened after that was the responsibility of the king he left in his wake.

Beowulf's actions as an authority figure in the poem work neither for nor against the mythemes regarding comparable figures in superhero mythology. The relation of Beowulf to authority figures is fairly clearly delineated by his experience in Heorot. Regarding Unferth, he is as much of an *antagonistic authority figure* as any in the work. However, he only fills the mytheme problematically at best. Unferth, "who sat at the feet of" Hrothgar has an unclear position of power.[39] Some have argued that he serves as an advisor, much in the way Grima Wormtongue does for Theoden in *The Two Towers*. Indeed, there is a strong argument to be made that Grima and Theoden were patterned after Unferth and Hrothgar respectively considering there is a strong connection between the society of *Beowulf* and Tolkien's riders of the Mark. Based on varying definitions of terms from the poem, others have suggested that Unferth was little more than a court jester figure.[40] Thus, his position of authority depends largely on questions of interpretation regarding his station. If Unferth was Hrothgar's official spokesman or representative then he does have enough authority to qualify, otherwise this mytheme goes largely unsatisfied.

Furthermore, though he taunts Beowulf with the story of his failed swimming race against Breca when he first meets the Geat, when the hero of the story prepares to face off against Grendel's mother, Unferth lends him "Hrunting, unique among ancient treasures [...] it had never failed any man who grasped it in his hands for battle."[41] Letting Beowulf take a prized sword into an uncertain conflict is not the act of an antagonistic character. Potentially, we could argue that Unferth belongs to a class of those won over by the hero's exploits, but it seems more likely that his antagonism toward Beowulf was not as deep and vitriolic as the trope requires. Indeed, his original taunting of Beowulf could have simply been a demonstration of *flyting*, a traditional ritual of challenge and response through insults common in the time period. On the other hand, it nearly goes without saying that Hrothgar easily fulfills the role of the *cooperative authority figure*. From the lavish gift-giving to the joyous welcomes to the long speeches in Beowulf's honor, Hrothgar clearly appreciates Beowulf's presence in his court and appreciates his help in resolving the troubles he faces.

Finally, though *Beowulf* still maintains an influence in our popular society, Beowulf himself still lacks any sort of real *chevron*. Though his fight against Grendel is certainly an iconic moment in literature, this type of folkloric iconicity is a different sort than that which we associate with the superhero. There is no iconic visual component to Beowulf. Divergent depictions of Beowulf share little to no similarity with each other. Whereas most superheroes can be identified by those who know their mythology from usually only the barest of visuals, Beowulf requires textual context for a positive identification. Furthermore, we have absolutely no sense that he utilizes any sort of *codename*. He is Beowulf and has no other name by which he deigns being called, except, perhaps, the son of Ecgtheow, which also fails to establish a codename in any way. In the myth of the English speaking world as a whole, *Beowulf* does have a sort of iconic status but it is different in kind than the iconicity—in costume, chevron, or codename—that the superhero mythology demands.

The lack of several pertinent mythemes in this examination of *Beowulf* helps develop the sense that the superhero is a very particular mythology. In the case of *Beowulf*, not only is it removed from the center of the superhero bull's-eye by virtue of coming into existence prior to the development of the mythology but it also was created outside of the culture that dominates the formation of superheroes. "Truth, justice, and the American way" is more than just hyperbole. Despite recent efforts and discussions regarding universalizing superheroes, they were and are and most likely always will be tied specifically to American traditions, folklore, and ideals. The physical ideals,

5. The Superhero Before the Superhero   167

the presentations of beauty, even the sense of superiority tied to superheroes all are more closely aligned with the worldview of the United States of America than that of any other society. This has been lampooned and deconstructed by some writers, including work done by several British writers like Neil Gaiman, Frank Quitley, and especially Alan Moore. There have been relatively successful efforts to diversify the pantheon of superheroes, but the fact remains that they still principally reflect a very American world view. The examination of *Beowulf* underscores this fact. Nearly every deviation between Beowulf's epic and the myth of the superhero can be connected to differences in culture between Old English and American societies. This is indicative of the way the society which produced the text had no real connection to many of the ideals which inform the superhero. Though there is still much in common between Beowulf and members of the pantheon of superheroes, he will always stand outside the genre and certainly not at the center of superhero mythology.

6

The Superheroic Structure
Examining the Mythological Character of the Superhero

The preceding chapters have examined the tropes of the superhero without a necessary connection to a part of the myth requisite for the myth to exist. Though there is a clear implied connection between certain mythemes and the character central to the myth, the superhero as a specific element has been left undiscussed. The implied connection may be sufficient in some ways, but central to superhero mythology is the character of the superhero. Speaking generically, Peter Coogan suggests that "[d]efining the superhero character is a necessary part of defining the superhero genre."[1] While it may be less necessary in the mythology, even series that take place in a superhero mythos can't shake the shadow of the superhero. Recent series like *Gotham Central* or the new television series *Gotham* that center on Gotham City's police department go to lengths to absent Batman from the stories, even though his presence is a constant background to the events of the stories told. The lexicon examined in this book is a broad list. It attempts to recognize the mythemes integral to superhero mythology though not necessarily exclusive thereto. Some are part of a broader heroic mythology. Others are more exclusive to the superhero. Some are exclusive in application if not in type. This chapter turns the focus to the character and those mythemes that establish a key component to any superhero structure, whether it be generic, mythological, psychological, or otherwise.

It is worth pointing out at this stage that any mythology is subject to flux and change. In the introduction to *The Hero in Transition*, Marshall W. Fishwick says, "When an old mythology disintegrates, a new one originates—along with new heroes. Instead of *discovering* a new mythos, we find ourselves *participating* in it."[2] He explains, "Cultural relocation and heroic transformations always go hand in hand. Freed by technology, fed by media" we are engaged in

6. The Superheroic Structure

re-making images to fulfill the mythological needs of society."[3] Steven Spielberg, when asked about the potential shift in Hollywood's "mega-budget" movies argued that "there will be a time when the superhero movie goes the way of the Western. It doesn't mean there won't be another occasion where [...] the superhero movie someday returns. Of course, right now the superhero movie is alive and thriving. I'm only saying that these cycles have a finite time in popular culture. There will come a day when the mythological stories are supplanted by some other genre."[4] His statement occasioned comments by many voices online, including the likes of Zack Snyder[5] and Kevin Feige,[6] two major influences over the current status of the superhero in cinema. Most commenters seem to be upset at Spielberg's comments and argue that his comments don't apply to superheroes in some way. However, the immutability of the superhero myth seems as unlikely as that of any other. If it fails to successfully meet the needs of the culture(s) that feed it, it will be replaced by something that fills the void.

Because the superhero is part of a living mythology, being reimagined in various media from mainstream and independent comics to television, film, and the Internet the framework of the superhero must be flexible enough to adapt as the myth evolves yet rigid enough to give us some structure by which we can identify and discuss the myth and its implications. This will be so at least until the hypothetical future moment suggested by Spielberg when the myth evolves into something so far removed from the current concept of superhero mythology that it becomes a new kind of myth or it is simply supplanted by a myth that serves the needs of the community.

Until that time comes, however, the superhero is a key character to mythology and needs to be understood as such. The most prevalent examination of the superhero as a character appears in Peter Coogan's *Superhero: The Secret Origin of a Genre*. Though his book is interested in superheroes as a generic convention, his approach to defining the superhero serves as a valuable starting point for the mythological conception of the superhero as well. Coogan argues that a superhero can be located and defined by the character's mission, powers, and identity, or MPI. He explains that a superhero's mission must be "prosocial and selfless, which means that his fight against evil must fit in with existing, professed mores of society and must not be intended to benefit or further his own agenda."[7] The powers "or superpowers, to emphasize the exaggeration inherent in the superhero"[8] are one of the most recognizable aspects of the superhero. The identity element of Coogan's definition "comprises the codename and costume, with the secret identity being a customary counterpart to the codename."[9] He further argues, "The identity convention most clearly marks the superhero as different from his predecessors"[10] and arguably from other characters who may fit the mythology in some ways, but not the genre. In Coogan's definition, all three elements of the MPI must be there, but especially the aspects that make up an identity. If a character has no codename or costume, if a character doesn't participate in the premise of a secret identity, then that character is almost certainly not a superhero.[11]

That generic distinction is important in Coogan's book. His MPI definition is the standard by which scholars define the superhero. Generically, it makes sense and strengthens our ability to recognize the superhero. Mythologically, it still serves as a strong core, but it is insufficient to recognize the broader context of the mythology. For his approach

> if a character fits the MPI conventions, even with some significant qualifications, and cannot be easily placed into another genre, the character is a superhero. On the reverse side, if a character largely fits the MPI qualifications of the definition, but can be firmly and sensibly placed within another genre, then the character is not a superhero.[12]

This is the point at which this work differs from Coogan's. To participate in the mythology a character only has to have a definite connection to several significant mythemes in the lexicon. The mythology is, by nature, much broader and more inclusive than the genre. However, because the mythology is present does not necessarily make a character a superhero. Though *Gotham* certainly participates in the mythology, thus far the show hasn't produced a superhero. Batman waits within Bruce Wayne, but he hasn't been brought from the shadows. Nor does it appear that the Caped Crusader will be a significant part of the actual narrative for some time yet.

Because of the difference between the genre and the mythology, the construct of the superhero as a character in the mythology draws clearly from but is different than that proposed in Coogan's work. Mythology is typically expressed through narrative, thus the mythological construct of the superhero also derives from a more narrative definition. The foundational facet of the superhero lies in the origin. Whether this origin is clearly expressed, as was the case with Superman early on, or unexpressed, as was the case with Wolverine until 2001–2002's *Origin* storyline, the implication remains that the superhero's origins are a critical foundation upon which the character is built. The origin establishes the groundwork for expressing a superhero's mission and powers and is also commonly a source for establishing the identity. Because of this, the origin is central to a mythological understanding of the character. Typically, the origin creates the *powers* and is integral to developing a superhero's sense of purpose. Once a superhero has a sense of purpose and powers, the character draws on this to create a *codename, costume,* and *chevron.* The three correlate with Coogan's identity clearly and share a circle of importance in this construction. In essence, this framework flows from the origin to purpose and powers to a triad that expresses identity. Thus, the center circle is focused on the origin, the second on the mission and means of accomplishing it, and the third with the representation of the identity of the character. Coogan's influence should be clear, but this construction adjusts the application of a definition in a way that is important to the mythological construct.

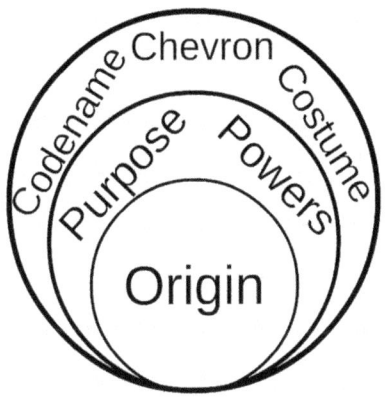

The bottom small circle is focused on the origin, the next out on the mission and means of accomplishing it, and the third with the representation of the identity of the character.

The advantage of this construction or definition for the superhero within the mythology is that it connects clearly to key mythemes and allows for the superhero to shift when a shift is necessary within a specific character's mythos. De Saussure's semiological system[13] constructs meaning in language as a combination of signifier and signified. Occasionally, signifier and signified can shift and slide, creating a dynamic, movable sign. By connecting a character to the foundational origin; constructive powers and purpose; and the encapsulating codename, costume and symbol; superheroes can change and adapt as their origins are adjusted to fit the needs of the mythology, as identities flux to recognize changes in mission, and even to recognize those times when a superhero's powers go through alterations. As the elements shift and interact, the character of the superhero can flex to adapt and adjust until the time when one or more elements of the superhero are removed or changed enough to move the character out of the construct completely—whether temporarily or permanently.

Further, this definition of the mythological superhero directly connects to some mythemes, demonstrating the priority several have in determining the strength of the myth in a given situation. In the superhero's origin, we can of course recognize the *spectacular origin* and the *traumatic trigger*. However, the situation of the superhero as *outsider* and *orphan* is closely tied to the origin. The groundwork for a superhero's need to *please the father* is usually established in the origin and frequently informs the character's purpose. This purpose further connects to *no killing, justice over law,* and significantly, *moral code* the element wherein the mission is frequently most clearly expressed for a given superhero. The mission further informs how superheroes will understand their specific connection to the *power and responsibility* mytheme. Naturally, this mytheme also has direct connections to powers. In the most clearly direct connection between an element of this definition and the mytheme, the second circle powers correlates to the *powers* mytheme. The third circle of the superhero comprises the *costume, chevron,* and *codename*. It also implies a link to the *alter ego* and recognizes the *strong visual component* of the mythology. It is also in this circle that the *amazing physique* can be recognized. The superhero is a key a component in the mythology. The myth can exist without a clearly defined superhero, but in those cases we find ourselves on the outskirts of the mythology rather than in the center. Even in these cases, the superhero tends to be an undefined but still recognizable presence in the background fabric of the narrative.

In several ways, Christopher Nolan's *Batman Begins* exemplifies the way this construct works to define the character of the superhero. The majority of the first seventeen minutes of the film are the story of a young Bruce Wayne and the trauma that creates within him the core of the character. The first scene results in him falling down a dry well where he disturbs a nest of bats. Their escape from the cave connected to the well causes Wayne's fear of bats. Later, this fear of bats is the reason the Waynes leave the opera early, which results in the death of Bruce's parents.[14] These two scenes are vital to Nolan's take on Batman. When Joe Chill is set free in a later scene, it creates a series of events that lead Bruce Wayne into developing his powers. His purpose also has its impetus in the results of his efforts to develop who he feels he must be. It is only after his powers and purpose have crystallized that he crafts his costume and chevron. When Alfred asks him why he chooses bats, Wayne explains, "Bats frighten me. It's time my enemies share my dread." His origin clearly controls his costume and chevron in this case. The costume causes his codename in this film. His costume further develops in *Batman Begins* to reflect his needs as he strives to achieve his purpose. The cape becomes a result of his desire for more maneuverability over the rooftops. His utility belt without a shoulder harness develops from a similar impetus. The contoured body armor, giving him the classic sculpted look, is designed to protect him from injury. Though the entire film could rightly be construed as an origin story, demonstrating the need for this construct to be flexible in application, the key elements that develop the character of the mythological superhero are manifest in the narrative.

The move from origin, through powers and purpose to identity is typical in superhero mythology. However, for many who become interested in the myth, their first introduction to the character is through their costume, codename, and chevron. Typically, they will then come to understand the character's power and purpose, until they finally come to recognize their origin.

6. The Superheroic Structure

Though the prevalence of the origin story in film has complicated this trajectory somewhat, it is still common for people interested in specific superheroic mythemes to start outward and work their way in.

This reading of the mythological character of the superhero identifies several of the issues with Beowulf's place in the mythology. While the epic does match up with superhero mythemes,[15] the character connects to the mythology less clearly. We get hints at Beowulf's origin, but there are holes in the narrative that lead to some apparent inconsistencies. At one point, the narrator explains

> He had been poorly regarded
> for a long time, was taken by the Geats
> for less than he was worth: and their lord too
> had never much esteemed him in the mead-hall.
> They firmly believed that he lacked force,
> that the prince [Beowulf] was a weakling[16]

However, immediately afterward we are told that "every affront to his deserving was reversed."[17]

Though this same section of the poem talks of Beowulf's "God-sent strength"[18] and "his outstanding natural powers"[19] there is no clear connection between his powers and any implied origin. However, the lack of esteem shown to him in this brief passage may hint at a motivation behind his purpose. In this reading, Beowulf's engagement in both the swimming race and the fight against Grendel are means by which he seeks to prove his value, that he is not a weakling and did, in fact, have worth in the Norse world.

Though this purpose is one that we can recognize, it hardly fits in with Coogan's prosocial ideal. It also doesn't establish much in the way of a *moral code* or a connection to *justice over law*. This mission is an egocentric goal of gaining recognition, certainly familiar to the Anglo-Saxons of the time, but not something that relates well to the superhero myth. Though this purpose itself connects to his powers, the powers bear no clear connection to the origin, largely because there isn't a clear origin, fragmenting any solid connection between the three elements. Nor do they work together in any significant way to establish an identity for Beowulf. As a literary figure, Beowulf does have a recognizable identity, but it fits poorly with the type of identity expected of a superhero. The iconic scene where he strips off his armor to fight Grendel might hint at a costume, but it establishes nothing that compares to a superhero's garb. Nor does it really show any consistency in costume since each subsequent fight requires more gear. He doesn't have any sort of codename. He promotes his singular identity as the heroic monster slayer. Further, there is absolutely no indication of a chevron for Beowulf.

Thus, *Beowulf* gives us a potential connection between its titular character and his origin. However, the connection is only tenuous. His purpose doesn't set him apart from the typical warrior of the time, and is poorly articulated in any case. His powers are fairly clear, but no connection is established between the powers and any previous element. In the sphere of identity, even the most tenuous connection falls apart. He has no chevron, no codename, and no real costume. Essentially, Beowulf lacks a superheroic identity that fulfills this vital element of the superhero construct.

Alphas runs into similar issues relating to the idea of identity. Though each character has specific personalities, and their clothing matches well with their personalities, there is no solid sense of costume or codename to speak of. Nor does the group as a whole, nor any individual have a chevron to speak of. Again, they are iconic in ways typical in their medium, but not in mythologically significant ways. Dr. Rosen presents as the sort of slightly disheveled professor, Gary as a man-child[20] in his long sleeved t-shirts and sneakers, and Cameron Hicks epitomizes the sexy scruffy man in his dress and grooming. While the characters do conform to television character tropes, their clothing doesn't have significant connection to their powers, with the possible exception of Nina who uses her powers to acquire the finer things in life, with an implication that this would include clothing. Harken's suits do connect to his origin as a member of the FBI, and in that way they could have some connection to his purpose, but they establish no real connection to his powers. While Rachel's more reserved personality connects her hypersensitivity to her identity insofar as she interacts with the world in a specific way because of her powers, it doesn't really satisfy the overall connectivity of the superhero character construct.

In fact, taking the show as a whole, each character tenuously connects some elements of origin, purpose, powers, and broad strokes of the identity circle to each other, but they fail to satisfactorily do so as a whole. By way of example, Rachel Pirzad has an origin that seems tied to her role in a traditional family. Her family owns a dry cleaning business. Her father seems to have "traditional" expectations for his daughter, mentioning in the pilot episode that he's concerned that "her condition" will keep her from getting a husband. She is the most reserved and shy of the Alpha's team. Her shyness is coupled, apparently, to both her family situation and the fact that her ability tends to lead to overwhelming sensory input when she doesn't keep control of her hypersensitivity. Thus, her powers, her origin, and her basic identity share some commonality, but it's not overtly clear, nor is it consistent. At one point in season one, when she is on a date with an unnamed man, their kiss overwhelms her senses and she sends him away, withdrawing from any contact with him.²¹ However, by season two she has become confident enough that she initiates a relationship with John Bennett, the government's liaison with the team.

Even the purpose of the team in the series is somewhat unclear. Originally, their mission is to find more Alphas, but they soon recognize that the ends behind this endeavor are problematic. Their commitment to the mission quickly fragments as the team members no longer share a common purpose. Even before they are drawn together as a team into the original mission their origins are diverse. Nina, Harken, and Hicks have origins that do connect to their powers, but not as clearly to their purpose. In fact, Harken's ability costs him his job at the FBI, making his power a roadblock to his purpose of rejoining the FBI.²² None of their powers connect satisfactorily to a superheroic sense of identity. None of them have a codename, none have a chevron, and their costumes are more standard TV character cliché than superheroic in nature and development. In fact, though the series does clearly engage with superhero mythology, the characters are removed from being truly superheroic characters. This is probably by design. Regardless of the intention, the fact that they tend to be less connected to the construct of the superhero character emblematizes the value of the superhero as character in establishing a concrete connection between a particular mythos and the center of superhero mythology. *Alphas* participates in the mythology, but is not a superhero story in any real, solid way. The series doesn't qualify by Coogan's generic definitions. The lack of the mythological character is largely at fault for this, indicating the value of being aware of how genre and mythology work together while still maintaining divergent methods of connecting to the superhero.

Buffy runs into similar issues regarding costume and codename. Though Buffy is frequently called the Slayer, suggesting a codename of sorts, its application is inconsistent and doesn't really promote an *alter ego* the way codenames tend to do. Further, she doesn't establish a costume with any consistency. The series and subsequent comics may arguably have a chevron in the stylized "Buffy" logo that was part of the opening credits for the television shows and is still used on the cover of the comics. However, this chevron— as much as it may be one—is never applied specifically to Buffy Summers. On the level of identity, then, Buffy has far more in common with the typical high school show than she does with the superhero. However, she does have a stronger connection between her powers and her origin than either *Alphas* or *Beowulf*. Perhaps this is a large part of why she still has proponents of the idea that she *is* a superhero despite arguments to the contrary. Her origin is established in the film, though problematically and with some adjustment by the television series. Because of the import of her origin as a reluctant slayer has on her powers, her connection to the character of the superhero is strengthened. Further, though she is resistant to the responsibility of her powers at first, as the series progresses she becomes devoted to her purpose as the slayer.

Buffy's purpose and powers draw directly from her origin, making a strong connection within the first two circles of the superhero construct. Her powers are thrust upon her during this origin, and that connection strengthens her connection to the mythology in a way that is lacking from Coogan's MPI definition. In his generic approach to the definition of the superhero, Buffy is not. Coogan allows that Buffy has a mission and powers, and even an identity as the Slayer. He argues, however, "this identity is not separate from her ordinary identity the way Superman is from Clark Kent [...]. The Slayer is not a public identity in the ordinary superhero sense."[23] While he is right, Buffy doesn't have a costume or chevron in typical superhero fashion, the addition of the origin as a foundational element of the mythological character of the superhero serves to strengthen Buffy's connection to that character. This is not to argue that Buffy is a superhero. For this work that's an unnecessary determination. What is significant in the mythology is her engagement, the level of immersion into the mythology rather than an absolute distinction. For the purposes of the genre, lines have to be drawn. For the myth, the more valuable consideration is levels of engagement. In this regard, Buffy fits into the mythology. She doesn't have a comfortable place in the deep waters of the mythology, near the center, but she does manifest some strong connections to the character of the superhero. Of the characters discussed thus far, she shows the strongest connection to the mythology.

A character like Green Arrow, by comparison, demonstrates that Buffy is not as close to the center as some may want to argue. Though his origin has shifted over time, it has largely solidified to incorporate the idea that Oliver Queen is stranded on an island and must develop his archery skills as a means to survive. The Silver Age Emerald Archer learned to use a bow to hunt game, and developed some of his trick arrows to help in this endeavor. Later on, the island where Queen was shipwrecked was expanded to include a drug plantation. In *Arrow*, the island became a sort of Chinese prison, a mercenary base of operations, and a secret A.R.G.U.S. prison. Since Jack Kirby created the island experience, it has been an integral part of Green Arrow's origin story. Because of this, Queen's powers are tied directly and significantly to his origin. *Arrow* makes a clear connection between his origin and his purpose. The impetus for his efforts to clean up Starling City is a result of the final conversation he had with his father, Robert Queen. Just before he shoots himself, Robert Queen tells his son to "right [the] wrongs" he did to their city, confessing that he had failed their city, giving his son the catchphrase, "You have failed this city."[24] Oliver's purpose in the series begins with righting the wrongs done by Robert, to *please the father* and redeem Starling City and his family name. While this purpose evolves through the run of the show, his purpose is still tied to his origin in the series.

Arrow also has an interesting take on the costume and codename. Though he begins without a codename, his costume harkens back to his origin with the hood he wears. Eventually, people in Starling City, especially Detective Lance, begin calling him the Vigilante and the Hood. His costume changes slightly for the second season when he vows to try to live by the *no killing* mytheme. This change also comes with his identification as the Arrow. Finally, when he returns to Starling City—now known as Star City—in the opening episode of season four he wears a slightly brighter costume and self identifies as the Green Arrow.[25] In the series, costume and codename are very interrelated. Each change in one suggests a change in the other. However, in the series and in the comics Green Arrow doesn't have the sort of iconic chevron expected of a superhero. Certain comics do incorporate an arrowhead in the title design, but the style varies enough so that a specific, clear chevron is not identifiable. *Arrow* continues the arrowhead styling, superimposing the show's title over an arrowhead. The placing of the arrowhead is more consistent in the television series than in the comics, but the style changes between episodes. In this way, strangely enough, *Arrow* shares a commonality with *Buffy*. In both series the title character survives without a chevron. This lack of a chevron may be part of why the Green Arrow is pushed to the edge of the central circle of the mythology, a place he seems to enjoy, depending on the writer.

Despite the lack of a chevron, Green Arrow does show a stronger connection between the three circles of the superheroic character than Buffy, Beowulf, or the cast of *Alphas*. His origin is clearly tied to his powers, and has strong connections to his purpose. This sense of purpose in *Arrow* is echoed in *Green Arrow: Year One*. In a final standoff between China White and Oliver Queen, he references Robin Hood, "Rich dude. Gave it all up to fight the power, help the poor. Free the oppressed. Like that."[26] Later, as he prepares to return home, he says,

> I kinda like the idea of living a shadowy double life, y'know? By day, a wastrel billionaire playboy, while by night, [....] Lets just say, maybe I've finally figured out what I want to do with my life ... and maybe there's more I can do to help the little guy than turn up drunk at the occasional charity fund-raiser.[27]

So, even when he doesn't have his father to urge him to action, the time on the island propels Oliver Queen to his purpose, to becoming a modern day superhero version of Robin Hood. His powers and purpose come directly from his origin. His connection to Robin Hood as part of his purpose and powers bears direct influence on his costume. For a time, his costume bore the same hat as the cinematic Errol Flynn version of Robin Hood. However, even the more recent hood has ties to a more historic costume for the archer. Besides the headgear, the Merry Men were famed for their Lincoln green clothing, a color Queen picks up on practically regardless of the *iteration* of the character. His codename also bears a direct link to his powers. Even though CW dropped the reference to color from the show's title, the series still reflects the nature of the character's codename and powers.

In the end, the more closely related the circles of origin, mission, and identity are to each other the more likely the character will be recognizably a superhero. While narratives can certainly interact with the superhero myth without a clearly defined superhero at the center of the story, the myth is most fully realized when the character of the superhero is recognizably present. The preceding chapters indicate the way superhero mythology resonates across various genres and eras. The central mythemes are designed to allow for a clearer means of explaining why we find echoes and resonances of the superhero in texts from *Gilgamesh* to *Star Wars*. Some of this comes from the shared nature of epic storytelling. The hero's journey is, after all, the hero's journey. That journey is an integral part of the superhero mythology, making the myth recognizable to others. However, the superhero mythology is unique in many aspects. Mythemes like *orphan* and *please the father* are prevalent outside the mythology. Mythemes like *powers, costume, the lair,* and *supervillain* are more clearly related specifically to the myth of the superhero. Those mythemes frequently found outside the mythology are still integral thereto and are included in the lexicon because of this importance. The more of these mythemes that are present in a narrative, the closer that narrative is to the center of the mythology.[28] The framework laid out in this chapter helps to further solidify the center of the mythology.

It is vital to understand that neither framework should be used as a hard and fast method to eliminate texts from consideration as part of the mythology. This book is intentionally designed not to be exclusionary in its efforts. Even texts on the outer edges of the mythology share resonances that are worth considering and exploring. Certainly, Beowulf may not be a superhero by generic constraints, but if readers see the superhero mythology in his story there is value in understanding that and letting that be a part of our conversations about the mythology and how it works in the cultures wherein it exists. The more we recognize the ebb and flow of the myth in the narratives around us the more capable we will be to comprehend how the mythology works to serve as a central database for discussing key aspects related to the values of society.

The central aspect of this work is Chapter 1's lexicon of superhero mythemes. TVtropes.org certainly has a more exhaustive list of elements related to the superhero, sometimes to the point of ridiculousness. Consider "Cut Lex Luthor a Check" and "Magic Pants." While both are potential tropes in superhero mythology, they aren't central to the core of the myth. It's an entertaining and valuable resource, but not specific in their focus on key parts of the mythology. It's not their purpose, which is why there is a need to codify tropes central to the mythology. The expectation is that this will be a first step in codifying the rich world of the mythology that has been a key factor in popular culture for decades and has recently had a sharp rise in prominence. Though superheroes have been with us for over fifty years, until recently they have only been studied tangentially, or with a specific agenda, bending the study to prove a preconceived idea. Recent studies have begun to deal with superheroes through generic and psychological analyses. The goal here is to forward an attempt to recognize the mythological role superheroes play in current society. This work creates a framework from which a character can be identified for its connection or lack thereof to the myth. Though most who recognize the superhero accept that there is a mythological aspect to the characters and the stories, there has been no study previously that attempts to codify what exactly the myth is and how it functions in our society. This book is a first step to develop a framework through which these discussions can be had to a fuller degree.

Appendix

Superhero Tropes

Arguably, the most complete database of tropes that exists regarding superheroes can be found at tvtropes.org. What follows is a list of the tropes that is included under the heading of "superhero tropes." This list helped inform the list found in the first chapter, but is far more comprehensive and specific than what is found in this book. Several of these tropes fall under the broader scope of mythemes introduced in the book, and some are too specific to a specific mythos for inclusion in the overarching mythology. However, their trope names and descriptions of the tropes are entertaining and insightful. The website is certainly worth exploring to gain a broader sense of the vast quantity of codified elements related to the superhero.

Tropes

Adaptation Origin Connection
Adaptive Armor
The Adjectival Superhero
Alliterative Name
Alternate Company Equivalent
Alternate Continuity
Alternate Universe Reed Richards Is
Animal Superheroes
Animal-Themed Superbeing
Anti-Climactic Unmasking
Awesome
Badass Cape
Badass Normal
Bat Signal
Beware the Superman
Boxing Lessons for Superman
Brought Down to Badass
Brought Down to Normal
Brought to You by the Letter "S"
Bruce Wayne Held Hostage
Building Swing

Bus Full of Innocents
By the Power of Grayskull!
The Cape
Cape Busters
Captain Ersatz
Captain Ethnic
Captain Geographic
Captain Patriotic
Captain Superhero
Charles Atlas Superpower
Chest Insignia
Chrome Champion
Civvie Spandex
Clark Kenting
Clingy Costume
Coat, Hat, Mask
Code Name
Codenames
Color Character
Comes Great Responsibility
Comic Book Movies Don't Use

Appendix

The Commissioner Gordon
Corporate-Sponsored Superhero
Cover-Blowing Superpower
The Cowl
Create Your Own Villain
Cut Lex Luthor a Check
Dark Age of Supernames
Dating Catwoman
Deadly Training Area
Death-Activated Superpower
Differently Powered Individual
Disability Superpower
Disposable Superhero Maker
Domino Mask
Dork Age
Enlightenment Superpowers
Evil Costume Switch
Fad Super
Fight Off the Kryptonite
Fights Like a Normal
Flaming Emblem
Freak Lab Accident
Future Spandex
Going for the Big Scoop
The Good Captain
Good Thing You Can Heal
Gratuitous Animal Sidekick
Heart Is an Awesome Power
Henshin Hero
Hero Does Public Service
Hero with Bad Publicity
Heroic Build
Heroic Fatigue
Heroic Host
Heroic Vow
Hero's First Rescue
Holding Out for a Hero
How Do I Shot Web?
How to Give a Character Superpowers
I Believe I Can Fly
I Just Want to Be Normal
Identity Impersonator
Idiosyncrazy
I'm Not a Hero, I'm…
Imagination-Based Superpower
In a Single Bound
Innocent Bystander Series
Instant Costume Change
The Jailer
Keep the Home Fires Burning
Kid Sidekick
Kryptonite Factor
Kryptonite Is Everywhere
Kryptonite-Proof Suit
Kryptonite Ring
Lamarck Was Right
Legacy Character
Legacy Implosion
Legacy Launch
Leotard of Power
Lighthearted Rematch
Magic Pants
Magical Girl Warrior
Man of Kryptonite
Marked Change
The Masquerade Will Kill Your Dating Life
Mass Super-Empowering Event
Meta Origin
Military Superhero
Monster Modesty
Morally Ambiguous Doctorate
Most Common Super Power
Movie Superheroes Wear Black
Mutant Draft Board
My Significance Sense Is Tingling
Never Be a Hero
New Powers as the Plot Demands
Nineties Anti-Hero
Non-Powered Costumed Hero
Normal Fish in a Tiny Pond
Not the Fall That Kills You
Not Wearing Tights
One Person, One Power
One Super, One Power Set
Pedestrian Crushes Car
Personality Powers
Phlebotinum Battery
Power Creep, Power Seep
Power Incontinence
Power Nullifier
Premature Empowerment
Proto-Superhero
Psychic Nosebleed
Psychic Radar
Psychosomatic Superpower Outage
Puberty Superpower
Randomly Gifted
Reckless Sidekick
Recruit the Muggles
Reed Richards Is Useless
Re-Power
Required Secondary Powers
Rich Idiot with No Day Job
Rogues Gallery

Rogues Gallery Showcase
Rogues-Gallery Transplant
Run the Gauntlet
Samaritan Syndrome
Second Super-Identity
Secret Chaser
Secret Identity
Secret Identity Apathy
Secret Identity Change Trick
Secret Identity Identity
Secret Keeper
Secret Public Identity
Semantic Superpower
Sentai
Shooting Superman
Sidekick
Sidekick Glass Ceiling
Sidekick Graduations Stick
Single-Power Superheroes
Slave to PR
Something Person
Spandex, Latex, or Leather
Star-Spangled Spandex
Steven Ulysses Perhero
Stock Superhero Day Jobs
Stock Superpowers
Strong as They Need to Be
Super Empowering
Super Fic
Super Hero Gods
Super Hero Origin
Super Human Trafficking
Super Power Meltdown
Super Powers for a Day
Super Registration Act
Super Robot Genre
Super Rug Pull
Super Serum
Super Zeroes
Superhero Movie Villains Die
Superhero Packing Heat
Superhero Paradox
Superhero Prevalence Stages
Superhero School
Superhero Sobriquets
Superhero Speciation
Superhero Trophy Shelf
Superheroes in Space
Superheroes Stay Single
Superheroes Wear Capes
Superheroes Wear Tights
Superhuman Transfusion
Superman Stays out of Gotham
Superpower Lottery
Superpower Silly Putty
Superpowered Alter Ego
Superpowered Date
Superpowered Evil Side
Supervillain
Swiss Army Superpower
Thematic Rogues Gallery
Thememobile
Thou Shalt Not Kill
Trainstopping
Traumatic Superpower Awakening
Trick Arrow
Triple Shifter
Two First Names
The Unmasking
Un-Sorcerer
Up, Up and Away!
Utility Belt
Villain Team-Up
Wall Crawl
We Can Rebuild Him
Weaksauce Weakness
West Coast Team
What Kind of Lame Power Is Heart, Anyway?
Where Does He Get All Those Wonderful Toys?
With Great Power Comes Great Perks
Wonder Twin Powers
World's Strongest Man
X-Ray Vision

More tropes can be found under the categories listed on the same webpage and further the tropes in specific and valuable ways. They include: The Ages of Super Hero Comics, Standard Superhero Suits, and Stock Superpowers. In all cases, the connections between many of these tropes and the broader mythemes found in Chapter 1 should be apparent. To explore these tropes more fully, see tvtropes.org/pmwiki/pmwiki.php/Main/SuperheroTropes.

Chapter Notes

Introduction

1. Gloria Steinem, "Introduction," in *Wonder Woman* (New York: DC Comics, 1972).
2. Les Daniels, *Superman: The Complete History* (New York: DC Comics, 1998), 19.
3. Daniels, *Superman*, 11.
4. Jerry Siegel and Joel Shuster, "The Origin of Superman & His Powers," in *Superman: The Greatest Stories Ever Told* (New York: DC Comics, 2004) 10.
5. Siegel and Shuster, "Origin," 11.
6. Red Tornado is especially interesting. Though now recognized as an android member of the DC pantheon, the original character is one of the earliest superhero parodies. Ma Hunkle wore the moniker of the Red Tornado (or sometimes just the Tornado) as an early female superhero and fought crime with a cooking pot on her head.
7. Amy Kiste Nyberg, *Seal of Approval: The History of the Comics Code* (Jackson: University Press of Mississippi, 1998), 3.
8. Nyberg, *Seal of* Approval, 56–57.
9. Ibid., 53.
10. Ibid., 124–125.
11. Ibid., 136.
12. Ibid., 136.
13. *Batman*, directed by Tim Burton (Hollywood: Warner Bros., 1989), DVD.
14. Arthur C. Clarke, *Profiles of the Future: An Inquiry Into the Limits of the Possible* (New York: Holt, Rinehart and Winston, 1984), 36.
15. *Thor*, directed by Kenneth Branagh (Burbank: Marvel Studios, 2011), DVD.
16. Indeed, the balance between the scientific and the magical within superhero stories can be a touchstone to looking at the abstract sensibilities of the creators and consumers of superhero mythology at a given point in its history.
17. J. R. R. Tolkien, "*Beowulf*: The Monsters and the Critics," *Beowulf: A Verse Translation*, ed. Daniel Donoghue (New York: W. W. Norton & Company, 2002), 112.
18. Richard Slotkin, *Regeneration Through Violence: The Mythology of the American Frontier 1600–1860* (Norman: University of Oklahoma Press, 1973), 6.
19. William G. Doty, *Mythography: The Study of Myths and Rituals* (Tuscaloosa: University of Alabama Press, 1986), 28.
20. Doty, *Mythography*, 29.
21. Ibid., 33.
22. Ibid., 33–34.
23. Robert A. Segal, *Myth: A Very Short Introduction* (New York: Oxford University Press, 2004) 4–6.
24. Segal, *Myth*, 5.
25. Terri Windling, "Introduction," *The Coyote Road: Trickster Tales*, ed. Ellen Datlow and Terri Windling (New York: Firebird, 2009).
26. Segal, *Myth*, 6.
27. Roland Barthes, *Mythologies*, trans. Richard Howard and Annette Lavers (New York: Hill and Wang, 2013), 3.
28. Barthes, *Mythologies*, 3.
29. Ibid., 4–5.
30. Segal, *Myth*, 6.
31. Though he makes no claim to superpowers of his own, the RLSH who calls himself Super Hero argues in favor of Master Legend's superpowers in the documentary *Superheroes*.
32. *Superheroes*, directed by Michael

Barnett (Los Angeles: Theodore James, 2011).

33. Joshua Bearman, "The Legend of Master Legend," *Rolling Stone*, December 17, 2008, www.rollingstone.com/culture/news/the-legend-of-master-legend-20081217.

34. Segal, *Myth*, 6.

35. Slotkin, *Regeneration Through Violence*, 6.

36. Ibid., 6.

37. Ibid., 8.

38. Ibid., 7–8.

39. Ibid., 8.

40. Ibid., 8.

41. Ibid., 19.

42. Ibid., 8.

43. Ibid., 9.

44. Barthes, *Mythologies*, 217.

45. Ibid., 217.

46. Ibid., 224.

47. Ibid., 224.

48. Scott McCloud, *Understanding Comics: The Invisible Art* (New York: Harper Perennial, 1994), 188.

49. Doty, *Mythography*, 463, emphasis added.

50. Ibid., 463.

51. Paladin87, "This kid had lost his dad in the crowd, and freaked out until he saw the Flash and Wonder Woman. He went up to the Flash to ask for help, because he knows him," reddit.com, https://www.reddit.com/r/pics/comments/iqgah/this_kid_had_lost_his_dad_in_the_crowd_and/.

52. Tom Hiddleston, "Superheroes Movies Like Avengers Assemble Should Not Be Scorned," *The Guardian*, April 19, 2012, www.theguardian.com/film/filmblog/2012/apr/19/avengers-assemble-tom-hiddleston-superhero.

53. Terrence Wandtke, *The Meaning of Superhero Comic Books* (Jefferson, NC: McFarland, 2012), 23.

54. Wandtke, *The Meaning of Superhero Comic Books*, 23.

55. Ibid., 5.

56. Ibid., 25.

57. Ibid., 25.

58. Ibid., 25.

59. Ibid., 85.

60. Ibid., 80.

61. Ibid., 83.

62. Ibid., 85.

63. Ibid., 84.

64. Ibid., 84.

65. Ibid., 86.

66. Peter Coogan, *Superhero: The Secret Origin of a Genre* (Austin, TX: MonkeyBrain, 2006), 49.

67. "CMOHS.org—Specialist Fourth Class SABO, JR., LESLIE H., U.S. Army," Congressional Medal of Honor Society, Official Website of the Congressional Medal of Honor Society, accessed November 3, 2015, www.cmohs.org/recipient-detail/3481/sabo-jr-leslie-h.php.

68. Doty defines mythos as the "plot of a story or myth" and "a 'mythic sense,' or 'feeling, or plot' that is 'behind' or at the core of a particular narrative" (464). Here it is used to describe those narratives that exist somewhat independently, yet still intertwine within the broader scope of superhero mythology.

69. Coogan, *Superhero*, 47.

Chapter 1

1. Peter Coogan, *Superhero: The Secret Origin of a Genre* (Austin, TX: MonkeyBrain, 2006), 24.

2. Coogan, *Superhero*, 25.

3. Ibid., 30.

4. Ibid., 31.

5. Ibid., 31.

6. Ibid., 32.

7. Ibid., 55.

8. Eric Luke (w), Yanick Paquette (p), and Bob McLeod (i), *Wonder Woman 2*, no. 140, January 1999.

9. Granted, Wonder Woman's longevity in comics certainly has something to do with Marston's deal with DC that she consistently remain in print.

10. This conversation took place when he discovered that I was working on a dissertation on superhero mythology. That dissertation served as the basis for this book. Significantly, his identification of the tropes mentioned in this example was done without his knowledge of any of the mythemes I was developing as vital for the mythology. In essence, without being a superhero scholar in his own right, he was able to recognize and articulate the boundaries of superhero mythology.

11. For ease of identification, all mythemes listed in this chapter and mentioned elsewhere in the book will be set off with italics outside of their own entry in the lexicon.

12. For some, the only access they have to superhero narratives is through film. Others relish television, video games, and comics. Some participate in cosplay and fanfic. The kinds of adherents and their level of engagement vary widely.

13. William G. Doty, *Mythography: The Study of Myths and Rituals* (Tuscaloosa: University of Alabama Press, 1986), 79–80.

14. Anthony J. Ferri, *Willing Suspension of Disbelief: Poetic Faith in Film* (New York: Lexington, 2007), ix.

15. Though admittedly more the latter than the former.

16. Richard Reynolds, *Super Heroes: A Modern Mythology* (Jackson: University of Mississippi Press, 1992), 44.

17. Reynolds, *Super Heroes*, 44.

18. When established events in superhero continuity are changed, either by simply eradicating them or by establishing that things weren't as they originally seemed, these changes are referred to as retcons, or retroactive continuity changes.

19. Reynolds, *Super Heroes*, 27.

20. Ibid., 28.

21. Ibid., 29.

22. John Jennings, "Superheroes by Design," *What is a Superhero?*, eds. Robin S. Rosenberg and Peter Coogan (New York: Oxford University Press, 2013), 59.

23. Though this has changed some in recent years, the footwear used by Scarlett Johansson as Black Widow still has elevated heels. Selina Kyle, as portrayed by Anne Hathaway, had very tall heels in her Catwoman persona in *The Dark Knight Rises* as well.

24. The Hawkeye Initiative, Skjaldmeyja, last modified October 2014, thehawkeyeinitiative.com.

25. This concept is furthered in the discussion about the male gaze in the *androcentric* mytheme.

26. Laura Mulvey, "Visual Pleasure and Narrative Cinema," *The Film Theory Reader: Debates and Arguments*, ed. Marc Furstenau (New York: Routledge, 2010), 203.

27. Mulvey, "Visual Pleasure and Narrative Cinema," 204–205.

28. "FAQ: What is the 'Male Gaze'?" *Finally, a Feminism 101 Blog*, Tekanji, last modified August 26, 2007, https://finallyfeminism101.wordpress.com/2007/08/26/faq-what-is-the-"male-gaze"/.

29. In *Avengers: Age of Ultron*, there is a moment when Thor is seen shirtless in a pool of water, but it is less designed for a female gaze than his shirtless scene in *Thor*.

30. This image, known more popularly as an icon or symbol, was called a chevron by Jim Steranko, and Peter Coogan perpetuated the use of this term for academic purposes. Though the terms can be interchangeable to some extent, the use of the term chevron here maintains a valuable consistency in the conversation.

31. The character of Constantine is emblematic of the way some characters can resonate with superhero mythology without being a part of the genre. Though he is certainly not a superhero, Constantine still has connections to the mythology.

32. "The Sting Connection," *The Ultimate Hellblazer Index*, John Goodrich, May 5, 2000, www.qusoor.com/hellblazer/Sting.htm.

33. See Erik Lundegaard's "Truth, Justice and (Fill in the Blank)," *The New York Times*, June 30, 2006, for a brief discussion of Superman's history with the phrase.

34. Louise Simonson (w), Jon Bognadove (p), and Dennis Janke (i), *Superman: Man of Steel*, vol. 1, no. 20, DC Comics, February 1993.

35. Timely Comics officially became Marvel Comics in 1961.

36. Jack Kirby, *Captain America Comics* #1, Marvel Comics (formerly Timely Comics), March 1, 1941.

37. Recalledcomics.com, "Action Comics #309—JFK," Recalled Comics.com, accessed November 3, 2015, www.recalledcomics.com/ActionComics309.php.

38. *X2: X-Men United*, directed by Bryan Singer (Los Angeles: Twentieth Century Fox Home Entertainment, 2003), DVD.

39. Reynolds, *Super Heroes*, 26.

40. George Perez, *Tales of the Teen Titans* Vol. 1 #44, DC Comics, July 1984.

41. Robert Kirkman (w), Cory Walker (p), and Ryan Ottley (p), *Invincible: Ultimate*

Collection, vol. 1 (Berkeley: Image Comics, 2005).
  42. Reynolds, *Super Heroes*, 41.
  43. Ibid., 26.
  44. A. David Lewis, "Save the Day," *What Is a Superhero?* eds. Robin S. Rosenberg and Peter Coogan (New York: Oxford University Press, 2013), 32.
  45. Lewis, "Save the Day," 37.
  46. Rick Lowell, a comics shop owner, recalls that it was "[t]he first time [his shop] ever had a line of people waiting for us to open [...] That happened three days in a row, and then repeated every week for a month or so." Quoted in Matthew Price, "Death of Superman: 20 Years Later," *NewsOK*, April 22, 2013, newsok.com/article/3792784.
  47. *The Incredibles*, directed by Brad Bird (Burbank: Walt Disney Studios, 2004).
  48. Joss Whedon (w) and John Cassaday (a), *Astonishing X-Men: Dangerous* (New York: Marvel Comics, 2010).
  49. Matt Fraction (w) and David Aja (a), *Hawkeye: My Life as a Weapon* (New York: Marvel Comics, 2013).
  50. Another example of this mytheme is Brad Meltzer and Rags Morales' *Identity Crisis*. In this story, coincidentally, the primary narration is done by DC's archery based superhero, Green Arrow.
  51. Alex Ross and Jim Krueger, *Justice* vol. 1 (New York: DC Comics, 2005).
  52. Elliot Maggin (w), Curt Swan (p), and Murphy Anderson (i), "Must There Be a Superman?" *Superman: The Greatest Stories Ever Told* (New York: DC Comics, 2004), 76.
  53. Maggin, Swan, Anderson, "Must There Be a Superman?," 84.
  54. In Superman's early days, he did take on more real-world adversaries, usually in very mundane settings. However, that all changed in *Action Comics* #17, published on October 1939, with the first appearance of the Ultra-Humanite. Originally an opposite of the Man of Steel, Ultra was confined to a wheelchair but had an incredible intellect. With the introduction of what is arguably the first supervillain, real world issues took a back seat to more fantastically spectacular challenges.
  55. Neil Gaiman (w) and Andy Kubert (p), *Whatever Happened to the Caped Crusader?* (New York: DC Comics, 2010).
  56. Gaiman and Kubert, *Whatever Happened to the Caped Crusader?*.
  57. Ibid.
  58. "Joker's Favor," *Batman: The Animated Series*, directed by Boyd Kirkland (Hollywood: Warner Bros., September 11, 1992).
  59. Reynolds, *Super Heroes*, 15.
  60. Ibid., 15.
  61. Jeph Loeb (w) and Jim Lee (p), *Batman: Hush* (New York: DC Comics, 2009).
  62. Arthurian Camelot was a place of sanctuary for the knights of the round table. Heorot in *Beowulf* was a lair for the Danes that was desecrated by the attacks of Grendel. Even Bag End was a place of safety for the Baggins for most of the Middle-earth saga. Granted, many superhero mythemes have connection to the earlier romances and epics. They draw from the same traditions, but their implementation and details vary sufficiently to establish a new mythology.
  63. The Fortress of Solitude has a clear, distinct resonance with the Doc Savage pulp novels. In the pulp series, the titular character had a lair in the Arctic where he would retreat to study and store items which had value to him or needed his protection.
  64. Reynolds, *Super Heroes*, 41.
  65. This concept receives more attention in the discussion of the *power and responsibility* mytheme.
  66. Mark Millar (w) and Steve McNiven (p), *Marvel: Civil War* (Dubuque, IA: Marvel Worldwide, 2010).
  67. Joe Kelly (w), Doug Mahnke (p), and Lee Bermejo (p), "What's So Funny About Truth, Justice and the American Way?" *Superman: The Greatest Stories Ever Told* (New York: DC Comics, 2004).
  68. Earlier in his history, he had no compunction against killing, but this mytheme later became an integral part of his character. Even in *Batman: The Dark Knight Returns*, as brutal as he is, Batman still stops short of actual killing.
  69. "Rogue," *Smallville*, directed by David Carson (Burbank: Warner Bros. Television, January 15, 2002).
  70. Geoff Johns (w), John Romita Jr. (a),

and Klaus Janson (a), *Superman* #38, DC Comics, February 4, 2015.

71. The idea of the Other is a philosophical and literary term that defines someone as "not like us," divergent and different in significant ways. Commonly, the Other will also be an outsider, someone removed either literally or figuratively from the unified community.

72. *X2*.

73. See Anton Karl Kozlovic, "Superman as Christ Figure: The American Pop Culture Movie Messiah," *Journal of Religion and Film*, vol. 6, no. 1 (April 2002) and Sarah Kozloff, "Superman as Savior: Christian Allegory in the Superman Movies," *Journal of Popular Film and Television*, vol. 9, issue 2 (1981), among others.

74. Luke 2:49 (King James Version).

75. With some variation, this story resonates throughout nearly every *iteration* of Spider-Man's origin, Miles Morales being one obvious exception.

76. It is also the mytheme that is used as a reductively simplistic way of discovering and defining the superhero. It seems that "everyone knows" that superheroes have powers, but often, it never goes beyond that.

77. William Shakespeare, "Twelfth Night," in *The Complete Works of William Shakespeare* 4th ed., ed. David Bevington (New York: Longman, 1997), 2.5, 142–143.

78. Coogan, *Superhero*, 41.

79. Adam Smith, "Batman Begins: The Original Feature," *EmpireOnline*, July 2005, www.empireonline.com/movies/features/batman-begins/.

80. Others include the Golden Age Atom, Al Pratt, Wildcat, the Golden Age Black Canary, and the Punisher.

81. "Unbreakable," *Stan Lee's Superhumans*, directed by Anwar Mamon (Los Angeles: Off the Fence, October 27, 2011).

82. Reynolds, *Super Heroes*, 50–51.

83. Ibid., 51.

84. This concept is underscored in *Watchmen*. Ozymandias becomes the villain of the story when he decides to become proactive in his efforts to protect the world.

85. Ross and Krueger, *Justice*.

86. This is true even when the spouse is also a superhero. Reed Richard and Susan Storm-Richards and Hank Pym and Janet van Dyne exemplify the fact that even superhero marriages are fraught with these sorts of issues.

87. "Years End," *Arrow*, directed by John Dahl (Burbank: CW, December 12, 2012).

88. Reynolds, *Super Heroes*, 48.

89. Ibid., 48.

90. This is especially clear in the reboot of the Spider-Man series with *The Amazing Spider-Man*. Coming so quickly on the heels of Raimi's Spider-Man series, the origin didn't need to be retold except for the fact that Webb's take was different at least in detail if not in overarching scope.

91. Christopher Golden, *X-Men: Mutant Empire Book 1: Siege* (New York: Boulevard, 1996), 2.

92. Golden, *X-Men*, 3.

93. There is some evidence that this may be changing, but the change seems to be slow for now.

94. See artist Mauricio Abril's "Poor Spidey" (mauricioabril.deviantart.com/art/Poor-Spidey-455487489), for example. There are several memes that also poke fun at the fact that Spider-Man sat out during the destruction of New York during *The Avengers*.

95. Reynolds, *Super Heroes*, 24.

96. Others include Hawkeye, Catwoman, Rogue, Bane, Deadpool and Venom.

97. Joe Casey (w) and Chris Weston (p), *Fantastic Four: First Family*, vol. 1, no. 2, Marvel Comics, June 2006.

98. Though it's not always the case, it usually stands as true. Of course, part of the reason for this may have to do with the concern we have with seeing children placed into the kind of situation that superheroes face. However, this concern seems to be less of a problem for the *helper*.

99. *X-Men*, directed by Bryan Singer, written by David Hayter (Los Angeles: Twentieth Century Fox Home Entertainment, 2000), DVD.

100. Though not always true, the privileged iterations of Superman tend to agree on this, especially in the most recent *Man of Steel* and the 1978 *Superman* films.

101. Joseph Campbell, *The Hero With a Thousand Faces* (Princeton, NJ: Princeton University Press, 1973), 10.

102. Reynolds, *Super Heroes*, 19.

103. Reynolds, *Super Heroes*, 19.
104. Though only Gotham and Metropolis are patterned after the Big Apple.
105. Aldo J. Regalado, *Bending Steel: Modernity and the American Superhero* (Jackson: University of Mississippi Press, 2015), 102.
106. Ibid., 102.
107. See, for example: Rachel Edidin, "Grim, Violent *Man of Steel* Sells Superman's Soul for Spectacle," *Wired*, June 13, 2013, www.wired.com/2013/06/man-of-steel-movie-review/, and Matt Singer, "One Year Later: *Man Of Steel*," *The Dissolve*, June 25, 2014, https://thedissolve.com/features/one-year-later/632-one-year-later-man-of-steel. Even Mark Millar seems to think that the film went too far: Mark Millar, "How Man Of Steel Traumatised Me So Much I Created Huck by Mark Millar," *GamesRadar*, November 17, 2015, www.gamesradar.com/mark-millar-how-man-steel-traumatised-create-huck/.
108. There are some stories that do depart from this trend, but in the vast body of superhero literature they are fairly rare.

Chapter 2

1. Kevin Smith, *Green Arrow: Quiver* (New York: DC Comics, 2002), 21.
2. "Years End," *Arrow*, directed by John Dahl (Burbank: CW, December 12, 2012).
3. Green Arrow's goatee was a development by Neal Adams that debuted in September 1968 in *The Brave and the Bold* #85 and lasted until the New 52 relaunch in 2011.
4. "An Innocent Man," *Arrow*, directed by Vincent Misiano (Burbank: CW, October 31, 2012).
5. "Trust but Verify," *Arrow*, directed by Nick Copus (Burbank: CW, January 23, 2013).
6. Who, thanks to his exposure to *mirakuru*, actually does develop *powers*.
7. "Al Sah-Him," *Arrow*, directed by Thor Freudenthal (Burbank: CW, April 29, 2015).
8. Andy Diggle (w) and Jock (a), *Green Arrow: Year One* (New York: DC Comics, 2007), 23.
9. "Vendetta," *Arrow*, directed by Kenneth Fink (Burbank: CW, December 5, 2012).

10. Diggle, *Year One*, 127.
11. Brad Meltzer (w), Phil Hester (p), and Ande Parks (i), *Green Arrow: The Archer's Quest* (New York: DC Comics, 2003).
12. Diggle, *Year One*, 117
13. "Pilot," *Arrow*, directed by David Nutter (Burbank: CW, October 10, 2012).
14. "Darkness on the Edge of Town," *Arrow*, directed by John Behring (Burbank: CW, May 8 2013).
15. "City of Heroes," *Arrow*, directed by John Behring (Burbank: CW, October 9, 2013).
16. "City of Heroes."
17. Ibid.
18. Ibid.
19. "Broken Dolls," *Arrow*, directed by Glen Winter (Burbank: CW, October 23, 2013).
20. "Home Invasion," *Arrow*, directed by Kenneth Fink (Burbank: CW, April 24, 2013).
21. "Vendetta."
22. "Lone Gunmen," *Arrow*, directed by Guy Norman Bee (Burbank: CW, October 24, 2012).
23. "Vendetta."
24. Ibid.
25. "City of Heroes."

Chapter 3

1. Peter Coogan, *Superhero: The Secret Origin of a Genre* (Austin, TX: Monkeybrain, 2006), 46.
2. "Dead Man's Party," *Buffy the Vampire Slayer*, directed by James Whitmore, Jr. (Los Angeles: Twentieth Century Fox, October 6, 1998).
3. Danny Fingeroth, *Superman on the Couch: What Superheroes Really Tell Us About Ourselves and Our Society* (New York: Continuum, 2004), 26.
4. Roz Kaveney, *Superheroes! Capes and Crusaders in Comics and Films* (New York: I.B. Tauris, 2008), 204.
5. Matthew Pateman, *The Aesthetics of Culture in Buffy the Vampire Slayer* (Jefferson, NC: McFarland, 2006), 208–209.
6. "Normal Again," *Buffy the Vampire Slayer*, directed by Rick Rosenthal (Los Angeles: Twentieth Century Fox, March 12, 2002).

7. The temporary nature of these alternate realities is problematized by the fact that Xander and Willow both seem to carry over some latent changes from their time in alternate storylines, Xander from his time as a soldier in "Halloween" and Willow's bisexuality, which is hinted at first in "Doppelgangland."

8. "The Wish," *Buffy The Vampire Slayer*, directed by David Greenwalt (Los Angeles: Twentieth Century Fox, December 8, 1998).

9. "Normal Again."

10. Joss Whedon, "10 Questions for Joss Whedon," *The New York Times*, May 16, 2003, www.nytimes.com/2003/05/16/readers opinions/16WHED.html.

11. "Welcome to the Hellmouth," *Buffy the Vampire Slayer*, directed by Joss Whedon (Los Angeles: Twentieth Century Fox, March 10, 1997).

12. "Surprise," *Buffy the Vampire Slayer*, directed by Michael Lange (Los Angeles: Twentieth Century Fox, January 19, 1998).

13. It is also, unfortunately, the centerpoint for the Hellmouth.

14. "Passion," *Buffy the Vampire Slayer*, directed by Michael E. Gershman (Los Angeles: Twentieth Century Fox, February 24, 1998).

15. "What's My Line? Part 1," *Buffy the Vampire Slayer*, directed by David Solomon (Los Angeles: Twentieth Century Fox, November 17, 1997).

16. "Witch," *Buffy the Vampire Slayer*, directed by Stephen Cragg (Los Angeles: Twentieth Century Fox, March 17, 1997).

17. "Innocence," *Buffy the Vampire Slayer*, directed by Joss Whedon (Los Angeles: Twentieth Century Fox, January 20, 1998).

18. "Killed by Death," *Buffy the Vampire Slayer*, directed by Deran Sarafian (Los Angeles: Twentieth Century Fox, March 3, 1998).

19. "Innocence."

20. "Helpless," *Buffy the Vampire Slayer*, directed by James A. Contner (Los Angeles: Twentieth Century Fox, January 19, 1999).

21. "Ted," *Buffy the Vampire Slayer*, directed by Bruce Seth Green (Los Angeles: Twentieth Century Fox, December 8, 1997).

22. "Gingerbread," *Buffy the Vampire Slayer*, directed by James Whitmore, Jr. (Los Angeles: Twentieth Century Fox, January 12, 1999).

23. "Bad Girls," *Buffy the Vampire Slayer*, directed by Michael Lange (Los Angeles: Twentieth Century Fox, February 9, 1999).

24. Though the film is set during her senior year, the series retcons the timeline to allow for more time in high school at the beginning of the series.

25. David Dylan Thomas, "The Ten Best Tracking Shots Ever," *AMC Movie Blog*, September 2007, accessed November 9, 2015, www.amc.com/talk/2007/09/the-ten-best-tr.

26. "Witch."

27. "The Prom." *Buffy the Vampire Slayer*, directed by David Solomon (Los Angeles: Twentieth Century Fox, May 11, 1999).

28. "Nightmares," *Buffy the Vampire Slayer*, directed by Bruce Seth Green (Los Angeles: Twentieth Century Fox, May 12, 1997).

29. "When She Was Bad," *Buffy the Vampire Slayer*, directed by Joss Whedon (Los Angeles: Twentieth Century Fox, September 15, 1997).

30. "The Body," *Buffy the Vampire Slayer*, directed by Joss Whedon (Los Angeles: Twentieth Century Fox, February 27, 2001).

31. "Earshot," *Buffy the Vampire Slayer*, directed by Regis B. Kimble (Los Angeles: Twentieth Century Fox, September 28, 1999).

32. "Prophecy Girl," *Buffy the Vampire Slayer*, directed by Joss Whedon (Los Angeles: Twentieth Century Fox, June 2, 1997).

33. "The Gift," *Buffy the Vampire Slayer*, directed by Joss Whedon (Los Angeles: Twentieth Century Fox, May 22, 2001).

34. "Bargaining: Part 1," *Buffy the Vampire Slayer*, directed by David Grossman (Los Angeles: Twentieth Century Fox, October 2, 2001).

35. "Bargaining: Part 2," *Buffy the Vampire Slayer*, directed by David Grossman (Los Angeles: Twentieth Century Fox, October 2, 2001).

36. "After Life," *Buffy the Vampire Slayer*, directed by David Grossman (Los Angeles: Twentieth Century Fox, October 9, 2001).

37. However, the *Supergirl* television series shows signs of moving away from such a sexualized manifestation of the character.

38. Ken P., "An Interview with Joss Whedon," *IGN*, 23 June 2003, www.ign.com/

articles/2003/06/23/an-interview-with-joss-whedon.

39. Coogan, *Superhero*, 48.

Chapter 4

1. "Alphaville," *Alphas*, directed by Nick Copus (New York: SyFy, August 27, 2012).
2. "Pilot," *Alphas*, directed by Jack Bender (New York: SyFy, July 11, 2011).
3. "God's Eye," *Alphas*, directed by Matthew Hastings (New York: SyFy, October 22, 2012).
4. "Cause and Effect," *Alphas*, directed by Constantine Makris (New York: SyFy, July 18, 2011).
5. "Cause and Effect."
6. "If Memory Serves," *Alphas*, directed by Allan Kroeker (New York: SyFy, October 8, 2012).
7. "Alphaville."
8. "If Memory Serves."
9. "Cause and Effect"
10. "Blind Spot," *Alphas*, directed by Michael W. Watkins (New York: SyFy, September 12, 2011).
11. "Alpha Dogs," *Alphas*, directed by Nick Copus (New York: SyFy, August 6, 2012).
12. "When Push Comes to Shove," *Alphas*, directed by Omar Madha (New York: SyFy, August 13, 2012).
13. "Need to Know," *Alphas*, directed by Nick Copus (New York: SyFy, October 15, 2012).
14. "When Push Comes to Shove."
15. "Cause and Effect."
16. "The Devil Will Drag You Under," *Alphas*, directed by Matt Hastings (New York: SyFy, September 24, 2012).
17. "The Devil Will Drag You Under."
18. "Original Sin," *Alphas*, directed by Nick Copus (New York: SyFy, September 26, 2011).
19. "Original Sin."
20. "Catch and Release," *Alphas*, directed by Kevin Hooks (New York: SyFy, August 22, 2011).
21. "Pilot."
22. "Wake-Up Call," *Alphas*, directed by Matthew Hastings (New York: SyFy, July 23, 2012).
23. "Life After Death," *Alphas*, directed by J. Miller Tobin (New York: SyFy, October 1, 2012).
24. "Life After Death."
25. "Pilot."
26. "God's Eye."
27. "Gaslight," *Alphas*, directed by Leslie Libman (New York: SyFy, August 20, 2012).
28. "If Memory Serves."
29. "God's Eye."
30. "Pilot."
31. Ibid.
32. "Alphaville."
33. "A Short Time in Paradise," *Alphas*, directed by John F. Showalter (New York: SyFy, August 29, 2011).
34. Their limited wardrobe is a trope mentioned on tvtropes.com as applicable to the genre of the superhero.
35. "Bill and Gary's Excellent Adventure," *Alphas*, directed by Leslie Libman (New York: SyFy, August 15, 2011).

Chapter 5

1. J.R.R. Tolkien, "*Beowulf*: The Monsters and the Critics," *Beowulf: A Verse Translation*, ed. Daniel Donoghue (New York: W.W. Norton, 2002), 105.
2. *Beowulf*, trans. Seamus Haney, ed. Daniel Donoghue (New York: W.W. Norton, 2002), 1560–1561.
3. *Beowulf*, 1637–1639.
4. Ibid., 533–576.
5. Ibid., 1495.
6. Ibid., 69–70, 78.
7. Ibid., 2359–2362.
8. Ibid., 2818–2819.
9. Ibid., 3131–3133.
10. Ibid., 2208–2209.
11. Ibid., 669–674.
12. Ibid., 1441–1461.
13. Ibid., 2518–2539.
14. Ibid., 991–1001.
15. Ibid., 816–818.
16. Tolkien, "*Beowulf*: The Monsters and the Critics," 115.
17. Ibid., 115.
18. *Beowulf*, 1931–1953.
19. Ibid., 1072–1075.
20. Ibid., 1114–1118.
21. The only historically factual event in the poem is Hygelac's failed raid on the Franks around A.D. 521. *Klaebur's Beowulf*,

4th ed., eds. R. D. Fulk, Robert E. Bjork, John D. Niles (Toronto: University of Toronto Press, 2009), xxxix.

22. *Beowulf*, 1020–1053.
23. Ibid., 1175–1179.
24. Ibid., 104–113.
25. Ibid., 1265–1266.
26. Ibid., 1258–1262.
27. Ibid., 1278.
28. In Robert Zemeckis' take on the epic, the noise of the mead hall causes Grendel literal pain which he seeks to appease by silencing the noises. Sturla Gunnarsson's *Beowulf and Grendel* suggests that Grendel is seeking vengeance for Hrothgar's role in the death of his father. On the other hand, John Gardner's *Grendel* focuses on a nihilistic view of the entire conflict, beginning with a simple misunderstanding between Grendel and Hrothgar's band. The poem itself doesn't resolve the question of motivation for the monster, allowing for multiple motives to be assigned to his actions.
29. *Beowulf*, 1296–1297, 1309.
30. Ibid., 2183–2189.
31. Ibid., 457–458.
32. Ibid., 472.
33. Ibid., 677–687.
34. Ibid., 267–271.
35. Ibid., 409–432.
36. Ibid., 2511–2514.
37. Not all superheroes' motives are purely altruistic, however. Luke Cage began his career as a "hero for hire" and was later joined in that endeavor by Iron Fist. In the 2005 *Fantastic Four* film, Johnny Storm clearly uses his abilities for egocentric gains. Deadpool is rarely motivated by any sort of clear sense of responsibility.
38. *Beowulf*, 2910–3030.
39. Ibid., 500.
40. J.R. Clark-Hall's *A Concise Anglo-Saxon Dictionary* defines the Anglo-Saxon word used to describe Unferth, *þyle*, as "speaker, orator: jester."
41. *Beowulf*, 1457–1461.

Chapter 6

1. Coogan, *Superhero*, 24.
2. Marshall W. Fishwick, "Introduction," *The Hero in Transition*, eds. Ray B. Brown and Marshall W. Fishwick (Bowling Green, OH: Bowling Green University Popular Press, 1983), 7.
3. Fishwick, 12–13.
4. Jake Coil, "Fall Movie Preview: Spielberg Plunges into the Cold War," Associated Press, September 2, 2015, www.startribune.com /fall-movie-preview-spielberg-plunges-into-the-cold-war/323849331/.
5. Jen Yamato, "Zack Snyder: Sorry Marvel, 'Batman V. Superman' Transcends Superhero Movies," *The Daily Beast*, September 10, 2015, www.thedailybeast.com/articles/2015/09/10/zack-snyder-sorry-marvel-batman-v-superman-transcends-superhero-movies.html.
6. Terri Schwartz, "Marvel's Kevin Feige Responds to Steven Spielberg, Zack Snyder Superhero Genre Comments," *IGN*, October 1, 2015, www.ign.com/articles/2015/10/01/marvels-kevin-feige-responds-to-steven-spielberg-zack-snyder-superhero-genre-comments.
7. Coogan, 31.
8. Ibid.
9. Ibid., 32.
10. Ibid.
11. This includes a character like Tony Stark who doesn't keep his alter ego a secret, but who still differentiates in at least a small degree between Stark and Iron Man. The two are similar but different.
12. Coogan, 43.
13. See the Introduction for a more developed discussion of the semiological system.
14. This is a deviation from the more recognized origin where the Waynes leave a Zorro film before they are shot.
15. See Chapter 5.
16. *Beowulf*, trans. Seamus Haney, ed. Daniel Donoghue (New York: W. W. Norton, 2002), 2183–2188.
17. *Beowulf*, 2189.
18. Ibid., 2182.
19. Ibid., 2182–2183.
20. A type not uncommon for special needs characters in fiction.
21. "Never Let Me Go," *Alphas*, directed by Jeffrey G. Hunt (New York: SyFy, August 8, 2011).
22. However, he does later give up on this mission and seems to become satisfied with being a part of the team rather than returning to the FBI.

23. Coogan, *Superhero*, 48.
24. "Pilot," *Arrow*, directed by David Nutter (Burbank: CW, October 10, 2012).
25. "Green Arrow," *Arrow*, directed by Thor Freudenthal (Burbank: CW, October 7, 2015).
26. Andy Diggle (w) and Jock (a), *Green Arrow: Year One* (New York: DC Comics, 2007), 144.
27. Diggle (w) and Jock (a), *Green Arrow: Year One*, 151.
28. This also increases the likelihood that the narrative is also part of the generic definition of the superhero, but it is still no guarantee.

Bibliography and Television Shows and Films

Television show episodes are listed in chronological order

Abril, Mauricio. "Poor Spidey." Mauricioabril.deviantart.com/art/Poor-Spidey-455487489.

Alphas. "Pilot." Directed by Jack Bender. New York: SyFy, July 11, 2011.

———. "Cause and Effect." Directed by Constantine Makris. New York: SyFy, July 18, 2011.

———. "Never Let Me Go." Directed by Jeffrey G. Hunt. New York: SyFy, August 8, 2011.

———. "Bill and Gary's Excellent Adventure." Directed by Leslie Libman. New York: SyFy, August 15, 2011.

———. "Catch and Release." Directed by Kevin Hooks. New York: SyFy, August 22, 2011.

———. "A Short Time in Paradise." Directed by John F. Showalter. New York: SyFy. August 29, 2011.

———. "Blind Spot." Directed by Michael W. Watkins. New York: SyFy, September 12, 2011.

———. "Original Sin." Directed by Nick Copus. New York: SyFy, September 26, 2011.

———. "Wake-Up Call." Directed by Matthew Hastings. New York: SyFy, July 23, 2012.

———. "Alpha Dogs." Directed by Nick Copus. New York: SyFy, August 6, 2012.

———. "When Push Comes to Shove." Directed by Omar Madha. New York: SyFy, August 13, 2012.

———. "Gaslight." Directed by Leslie Libman. New York: SyFy, August 20, 2012.

———. "Alphaville." Directed by Nick Copus. New York: SyFy, August 27, 2012.

———. "The Devil Will Drag You Under." Directed by Matt Hastings. New York: SyFy, September 24, 2012.

———. "Life After Death." Directed by J. Miller Tobin. New York: SyFy, October 1, 2012.

———. "If Memory Serves." Directed by Allan Kroeker. New York: SyFy, October 8, 2012.

———. "Need to Know." Directed by Nick Copus. New York: SyFy, October 15, 2012.

———. "God's Eye." Directed by Matthew Hastings. New York: SyFy, October 22, 2012.

The Amazing Spider-Man. Directed by Marc Webb. Culver City: Sony Pictures Entertainment, 2012.

Arrow. "Pilot." Directed by David Nutter. Burbank: CW, October 10, 2012.

———. "Lone Gunmen." Directed by Guy Norman Bee. Burbank: CW, October 24, 2012.

———. "An Innocent Man." Directed by Vincent Misiano. Burbank: CW, October 31, 2012.

———. "Vendetta." Directed by Kenneth Fink. Burbank: CW, December 5, 2012.

———. "Year's End." Directed by John Dahl. Burbank: CW, December 12, 2012.

———. "Home Invasion." Directed by Kenneth Fink. Burbank: CW, April 24, 2013.

———. "Darkness on the Edge of Town." Directed by John Behring. Burbank: CW, May 8, 2013.

———. "City of Heroes." Directed by John Behring. Burbank: CW, October 9, 2013.

———. "Broken Dolls." Directed by Glen Winter. Burbank: CW, October 23, 2013.

_____. "Trust But Verify." Directed by Nick Copus. Burbank: CW, January 23, 2013.

_____. "Al Sah-Him." Directed by Thor Freudenthal. Burbank: CW, April 29, 2015.

_____. "Green Arrow." Directed by Thor Freudenthal. Burbank: CW, October 7, 2015.

Augustyn, Brian (w), Michael Mignola (p), P. Craig Russell (i). *Batman: Gotham by Gaslight*. New York: DC Comics, 1989.

The Avengers. Directed by Joss Whedon. Burbank: Marvel Studios, 2012. Blu-ray.

Avengers: Age of Ultron. Directed by Joss Whedon. Burbank: Marvel Studios, 2015. Blu-ray.

Barthes, Roland. *Mythologies*. Translated by Richard Howard and Annette Lavers. New York: Hill and Wang, 2013.

Batman. Directed by Tim Burton. Hollywood: Warner Bros., 1989. DVD.

Batman Begins. Directed by Christopher Nolan. Hollywood: Warner Bros., 2005. DVD.

Batman: The Animated Series. "Joker's Favor." Directed by Boyd Kirkland. Hollywood: Warner Bros., September 11, 1992.

Batman: Under the Red Hood. Directed by Brandon Vietti. Hollywood: Warner Bros., 2010.

Bearman, Joshua. "The Legend of Master Legend." *Rolling Stone*. December 17, 2008. www.rollingstone.com/culture/news/the-legend-of-master-legend-20081217.

Beowulf. Directed by Robert Zemeckis. Hollywood: Paramount Pictures, 2007. DVD.

Beowulf. Translated by Seamus Haney. Edited by Daniel Donoghue. New York: W.W. Norton, 2002.

Beowulf and Grendel. Directed by Sturla Gunnarsson. West Sussex: Movision, 2005. DVD.

Buffy the Vampire Slayer. Directed by Fran Rubel Kuzui. Los Angeles: Twentieth Century Fox, 1992.

Buffy the Vampire Slayer. "Welcome to Hellmouth." Directed by Joss Whedon. Los Angeles: Twentieth Century Fox, March 10, 1997.

_____. "Witch." Directed by Stephen Cragg. Los Angeles: Twentieth Century Fox, March 17, 1997.

_____. "Nightmares." Directed by Bruce Seth Green. Los Angeles: Twentieth Century Fox, May 12, 1997.

_____. "Prophecy Girl." Directed by Joss Whedon. Los Angeles: Twentieth Century Fox, June 2, 1997.

_____. "When She Was Bad." Directed by Joss Whedon. Los Angeles: Twentieth Century Fox, September 15, 1997.

_____. "Halloween." Directed by Bruce Seth Green. Los Angeles: Twentieth Century Fox, October 27, 1997.

_____. "What's My Line? Part 1." Directed by David Solomon. Los Angeles: Twentieth Century Fox, November 17, 1997.

_____. "Ted." Directed by Bruce Seth Green. Los Angeles: Twentieth Century Fox, December 8, 1997.

_____. "Surprise." Directed by Michael Lange. Los Angeles: Twentieth Century Fox, January 19, 1998.

_____. "Innocence." Directed by Joss Whedon. Los Angeles: Twentieth Century Fox, January 20, 1998.

_____. "Passion." Directed by Michael E. Gershman. Los Angeles: Twentieth Century Fox, February 24, 1998.

_____. "Killed by Death." Directed by Deran Serafian. Los Angeles: Twentieth Century Fox, March 3, 1998.

_____. "Becoming: Part 2." Directed by Joss Whedon. Los Angeles: Twentieth Century Fox, May 19, 1998.

_____. "Dead Man's Party." Directed by James Whitmore, Jr. Los Angeles: Twentieth Century Fox, October 6, 1998.

_____. "Band Candy." Directed by Michael Lange. Los Angeles: Twentieth Century Fox, November 10, 1998.

_____. "The Wish." Directed by David Greenwalt. Los Angeles: Twentieth Century Fox, December 8, 1998.

_____. "Gingerbread." Directed by James Whitmore Jr. Los Angeles: Twentieth Century Fox, January 12, 1999.

_____. "Helpless." Directed by James A. Contner. Los Angeles: Twentieth Century Fox, January 19, 1999.

_____. "Bad Girls." Directed by Michael Lange. Los Angeles: Twentieth Century Fox, February 9, 1999.

_____. "Doppelgangland." Directed by Joss Whedon. Los Angeles: Twentieth Century Fox, February 23, 1999.

———. "The Prom." Directed by David Solomon. Los Angeles: Twentieth Century Fox, May 11, 1999.
———. "Earshot." Directed by Regis B. Kimble. Los Angeles: Twentieth Century Fox, September 28, 1999.
———. "The Body." Directed by Joss Whedon. Los Angeles: Twentieth Century Fox, February 27, 2001.
———. "The Gift." Directed by Joss Whedon. Los Angeles: Twentieth Century Fox, May 22, 2001.
———. "Bargaining: Part 1." Directed by David Grossman. Los Angeles: Twentieth Century Fox, October 2, 2001.
———. "Bargaining: Part 2." Directed by David Grossman. Los Angeles: Twentieth Century Fox, October 2, 2001.
———. "After Life." Directed by David Grossman. Los Angeles: Twentieth Century Fox, October 9, 2001.
———. "Normal Again." Directed by Rick Rosenthal. Los Angeles: Twentieth Century Fox, March 12, 2002.
Butler, Judith. *Gender Trouble*. New York: Routledge, 1990.
Campbell, Joseph. *The Hero with a Thousand Faces*. Princeton: Princeton University Press, 1973.
Captain America: The First Avenger. Directed by Joe Johnston. Burbank: Marvel Studios, 2011. Blu-ray.
Captain America: The Winter Soldier. Directed by Anthony Russo and Joe Russo. Burbank: Marvel Studios, 2014. Blu-ray.
Casey, Joe (w), and Christ Weston (p). *Fantastic Four: First Family* 1 no. 2 (June 2006).
Clark-Hall, J. R. *A Concise Anglo-Saxon Dictionary*. 2008. "*pyle*."
Clarke, Arthur C. *Profiles of the Future: An Inquiry into the Limits of the Possible*. New York: Holt, Rinehart and Winston, 1984.
Coil, Jake. "Fall Movie Preview: Spielberg Plunges into the Cold War." Associated Press. September 2, 2015. www.startribune.com/fall-movie-preview-spielberg-plunges-into-the-cold-war/323849331/.
Congressional Medal of Honor Society. "CMOHS.org—Specialist Fourth Class Sabo, Jr., Leslie H., U.S. Army." Official Website of the Congressional Medal of Honor Society. Accessed November 3, 2015. www.cmohs.org/recipient-detail/3481/sabo-jr-leslie-h.php.
Constantine. Directed by Francis Lawrence. Hollywood: Warner Bros., 2005.
Coogan, Peter. *Superhero: The Secret Origin of a Genre*. Austin: MonkeyBrain, 2006.
Daniels, Les. *Superman: The Complete History*. New York: DC Comics, 1998.
The Dark Knight. Directed by Christopher Nolan. Hollywood: Warner Bros., 2008.
The Dark Knight Rises. Directed by Christopher Nolan. Hollywood: Warner Bros., 2012.
Diggle, Andy (w), and Jock (a). *Green Arrow: Year One*. New York: DC Comics, 2007.
Doty, William G. *Mythography: The Study of Myths and Rituals*. Tuscaloosa: University of Alabama Press, 1986.
Edidin, Rachel. "Grim, Violent *Man of Steel* Sells Superman's Soul for Spectacle." *Wired*. June 13, 2013. www.wired.com/2013/06/man-of-steel-movie-review/.
Fantastic Four. Directed by Tim Story. Los Angeles: Twentieth Century Fox, 2005. DVD.
Ferri, Anthony J. *Willing Suspension of Disbelief: Poetic Faith in Film*. New York: Lexington, 2007.
Fingeroth, Danny. *Superman on the Couch: What Superheroes Really Tell Us About Ourselves and Our Society*. New York: Continuum, 2004.
Fishwick, Marshall W. "Introduction." *The Hero in Transition*. Edited by Ray B. Brown and Marshall W. Fishwick. Bowling Green, OH: Bowling Green University Popular Press, 1983.
Fraction, Matt (w), and David Aja (a). *Hawkeye: My Life as a Weapon*. New York: Marvel Comics, 2013.
Gaiman, Neil (w), and Andy Kubert (p). *Whatever Happened to the Caped Crusader*. New York: DC Comics, 2010.
Gardner, John. *Grendel*. New York: Vintage, 1989.
Golden, Christopher. *X-Men: Mutant Empire Book 1: Siege*. New York: Boulevard, 1996.
Goodrich, John. "The Sting Connection." *The Ultimate Hellblazer Index*. May 5, 2000. www.qusoor.com/hellblazer/Sting.htm.
Grell, Mike (a). *Green Arrow: The Longbow Hunters*. New York: DC Comics, 2012.

Hale, Shannon. *Dangerous*. New York: Bloomsbury, 2014.

Haney, Bob (w), Neal Adams (p), and Dick Giordano (i). *The Brave and the Bold* 1 no. 85 (September 1969).

Hickman, Tracy. *Wayne of Gotham*. New York: HarperCollins, 2012.

Hiddleston, Tom. "Superheroes Movies like Avengers Assemble Should Not Be Scorned." *The Guardian*. April 19, 2012. www.theguardian.com/film/filmblog/2012/apr/19/avengers-assemble-tom-hiddleston-superhero.

The Incredibles. Directed by Brad Bird. Burbank: Walt Disney Studios, 2004.

Jenkins, Paul (w), Andy Kubert (p), and Richard Isanove (i and c). *Wolverine: Origin* 1 nos. 1–6 (November 2001-April 2002).

Jennings, John. "Superheroes by Design." In *What Is a Superhero?* Edited by Robin S. Rosenberg and Peter Coogan. New York: Oxford University Press, 2013.

Johns, Geoff (w), Gary Frank (p), and Jon Sibal (i). *Superman: Secret Origin*. New York: DC Comics, 2010.

Johns, Geoff (w), John Romita, Jr. (a), and Klaus Janson (a). *Superman* 3, no. 38 (April 2015).

Kaveney, Roz. *Superheroes! Capes and Crusaders in Comics and Films*. New York: I. B. Tauris, 2008.

Kelly, Joe (w), Doug Mahnke (p), and Lee Bermejo (p). "What's So Funny About Truth, Justice & the American Way?" *Superman: The Greatest Stories Ever Told*. New York: DC Comics, 2004. 151–189.

Kirbey, Jack. *Captain America Comics* 1, no. 1 (March 1, 1941).

Kirkman, Robert (w), Cory Walker (p), and Ryan Ottley (p). *Invincible: Ultimate Collection, Vol. 1*. Berkley: Image Comics, 2005.

Klaebur's Beowulf. 4th ed. Edited by R. D. Fulk, Robert E. Bjork, and John D. Niles. Buffalo: University of Toronto Press, 2009.

Kozloff, Sarah. "Superman as Savior: Christian Allegory in the Superman Movies." *Journal of Popular Film and Television* 9 no. 2 (1981).

Kozlovic, Anton Karl. "Superman as Christ Figure: The American Pop Culture Movie Messiah." *Journal of Religion and Film* 6, no. 1 (April 2002).

The Lego Movie. Directed by Phil Lord and Christopher Miller. Hollywood: Warner Bros., 2014. Blu-ray.

Lewis, A. David. "Save the Day." In *What Is a Superhero?* Edited by Robin S. Rosenberg and Peter Coogan. New York: Oxford University Press, 2013.

LoCicero, Don. *Superheroes and Gods: A Comparative Study from Babylonia to Batman*. Jefferson, NC: McFarland, 2007.

Loeb, Jeph (w), and Jim Lee (p). *Batman: Hush*. New York: DC Comics, 2009.

The Lord of the Rings: The Two Towers. Directed by Peter Jackson. Los Angeles: New Line Cinema, 2002.

Luke, Eric (w), Yanick Paquette (p), and Bob McLeod (i). *Wonder Woman* 2, no. 140 (January 1999).

Lundegaard, Erik. "Truth, Justice and (Fill in the Blank). *The New York Times*. June 30, 2006. www.nytimes.com/2006/06/30/opinion/30lundegaard.html.

Maggin, Elliot (w), Curt Swan (p), and Murphy Anderson (i). "Must There Be a Superman?" *Superman: The Greatest Stories Ever Told*. New York: DC Comics 2004. 69–85.

Man of Steel. Directed by Zack Snyder. Hollywood: Warner Bros., 2013.

McCloud, Scott. *Understanding Comics: The Invisible Art*. New York: HarperPerennial, 1994.

Megamind. Directed by Tom McGrath. Glendale: DreamWorks Animation, 2010.

Meltzer, Brad (w), Phil Hester (p), and Ande Parks (i). *Green Arrow: The Archer's Quest*. New York: DC Comics, 2003.

Millar, Mark. "How Man of Steel Traumatised Me So Much I Created Huck by Mark Millar." *GamesRadar*. November 17, 2015. www.gamesradar.com/mark-millar-how-man-steel-traumatised-create-huck/.

Millar, Mark (w), Dave Johnson and Andrew Robinson (a), Kilian Plunkett and Walden Wong (a). *Superman: Red Son*. New York: DC Comics, 2014.

Millar, Mark (w), and Steve McNiven (p). *Marvel: Civil War*. Dubuque: Marvel Worldwide, 2010.

Miller, Frank. *Batman: The Dark Knight Returns*. New York: DC Comics, 2002.

Miller, Frank (w), and David Mazzucchelli (a). *Batman: Year One*. New York: DC Comics, 2007.

Moore, Alan (w), and Dave Gibbons (a). *Watchmen*. New York: DC Comics, 1986.

Mulvey, Laura. "Visual Pleasure and Narrative Cinema." In *The Film Theory Reader: Debates and Arguments*. Edited by Marc Furstenau. New York: Routledge, 2010.

Nyberg, Amy Kiste. *Seal of Approval: The History of the Comics Code*. Jackson: University Press of Mississippi, 1998.

O'Neil, Dennis (w), and Neal Adams (a). *Green Lantern/Green Arrow*. New York: DC Comics, 2012.

P., Ken. "An Interview with Joss Whedon." *IGN*. 23 Jun3, 2003. www.ign.com/articles/2003/06/23/an-interview-with-joss-whedon.

Paladin87. "This Kid Had Lost His Dad In the Crowd, and Freaked Out Until He Saw the Flash and Wonder Woman. He Went Up to the Flash to Ask for Help, Because He Knows Him." reddit.com. Accessed November 11, 2015. https://www.reddit.com/r/pics/comments/iqgah/this_kid_had_lost_his_dad_in_the_crowd_and/.

Pateman, Matthew. *The Aesthetics of Culture in Buffy the Vampire Slayer*. Jefferson, NC: McFarland, 2006.

Perez, George. *Tales of the Teen Titans* 1, no. 44 (July 1984).

Price, Matthew. "Death of Superman: 20 Years Later." *NewsOK*. April 22, 2013. Newsok.com/articles/3792784.

Raglan, Lord. *The Hero: A Study in Tradition, Myth and Drama*. Mineola, NY: Dover, 2011.

Recalledcomics. "Action Comics #309—JFK." Recalledcomics.com. Accessed November 3, 2015. www.recalledcomics.com/ActionComics309.php.

Regalado, Aldo J. *Bending Steel: Modernity and the American Superhero*. Jackson: University of Mississippi Press, 2015.

Reynolds, Richard. *Super Heroes: A Modern Mythology*. Jackson: University of Mississippi, 1992.

Rollin, Roger B. "Beowulf to Batman: The Epic Hero and Pop Culture." *College English* 31 no. 5 (February 1970): 431–449.

Ross, Alex, and Jim Krueger. *Justice* 1. New York: DC Comics, 2005.

Ross, Alex, and Jim Krueger (s), John Paul Leon (p), and Bill Reinhold (i). *Earth X*. New York: Marvel Comics, 2010.

Sanderson, Brandon. *Steelheart*. New York: Delacorte, 2013.

Schwartz, Terri. "Marvel's Kevin Feige Responds to Steven Spielberg, Zack Snyder Superhero Genre Comments." *IGN*. October 1, 2015. www.ign.com/articles/2015/10/01/marvels-kevin-feige-responds-to-steven-spielberg-zack-snyder-superhero-genre-comments.

Segal, Robert A. *Myth: A Very Short Introduction*. New York: Oxford University Press, 2004.

Seigel, Jerry, and Joel Shuster. "The Origin of Superman & His Powers." In *Superman: The Greatest Stories Ever Told*. New York: DC Comics, 2004. 9–11.

_____. *Action Comics* 1, no. 17 (October 1939).

Shakespeare, William. "Twelfth Night." In *The Complete Works of William Shakespeare*, 4th ed. Edited by David Bevington. New York: Longman, 1997.

Simonson, Louise (w), Jon Bognadove (p), and Dennis Janke (i). *Superman: Man of Steel* 1 no. 20 (February 1993).

Singer, Matt. "One Year Later: Man of Steel." *The Dissolve*, June 25, 2014. https://thedissolve.com/features/one-year-later/632-one-year-later-man-of-steel.

Skjaldmeyja. The Hawkeye Initiative. Last modified October 2014. thehawkeyeinitiative.com.

Slotkin, Richard. *Regeneration Through Violence: The Mythology of the American Frontier, 1600–1860*. Norman: University of Oklahoma Press, 1973.

Smallville. "Rogue." Directed by David Carson. Burbank: Warner Bros. Television, January 15, 2002.

Smith, Adam. "Batman Begins: The Original Feature." *EmpireOnline*. July 2005. www.empireonline.com/movies/features/batman-begins/.

Smith, Kevin. *Green Arrow: Quiver*. New York: DC Comics, 2002.

The Sorcerer's Apprentice. Directed by Jon Turteltaub. Burbank: Walt Disney Pictures, 2010.

Spider-Man. Directed by Sam Raimi. Culver City: Sony Pictures Entertainment, 2002. DVD.

Spider-Man 2. Directed by Sam Raimi. Culver City: Sony Pictures Entertainment, 2004. DVD.

Stan Lee's Superhumans. "Unbreakable." Directed by Anwar Mamon. Los Angeles: Off the Fence, October 27, 2011.

Steinem, Gloria. "Introduction." In *Wonder Woman*. New York: DC Comics, 1972.

Suicide Squad. Directed by David Ayer. Hollywood: Warner Bros., 2016.

Superheroes. Directed by Michael Barnett. Los Angeles: Theodore James, 2011.

Superman. Directed by Richard Donner. Hollywood: Warner Bros., 1978.

Superman II. Directed by Richard Lester. Hollywood: Warner Bros., 1981.

Tekanji. "FAQ: What is the 'Male Gaze'?" *Finally, a Feminism 1010 Blog*. Last Modified August 26, 2007. https://finallyfeminism 101.wordpress.com/2007/08/26/faq-what-is-the-"male-gaze"/.

Thomas, David Dylan. "The Ten Best Tracking Shots Ever." *AMC Movie Blog*. Accessed November 9, 2015. www.amc.com/talk. 2007/09/the-ten-best-tr.

Thor. Directed by Kenneth Branagh. Burbank: Marvel Studios, 2011. DVD.

Tolkien, J. R. R. "*Beowulf*: The Monsters and the Critics." *Beowulf: A Verse Translation*. Edited by Daniel Donoghue. New York: W.W. Norton, 2002. 103–130.

Tvtropes. "Superhero Tropes." Tvtropcs.org. Accessed November 10, 2015. Tvtropes.org/pmwiki/pmwiki.php/Main/SuperheroTropes.

Waid, Mark (w), and Alex Ross (a). *Kingdom Come*. New York: DC Comics, 1997.

Waid, Mark (w), Barry Kitson (p), and Mark Farmer (i). *Amazing Spider-Man* 1 no. 583 (March 2009).

Waid, Mark (w), Bryan Hitch (p), and Paul Neary (i). *JLA: Heaven's Ladder*. New York: DC Comics, 2000.

Wandtke, Terrence. *The Meaning of Superhero Comic Books*. Jefferson, NC: McFarland 2012.

Whedon, Joss. "10 Questions for Joss Whedon." *The New York Times*, May 16, 2003. www.newyorktimes.com/2003/05/16/readersopinions/16WHED.html.

Whedon, Joss (w), and John Cassaday (a). *Astonishing X-Men: Dangerous*. New York: Marvel Comics, 2010.

Windling, Terri. "Introduction." *The Coyote Road: Trickster Tales*. Edited by Ellen Datlow and Terri Windling. New York: Firebird, 2009.

Wolfman, Marv (w), George Perez (p), Dick Giordano (i), Mike DeCarlo (i), and Jerry Ordway (i). *Crisis on Infinite Earths*. New York: DC Comics, 2000.

The Wolverine. Directed by James Mangold. Los Angeles: Twentieth Century Fox, 2013.

X-Men. Directed by Bryan Singer. Written by David Hayter. Los Angeles: Twentieth Century Fox, 2000.

X-Men: Days of Future Past. Directed by Bryan Singer. Los Angeles: Twentieth Century Fox, 2014.

X-Men: First Class. Directed by Matthew Vaughn. Los Angeles: Twentieth Century Fox, 2011.

X-Men Origins: Wolverine. Directed by Gavin Hood. Los Angeles: Twentieth Century Fox, 2009.

X2: X-Men United. Directed by Bryan Singer. Los Angeles: Twentieth Century Fox, 2003.

Yamato, Jen. "Zack Snyder: Sorry Marvel, 'Batman V. Superman' Transcends Superhero Movies." *The Daily Beast*. September 10, 2015. www.thedailybeast.com/articles/2015/09/10/zack-snyder-sorry-marvel-batman-v-superman-transcends-superhero-movies.html.

Index

Action Comics 3, 4, 5–6, 15, 42, 45, 52*n*54
Adams, Neal 7, 99*n*3
Ageless 28–30, 98–99, 123, 136, 153
Alphas 21, 27, 132–49, 174–175, 177
alter ego 30–33, 37, 50, 57, 58, 68, 78, 100, 105, 106, 108, 117, 147–48, 161, 172, 175
The Amazing Spider-Man 37, 55
androcentric 34, 34–36, 45, 97–98, 130, 148, 157–60, 163
Arrow (character) *see* Green Arrow
Arrow (television series) 49–50, 60–61, 74, 78–79, 82, 95–111, 133, 149, 176–77, 178
authority figure, antagonistic 36–38, 42, 100, 108–09, 118, 118–20, 139–40, 165–66
authority figure, cooperative 37, 42–43, 51, 108, 118–19, 138–39, 166
The Avengers 9, 17, 31, 36, 74, 84, 90, 93, 113
The Avengers: Age of Ultron 9, 76, 84, 86, 91

Barthes, Roland 1, 4, 11, 14–15, 16
Batman (character) 6, 7, 14–15, 20, 21, 26–27, 29, 35–36, 39, 42, 43–44, 45, 46, 50, 51–52, 53, 54–55, 56–57, 58, 63, 64, 65, 66, 67, 68, 71, 72, 73, 73–74, 74–75, 77, 80, 82, 83–84, 85, 87, 90, 95, 100, 103, 108, 114, 115, 133, 154, 155, 168, 170; *see also Batman Begins; Batman: Hush; Batman: The Animated Series; Batman: Under the Red Hood; Batman v. Superman: Dawn of Justice; Batman: Year One; The Dark Knight; The Dark Knight Returns; The Dark Knight Rises;* the Dark Knight trilogy
Batman Begins 32, 62, 80, 172
Batman: Hush 58, 61–62, 83, 87
Batman: The Animated Series 53–54
Batman: The Dark Knight Returns 50, 55, 63, 81, 84, 87, 98
Batman: Under the Red Hood 62
Batman v. Superman: Dawn of Justice 34, 84, 85, 87, 93
Batman: Year One 42
Beowulf (character) 21, 25, 27, 150–167, 173–174, 177, 178–179; *see also Beowulf* (film); *Beowulf* (poem)
Beowulf (film) 154

Beowulf (poem) 1, 150–167, 173–74, 175, 58*n*62
Buffy the Vampire Slayer (film) 112, 115
Buffy the Vampire Slayer (television series) 27, 112–131, 177
Butler, Judith 147–148

Campbell, Joseph 89
The Cape 27, *133*
Captain America 6, 29–30, 31, 34, 39, 40, 42, 46, 47, 57, 59–60, 73, 85, 93; *see also Captain America: The First Avenger; Captain America: The Winter Soldier*
Captain America: The First Avenger 36, 60, 142
Captain America: The Winter Soldier 31, 51, 142
chevron 38–40, 43, 44, 44–45, 99, 124, 146, 166, 170–171, **171**, 172, 173–77
codename 25, 30–31, 39, 40–42, 44, 79, 106, 123, 146, 166, 169–70, **171**, 171–72, 173–78
Coogan, Peter 1, 20, 22, 25, 43, 74, 112–13, 131, 168, 169–71, 173, 175, 176
costume 5, 6, 9, 15, 17, 25, 27, 31, 32, 35, 39, 40, 41, 43–46, 55, 73, 81, 82, 91, 92, 98, 105–06, 125, 131, 146, 154–55, 166, 169–72, **171**, 173–78
Crisis on Infinite Earths 54

The Dark Knight 56
The Dark Knight Rises 36
the Dark Knight trilogy 42, 49, 55, 57, 74, 84, 90, 115, 142; *see also Batman Begins; The Dark Knight; The Dark Knight Rises*
death, temporary 46–47, 103–04, 128–29, 135–36, 156–57
de Saussure, Ferdinand 14–15, 171
disbelief, willing suspension of 29–30
Doty, William G. 1, 8–9, 10, 15, 16, 29, 186*n*68
Dr. Horrible's Sing-Along Blog 124

Earth X 55
Eaters of the Dead 154
expository narration 47–50, 107, 124, 146, 161

Fantastic Four 6, 31, 47, 63–64, 84, 88, 164*n*37
Fingeroth, Danny 113
Finnsburh Fragment 156, 158
Fishwick, Marshall W. 168–69

201

Index

The Flash (character) 17, 110; *see also The Flash* (television series)
The Flash (television series) 50, 82, 96

Gender Trouble see Butler, Judith
Gilgamesh 1, 27, 91, 178
Gordon, James "Jim" 42, 42–43, 45, 55, 56–57, 61–62, 108
Gotham (city) 42, 43, 56–57, 66, 83, 90, 168
Gotham (television series) 168, 170
Gotham by Gaslight 54
Gotham Central 168
Grayson, Richard "Dick" 29, 43–44, 51, 65, 66
Green Arrow 6, 71, 72, 74, 75, 82, 90, 95–111; *see also* Arrow; *Green Arrow: The Archer's Quest; Green Arrow: The Longbow Hunters; Green Arrow: Year One; Green Lantern/Green Arrow; Quiver*
Green Arrow: The Archer's Quest 96, 99, 102, 104–05, 109–110
Green Arrow: The Longbow Hunters 96, 98, 99, 102, 110
Green Arrow: Year One 96, 98, 99, 100, 101–02, 103–04, 105, 110–11, 177–78
Green Lantern 7, 21, 40, 54, 59, 70–71, 77, 79, 82, 87, 95, 110, 142
Green Lantern/Green Arrow 7, 59

Harry Potter series 4, 27, 28
The Hawkeye Initiative 34
Hawkeye: My Life as a Weapon 49
helper 50–51, 100–01, 118, 146, 163
The Hero in Transition see Fishwick, Marshall W
Heroes 27, 132, 133
Hiddleston, Tom 17–18

identity, secret 25, 30, 32, 42, 112, 117, 169–70
The Incredibles 48
Invincible (character) 90; *see also Invincible* (comic)
Invincible (comic) 39, 44
Iron Man 31, 32, 57, 59, 74, 79, 93, 133, 142, 155; *see also* Stark, Tony
Iterations 11, 28–29, 44, 47, 53–56, 88–89, 96–97, 110–11, 115–17, 144–45, 153–54

Jennings, John 33
JLA: Heaven's Ladder 16–17
The Joker 53–54, 61, 62, 77, 85
Justice 52, 76
Justice League 16–17, 21, 52, 59, 66, 76, 83, 84, 95, 133
justice over law 56–57, 59, 60, 109, 127, 141–42, 163, 171, 173

Kaveney, Roz 113
Kent, Clark 28, 32, 33, 42, 50, 53, 62, 65–66, 66, 67, 78, 80, 88, 90–91, 96, 176; *see also Batman v. Superman: Dawn of Justice; Man of Steel; Smallville;* Superman (character);

Superman (film); *Superman: Secret Origin; Superman II*
Kick-Ass 93
Kingdom Come 55
Kirby, Jack 30, 176

the lair 27, 58n62, 57–59, 99, 117, 137, 141, 152, 161, 178
Lee, Stan 30, 95; *see also Stan Lee's Superhumans*
The Lego Movie 10
Lewis, A. David 46
Logan 43, 68–69, 80–81; *see also* Wolverine (character); *The Wolverine; X-Men Origins: Wolverine*
The Lord of the Rings: The Two Towers 165

Magneto 72, 81, 85–86, 86–87, 137
male gaze 35–36
Man of Steel 45, 53, 65–66, 80, 84, 93, 142
Marvel: Civil War 9, 41, 57, 60, 87
Master Legend 13
McCloud, Scott 15
The Meaning of Superhero Comic Books see Wandtke, Terrence
Megamind 66
Metropolis 32, 47, 90–91, 93, 104
The Misfits 132
moral code 57, 59–60, 62, 69, 87, 93, 106–07, 121–22, 147, 163, 171, 173
Mythography: The Study of Myths and Rituals see Doty, William G
Mythologies see Barthes, Roland

New York 59, 69, 73, 90, 93
Nightwing 29, 44, 45, 51, 72
no killing 61, 61–62, 105, 122, 135, 161, 171, 177
No Ordinary Family 27, 133
Nolan, Christopher *see Batman Begins; The Dark Knight; The Dark Knight Rises;* the Dark Knight trilogy

O'Neil, Denny 7, 59, 80, 83
Ong, Walter 18
Origin 68–69, 170
origin, spectacular 40, 64, 79–81, 110–11, 123, 144, 161, 171
orphan 27, 64–66, 103, 125–26, 143, 162, 171, 178
outsider 66–67, 102, 125, 143–44, 161–62, 163, 171

Parker, Peter 37–38, 41, 59, 73, 80; *see also The Amazing Spider-Man;* Spider-Man (character); *Spider-Man* (film); *Spider-Man 2*
Pateman, Matthew 113
physique, amazing 33–34, 35, 97–98, 129–30, 142–43, 151–52, 172
"please the father" 43, 67–69, 70, 103, 118–19, 120, 138–39, 162, 171, 177
power and responsibility 69–70, 72, 126, 145–46, 164, 171–72

Index

power, one per person 62–64, 70, 102, 114, 134, 153
powers 6, 7, 10, 12, 25, 27, 34, 37, 38, 41, 44, 45, 51, 52, 59, 60, 62–64, 66, 69–70, 70–75, 77, 78, 79–80, 82, 87–88, 89, 91, 101–02, 101n6, 109, 112, 114–15, 128, 132, 133–34, 138–39, 140, 145, 148, 151, 153, 164, 169–72, *171*, 173–78; pseudo-superpower 64, 69, 72, 73–75, 101, 114, 133–34, 151
promotes/maintains status quo 75–77, 109, 127–28, 141, 164–65
The Punisher 38, 60, 61, 72

Quiver 91, 96, 98, 99, 102, 104

real world problems, superheroes ineffective against 7, 51–52, 69, 108, 126–27, 141, 163–64
Reeve, Christopher 31–32, 53
Regalado, Aldo J. 92
Regeneration Through Violence see Slotkin, Richard
relationship struggles 77–79, 97, 120–21, 148–49, 162
retcon 22, 31, 31n18, 77, 129
Reynolds, Richard 1, 32, 45, 56, 59, 75–76, 79–80, 86, 90
Robin 6, 29, 47, 50–51, 58, 64, 65
Rogers, Steve 30, 31, 40, 72–73; *see also* Captain America; *Captain America: The First Avenger*; *Captain America: The Winter Soldier*
Rollin, Roger B. 150
The Runaways 65

semiology 4, 14–15, 16, 20–21, 146, 171
Serenity 125
Shuster, Joe *see* Siegel, Jerry
Siegel, Jerry 4–5, 8, 15, 45, 91
Silver Age 6–7, 102, 176
the Slayer *see Buffy the Vampire Slayer* (film); *Buffy the Vampire Slayer* (television series); Summers, Buffy
Slotkin, Richard 8, 13
Smallville 28, 53, 62, 82, 91, 96, 133, 149
The Sorcerer's Apprentice 27
Spider-Man (character) 38, 40, 41, 73; *see also The Amazing Spider-Man*; Parker, Peter; *Spider-Man* (film); *Spider-Man 2*
Spider-Man (film) 33–34, 70, 73
Spider-Man 2 30, 33, 37
Stan Lee's Superhumans 74
Stark, Tony 31, 32, 41, 51, 59, 74, 87, 90, 170n11; *see also* Iron Man
Steinem, Gloria 3
Suicide Squad 54
Summers, Buffy 4, 112–131, 175–176, 177; *see also Buffy the Vampire Slayer* (film); *Buffy the Vampire Slayer* (television series)
Superhero: The Secret Origin of a Genre see Coogan, Peter
Superman (character) 3, 4–8, 14–15, 20, 21, 26–27, 28–29, 39, 40, 42, 43–44, 45–46, 46–47, 50, 51, 52, 53, 56, 57–59, 61, 62–63, 64–66, 67, 71, 72, 78, 79, 81, 83, 84, 87, 90–91, 92, 95, 103, 104, 111, 131, 162, 170, 176; *see also Batman v Superman: Dawn of Justice*; Kent, Clark; *Man of* Steel; *Smallville*; *Superman* (film); *Superman: Red Son*; *Superman: Secret Origin*; *Superman II*
Superman (film) 32, 78
Superman: Red Son 84
Superman: Secret Origin 88
Superman II 33, 78
superteam 6, 64, 82–84, 95, 101, 118, 134, 153
supervillain 5, 27, 37, 38, 47–48, 52, 54, 60, 65, 76, 84–86, 97, 110, 114, 120, 128, 137–38, 152, 153, 160–61, 178
switching sides 86–87, 101, 120, 139–40, 163

Taming of the Shrew 158
The 13th Warrior 154
Thor (character) 10, 13–14, 34, 71, 76, 93; *see also Thor* (film)
Thor (film) 8, 17, 36, 142
Timely Comics 42, 42n35
Tolkien, J.R.R. 8, 150, 154, 156–57, 165
Toy Story 125
trigger, traumatic 87–89, 101–02, 115, 140, 153, 171
TVTropes.org 22,, 42–43, 179, 181–83

Understanding Comics: The Invisible Art see McCloud, Scott
urban 90–92, 102, 117–18, 144–45, 152

violence 6, 27, 35, 60, 61, 83, 92–93, 96, 104–05, 122–23, 135, 147, 156–59
visual component, strong 81–82, 91–92, 99, 124–25, 134, 155–56, 166, 172

Wandtke, Terrence 18–19, 54, 55–56
Watchmen 69–70, 76n84, 81
Wertham, Fredric 6
Whedon, Joss 27, 48–49, 112, 113, 115, 116–17, 123, 124, 125, 127, 130
Wolverine (character) 3, 34, 44–45, 48–49, 59, 63, 68, 80, 82, 84, 142, 170; *see also Logan*; *Origin*; *The Wolverine* (film); *X-Men Origins: Wolverine*
The Wolverine (film) 55
Wonder Woman 3, 6, 26–27, 34, 39, 58, 68, 71, 78, 95, 131
World War II 29–30, 31, 42, 47

X-Men (characters) 83, 133; *see also X-Men* (film); *X-Men: Days of Future Past*; *X-Men: First Class*; *X2: X-Men United*
X-Men (film) 3, 55, 63
X-Men: Days of Future Past 55
X-Men: First Class 55
X-Men Origins: Wolverine 55
X2: X-Men United 55

www.ingramcontent.com/pod-product-compliance
Ingram Content Group UK Ltd.
Pitfield, Milton Keynes, MK11 3LW, UK
UKHW042003140426
5217IPUK00015B/952